westermann

AF288596

William Shakespeare

The Tragedy of Hamlet, Prince of Denmark

Annotated
by Rudolph F. Rau

Tasks
by Ilka Kratz

Materialien zum Download

Materialien für Lehrkräfte mit didaktisch-methodischen Hinweisen, Hintergrundinformationen, Lösungsvorschlägen zu den Aufgaben der Textausgabe und einem Klausurvorschlag finden Sie online auf www.westermann.de. Geben Sie dafür in das Suchfeld auf der Startseite die Nummer 73068 ein. In der Rubrik „Ergänzende Materialien" können Sie das Material abrufen.

Bildquellen

|Alamy Stock Photo, Abingdon/Oxfordshire: Charles Walker Collection 7.2; Classic Image 38.1; Martin Thomas Photography 7.1. |Bridgeman Images, Berlin: © Tristram Kenton Titel. |Shutterstock.com, New York: Stocksnapper 6.1.

Textquellen

8-9   "Shakespeare's Danish Links" by Rodney Bolt in *The Telegraph*, 15 April 2014
        © Rodney Bolt / Telegraph Media Group Limited 2014.
192   "The Wheel of Fortune" by Andrea Wilson,
        http://wilsonsbritworld.weebly.com/uploads/7/0/9/1/7091916/theelizabethanworldview.pdf.
193   "The Great Chain of Being", *BBC Bitesize: Beliefs and Superstitions*,
        https://www.bbc.co.uk/bitesize/guides/zmjnb9q/revision/2.

westermann GRUPPE

© 2021 Westermann Bildungsmedien Verlag GmbH, Georg-Westermann-Allee 66, 38104 Braunschweig
www.westermann.de

Druck A^2 / Jahr 2022
Alle Drucke der Serie A sind im Unterricht parallel verwendbar.

Redaktion: Thorsten Schimming, Caitlin Gray, Angela Wesser
Layout: Harald Thumser, Frankfurt am Main
Druck und Bindung: Westermann Druck GmbH, Georg-Westermann-Allee 66, 38104 Braunschweig

ISBN 978-3-425-**73068**-4

Contents

Introduction

The Tragedy of Hamlet, Prince of Denmark is Shakespeare's most famous play and the one which is most often performed. It has seen numerous film adaptations. Records show the first performance to have taken place in or shortly before 1602. There is a consensus that Shakespeare actually wrote the play in 1601.

There are basically three early printed versions of the play. The version of 1603 seems to be based on actors recalling an early performance, and is considered unreliable. A year later a longer version was printed, which was lauded as a much more accurate version. Another version, known as the Folio, was published in 1623. It is the Folio version that is now usually used for publication, with modern spelling and punctuation. Where there is doubt whether a passage or expression is authentic Shakespeare, scholars make comparisons with the other versions of the text and Shakespeare's other plays.

The plot has its source in a Scandinavian folk tale from the twelfth century, *Historia Danica*, written in Latin by the Danish author Saco Grammaticus. A version translated into French appeared in 1580.

There seems to have been an earlier English version of the play in 1589 that might have actually been performed, but all traces of it have disappeared.

The setting of the play is Denmark during the Middle Ages, at a time when England was a comparatively weak country still dominated by the Anglo-Saxons. Denmark (and Norway) were militarily and politically stronger, as evidenced by the English having to pay tribute to Denmark as mentioned in the play. But *Hamlet* contains many allusions to the contemporary cultural, political, and religious situation of Elizabethan England as well, no doubt to make the play more appealing to audiences at that time.

Introduction to this edition

This edition of William Shakespeare's *Hamlet* focuses on three key themes throughout the play:

→ Fate vs. free will
→ The role(s) of women
→ Questions of morality

Relevant passages relating to these themes are highlighted:

145 **HORATIO**   ↻ Fate vs.
    That can I.   free will
    At least the whisper goes so: Our last King,
    Whose image even but now appeared to us,
    Was, as you know, by Fortinbras of Norway,

Every scene is followed by a short summary of the action and some tasks.

In addition to these tasks, you will find pre-reading tasks on pages 7-9 and post-reading tasks, relating to the three key themes, from page 191 onwards.

The text of *Hamlet* is complimented by a wealth of useful annotations to help you understand both the language used, and the deeper meaning of the text. In addition to these annotations, you will find additional notes towards the back of the book on pages 200-207. Words and phrases in the text which have a corresponding additional note are marked with an asterisk (*).

William Shakespeare: a short biography

Our knowledge of what Shakespeare's life was like is rather sketchy. At the time few extensive records of peoples' lives apart from the nobility were kept. Most of the information about Shakespeare's life is drawn from church and legal documents, and occasional references to him by his contemporaries.

According to church records, he was baptized on 26 April 1564 in Trinity Church in Stratford-upon-Avon and buried there on 25 April 1616. His father, John Shakespeare was a well-to-do glove maker in Stratford, who held numerous municipal offices. His mother, Mary Arden came from a wealthy family of landowners. We can assume that his father was able to afford to send his son to a Grammar School, where he probably learned Latin and some ancient Greek, and came into contact with Greek and Roman literature. However, William Shakespeare was not university-trained.

In 1582 he married Anne Hathaway. Their first child was born in 1583. The twins, Hamnet and Judith, were born five years later.

What happened between 1585 and 1592 remains a blank, but we can assume Shakespeare moved to London at some point to begin a career as a playwright and actor. Turning more to playwriting, he became full owner of his acting company, the Lord Chamberlain's Men, later with the approval of King James I, the King's Men. He was also part owner of the Globe Theatre and Blackfriars Theatre.

Apparently, he became financially so well situated that he could afford to purchase a large house in Stratford, where he probably spent most of his remaining life.

Pre-reading

1. The story of *Hamlet*

Who has not heard of *Hamlet*? Surely, everybody associates the famous line "To be or not to be" with this play. But what is the play about? And what does the line mean?

a) Tell the story of *Hamlet* using the keywords below, even if you do not know anything about it.

> Denmark – new king – ghost of the old king – revenge – love – to deceive – mad – players – performance of a play – to murder – to commit suicide – fencing match – poison

b) Speculate what the famous line "To be, or not to be, that is the question" means.

2. Where did Shakespeare get his *Hamlet* from?

Group work (3): Shakespeare was not the first author to come up with a character named Hamlet. Do some research on the following authors and their works and exchange your results with your group members:
- Saxo Grammaticus
- Thomas Kyd
- François de Belleforest

3. The setting

a) Describe the two pictures below and the atmosphere they convey.

b) Pair work: Speculate why Shakespeare used this setting for his tragedy.
c) Have you ever wondered why William Shakespeare set his play in a country he never visited? Where did he get all the details about the castle from? Did he make them up?
Read the extract on pages 8 and 9 from an article by Rodney Bolt published in *The Telegraph* in 2014 and outline the main ideas.

Shakespeare's Danish Links

by Rodney Bolt, 15 April 2014

to elicit to get a reaction from sb

"Which room did Shakespeare write Hamlet in?" was a frequent question when tourists were first admitted to Kronborg Castle in Elsinore, in the 1920s. The line elicits knowing chuckles from present-day visitors to what is now one of Denmark's top tourist attractions. We, of
5 course, know the Bard never visited Denmark, and that the Elsinore castle he specifies as the setting of Hamlet is based on pure imagination. Or is it?

strand one of the different parts of an idea

low-down true facts about sth
coincidental happening by chance

I'm not so sure. In the course of researching an historical novel, I'd come across curious strands of insider information about Kronborg
10 Castle in Shakespeare's play. Somebody, it seemed, had given the playwright the low-down on castle life. Were these details purely coincidental? [...]

to roam to travel around
to wow to impress sb very much

downright absolute, complete
tumbler acrobat
codpiece a piece of decorative cloth attached to a man's lower clothing and covering his genitals

In Shakespeare's time, travelling bands of English players roamed the Continent. They were hugely popular. The actors wowed the crowds
15 with their acrobatic style, sumptuous costumes (often court castoffs), and downright sexiness. One contemporary poem celebrated a "tumbler" from such a troupe: "His hose they fitted him so tight / His codpiece was a lovely sight". Language was apparently no barrier. Fynes Moryson, an English traveller of the time, noted that men
20 and women "flocked wonderfully to see gesture and Action, rather than heare them, [as they speak] English which they understand not". Richer courts sometimes employed a simultaneous interpreter, rather like live subtitles.

Leicester's Men one of the major acting companies in Renaissance England, under the patronage of the Earl of Leicester

to flock to come together in large numbers

In 1586, about 15 years before the first production of Hamlet at the
25 Globe, one group of English players, most likely Leicester's Men, visited Elsinore, performing at the inaugural celebrations of a newly rebuilt Kronborg Castle. They also played in the courtyard of the Elsinore Town Hall, to which the crowds flocked so wonderfully that they knocked down a courtyard wall. Among the players was one
30 Wilhelm Kempe, now commonly acknowledged as being Will Kempe, "my Lord of Lester's jesting player". Kempe went on to become one of Shakespeare's most popular clowns, playing Dogberry and probably Falstaff.

Sound the stretch of water between Denmark and Sweden

to swam to move around in a large group
bound back likely to go back

"I think Kempe could very likely have given Shakespeare the detail
35 he needed," says local Hamlet expert William Jansen, standing on the castle "platform", the cannon-lined bastion overlooking the Sound. "But there's another very likely source of information. The Sound provided the main sea access to the Baltic. Elsinore at the time would have been swarming with English merchants, many bound back for

40 London." But merchants are less likely to have known the inside layout of the castle, rooms that players had readier access to. Kronborg is
ranged around a square central courtyard – royal apartments occupy-
ing the north wing, chapel and great hall in the south, the east and
west wings a hotchpotch of personal chambers and reception rooms.

hotchpotch a number of things mixed together

45 The courtyard walls are clad in pale grey sandstone, breaking out
here and there into fripperies of Renaissance carving. [...]

fripperies objects, decorations that are considered unnecessary and expensive

Other revelations follow: Shakespeare, alone among his English contemporaries correctly uses the Danish word Dansker, to mean Dane;
the dumb show that precedes the play-within-a-play, when the trav-
50 elling players perform for the king, was a Danish and not an English
custom. Most intriguingly, Hamlet's two university friends, Rosencrantz and Guildenstern, would appear to come from two notable
local families. The Guildensterns even have their own chamber at the
castle.

55 Farfetched? Possibly. Pure coincidence? Perhaps so. Or maybe the diligent playwright did indeed consult Will Kempe for the sake of accuracy
and a little local colour. "However you view things, I think there is no
doubt that Shakespeare made a concerted effort to place Hamlet here,"
says Jansen. He believes that the canny Bard was playing a careful card

diligent showing care and effort

concerted done in a planned and deter-mined way

60 to flatter the future King James I, whose wife, Anne, was sister to the
Danish king, and who had lived at the castle. James also stayed here,
soon after they were married, some years before Hamlet was written.

canny intelligent

With much to ponder, I make my way back to the station – built,
incidentally, by the Rosencrantz family. [...]

incidentally in a way that was not planned

4. Who is who in *Hamlet*?

Have a look at the *Dramatis Personae* on the next page in order to find out about the characters involved in the
play. Start a character map in which you show the relationships between the characters. Add information to the
map while you read the play.

Dramatis Personae

Ghost of the late King of Denmark, King Hamlet
Claudius, King of Denmark, brother of the late King Hamlet
Gertrude, Queen of Denmark, mother of Prince Hamlet, widow of King Hamlet, now the wife of Claudius
Prince Hamlet, son of King Hamlet and Queen Gertrude and nephew of King Claudius
Polonius, Lord Chamberlain
Laertes, son of Polonius
Ophelia, daughter of Polonius
Reynaldo, servant of Polonius

Horatio
Rosencrantz } friends of Prince Hamlet
Guildenstern

Francisco
Bernardo } soldiers
Marcellus

Voltimand
Cornelius } courtiers
Osric

Gentlemen
A Priest
Two Clowns, a gravedigger and his companion
Fortinbras, Prince of Norway
A Captain in his army
Ambassadors from England
Players, who play the parts of the **Prologue, Player King, Player Queen** and **Lucianus** in *The Mousetrap*
Lords
Messengers
Attendants
Guards
Soldiers
Followers of Laertes
Sailors

Lord Chamberlain chief officer of the household of a king, adviser

courtier [ˈkɔːtiə] person who is constantly present at the court of a king, often influential

ambassador *Botschafter*

attendant person or servant present at a court with various functions

ACT I

SCENE I. Elsinore Castle, Denmark. A platform before the castle.

Enter two sentinels, first FRANCISCO, then BERNARDO, who approaches him.

sentinel soldier whose job it is to guard s.th.

BERNARDO
Who's there?
5 **FRANCISCO**
Nay, answer me. Stand, and unfold yourself.

Nay, answer me. i.e. Rather, answer *me*.
unfold yourself (fig.) reveal who you are

BERNARDO
Long live the King!
FRANCISCO
10 Bernardo?
BERNARDO
He.
FRANCISCO
You come most carefully upon your hour.

come most carefully upon your hour
   come perfectly on time to begin your
   duty

15 **BERNARDO**
'Tis now struck twelve. Get thee to bed, Francisco.
FRANCISCO
For this relief much thanks. 'Tis bitter cold,
And I am sick at heart.

'Tis (archaic) (here) It has
Get thee (archaic) get yourself
relief i.e. your coming to replace me
'Tis (archaic) It is
sick at heart depressed

20 **BERNARDO**
Have you had quiet guard?
FRANCISCO
Not a mouse stirring.

to stir to move

BERNARDO
25 Well, good night.
If you do meet Horatio and Marcellus,
The rivals of my watch, bid them make haste.

rivals of my watch my partners as sentinels
bid them ask them
to make haste (archaic) to hurry up

FRANCISCO
I think I hear them. Stand! Who's there?

30 *Enter HORATIO and MARCELLUS*

HORATIO
Friends to this ground.

ground country

MARCELLUS
And liegemen to the Dane.

liegeman loyal follower
to the Dane of the Danish King

35 **FRANCISCO**
Give you good night.

Give you good night. May God give you a
   good night.

MARCELLUS
O, farewell, honest soldier.
Who hath relieved you?

farewell goodbye
hath (archaic) has
to relieve (here) to replace

40 **FRANCISCO**
Bernardo has my place. Give you good night.

Exit

MARCELLUS

Holla earlier form of "hello"

Holla! Bernardo!
45 **BERNARDO**
Say, what, is Horatio there?
HORATIO

a piece of him (meant to be humorous)

A piece of him.
BERNARDO
50 Welcome, Horatio. Welcome, good Marcellus.
MARCELLUS
What, has this thing appeared again tonight?
BERNARDO
I have seen nothing.
55 **MARCELLUS**

but only

Horatio says 'tis but our fantasy,
And will not let belief take hold of him

touching in Bezug auf • **dreaded** terrible

Touching this dreaded sight, twice seen of us.

to entreat s.o. to ask s.o. earnestly to do s.th.

Therefore I have entreated him along

along to come along
apparition ghost
approve our eyes confirm what we saw

60 With us to watch the minutes of this night;
That, if again this apparition come,
He may approve our eyes and speak to it.
HORATIO

tush (archaic) expression of disapproval
'twill it will

Tush, tush, 'twill not appear.
65 **BERNARDO**
Sit down awhile,

to assail (fig.) to attack

And let us once again assail your ears,

fortified against i.e. unwilling to believe

That are so fortified against our story
What we have two nights seen.
70 **HORATIO**
Well, sit we down,
And let us hear Bernardo speak of this.
BERNARDO

last night of all just last night

Last night of all,

yon (archaic) that • **pole** northern star

75 When yon same star that's westward from the pole

to illume (archaic) to illuminate *(erleuchten)*

Had made his course to illume that part of heaven
Where now it burns, Marcellus and myself,
The bell then beating one –

Enter GHOST

80 **MARCELLUS**

Peace, break thee off. Be silent.

Peace, break thee off. Look, where it comes again!
BERNARDO
In the same figure, like the King that's dead.

MARCELLUS
85 Thou art a scholar. Speak to it, Horatio.

thou art (archaic) you are
scholar student at a university

BERNARDO
Looks it not like the King? Mark it, Horatio.

mark it take a close look

HORATIO
Most like. It harrows me with fear and wonder.

to harrow to torture

90 **BERNARDO**
It would be spoke to.

would be spoke to wishes to be spoken to

MARCELLUS
Question it, Horatio.

HORATIO
95 [*to the GHOST*]
What art thou that usurp'st this time of night,
Together with that fair and warlike form
In which the majesty of buried Denmark
Did sometimes march? By heaven I charge thee, speak!

that usurp'st this time […] sometimes march? that has taken over this time of night and taken on the form of the body of the dead King of Denmark, looking majestic in the armour (*Rüstung*) he used to wear in battle?
to charge (archaic) to order
thee (archaic) you

100 **MARCELLUS**
It is offended.

BERNARDO
See, it stalks away!

to offend *beleidigen*
to stalk to walk stiffly

HORATIO
105 [*to the GHOST*]
Stay, speak, speak, I charge thee speak.

Exit GHOST

MARCELLUS
'Tis gone, and will not answer.

110 **BERNARDO**
How now, Horatio, you tremble and look pale.
Is not this something more than fantasy?
What think you on't?

to tremble to shake

on't on it (archaic) of it

HORATIO
115 Before my God, I might not this believe
Without the sensible and true avouch
Of mine own eyes.

before I swear before
avouch evidence
mine (archaic) my

MARCELLUS
Is it not like the King?

120 **HORATIO**
As thou art to thyself.
Such was the very armour he had on
When the ambitious Norway combated.
So frowned he once, when, in an angry parley
125 He smote the sledded Polacks on the ice.
'Tis strange.

thyself (archaic) yourself
very same
Norway King of Norway
to combate (archaic) to start a battle
to frown to make an angry face
parley negotiation
to smite, smote, smitten to strike with a heavy blow
sledded with sleds (*Schlitten*)
Polacks Poles

MARCELLUS
Thus twice before, and just at this dead hour,
With martial stalk hath he gone by our watch.

dead hour midnight
martial stalk military manner of walking

In what [...] to work What precise theory to follow
know not (archaic) don't know
in the gross and scope of my opinion in my general opinion
bodes *lässt erahnen*
eruption major disaster
nightly toils the subject of the land makes the subjects *(Untertanen)* of Denmark work so hard even at night
cast production
brazen made of brass *(Messing)*
foreign mart spending money in foreign countries
implements weapons
impress forced labour
shipwright ship builder · **sore** urgent
Does not [...] from the week also requires work on Sundays
toward anticipated
sweaty haste hard labour requiring speed
Doth make [...] with the day requires workers working day and night
is't is it · **whisper** rumour
Thereto [...] emulate pride incited *(angestiftet)* to go to war by a competitive sense of honour
to dare *herausfordern* · **valiant** brave
this side of our known world all of Europe
to esteem *einschätzen*
to slay to kill
by heraldy because he lost the war
to forfeit [ˈfɔːfɪt] to lose
stood seized of legally owned
moiety competent an equal portion of land
to gage (archaic) to wager, to risk s.th. of value on s.th.
had returned would have gone
inheritance ownership
vanquisher person who wins
convenant treaty, contract
carriage [...] designed execution of the contract's provisions
his his land
unimproved untested · **mettle** bravery
skirts outskirts
sharked up gathered · **list** group
resolutes desperate men
for food and diet paid with food
stomach courage to fight · **well** obviously
by strong hand by force
terms compulsatory conditions that are forced on you when you are defeated
head origin
post-haste and romage *eilige Unruhe*
e'en even · **sort** be fitting
portentous indicating an important future event

HORATIO
In what particular thought to work I know not,
But in the gross and scope of my opinion,
This bodes some strange eruption to our state.
MARCELLUS
Good now, sit down, and tell me, he that knows,
Why this same strict and most observant watch
So nightly toils the subject of the land,
And why such daily cast of brazen cannon,
And foreign mart for implements of war,
Why such impress of shipwrights, whose sore task
Does not divide the Sunday from the week,
What might be toward that this sweaty haste
Doth make the night joint-labourer with the day?
Who is't that can inform me?
HORATIO
That can I.
At least the whisper goes so: Our last King,
Whose image even but now appeared to us,
Was, as you know, by Fortinbras of Norway,
Thereto pricked on by a most emulate pride,
Dared to the combat, in which our valiant Hamlet
(For so this side of our known world esteemed him)
Did slay this Fortinbras, who by a sealed compact
Well ratified by law and heraldry,
Did forfeit, with his life, all those his lands
Which he stood seized of, to the conqueror;
Against the which, a moiety competent
Was gagèd by our King, which had returned
To the inheritance of Fortinbras,
Had he been vanquisher, as, by the same covenant
And carriage of the article designed
His fell to Hamlet. Now, sir, young Fortinbras,
Of unimprovèd mettle hot and full,
Hath in the skirts of Norway here and there
Sharked up a list of lawless resolutes,
For food and diet to some enterprise
That hath a stomach in't, which is no other –
As it doth well appear unto our state –
But to recover of us, by strong hand
And terms compulsatory, those foresaid lands
So by his father lost. And this, I take it,
Is the main motive of our preparations,
The source of this our watch and the chief head
Of this post-haste and romage in the land.
BERNARDO
I think it be no other but e'en so.
Well may it sort that this portentous figure

⊘ Fate vs. free will

Comes armèd through our watch so like the King
That was and is the question of these wars.

180 **HORATIO**
A mote it is to trouble the mind's eye.
In the most high and palmy state of Rome,
A little ere the mightiest Julius fell,
The graves stood tenantless and the sheeted dead
185 Did squeak and gibber in the Roman streets*:
As stars with trains of fire and dews of blood,
Disasters in the sun; and the moist star
Upon whose influence Neptune's* empire stands
Was sick almost to doomsday with eclipse:
190 And even the like precurse of feared events,
As harbingers preceding still the fates*
And prologue to the omen coming on,
Have heaven and earth together demonstrated
Unto our climature and countrymen.
195 But soft, behold! Lo where it comes again!

Re-enter GHOST

I'll cross it, though it blast me. Stay, illusion!

The GHOST spreads his arms.

If thou hast any sound, or use of voice,
200 Speak to me.
If there be any good thing to be done,
That may to thee do ease and grace to me,
Speak to me.
If thou art privy to thy country's fate,
205 Which happily foreknowing may avoid,
O, speak!
Or if thou hast uphoarded in thy life
Extorted treasure in the womb of earth –
For which, they say, you spirits oft walk in death –

210 *The cock crows.*

Speak of it. Stay, and speak!
Stop it, Marcellus.

MARCELLUS
Shall I strike at it with my partisan?
215 **HORATIO**
Do, if it will not stand.
BERNARDO
'Tis here!

Comes armèd carrying weapons
question cause

mote bit of dust
palmy at the height of its development

train trail · **dew** *Tau*
disasters evil influences (astrology)
moist star i.e. the moon which influences the tide
was sick almost to doomsday with eclipse the moon was in total eclipse, i.e. completely blacked out, as if it signified the return of Christ on Judgement Day
like precurse similar to warning signs
harbinger messenger · **still** (here) always
omen (here) disastrous event
climature (archaic) region
soft be quiet · **behold lo** (archaic) look

cross it cross its path · **blast** destroy

may to thee do ease let you rest in peace
grace to me be considered a virtuous act on my part
to be privy to to know about
thy [ðaɪ] (archaic) your
happily perhaps
foreknowing knowing ahead of time
uphoarded accumulated
extorted wrongfully obtained
womb [wuːm] (fig.) *Gebärmutter*, i.e. deepest part
cock *Hahn* · **to crow** *krähen*

partisan sharp long weapon

HORATIO
220 'Tis here!

MARCELLUS
'Tis gone!

Exit GHOST

We do it wrong, being so majestical,
225 To offer it the show of violence;
For it is as the air invulnerable,
And our vain blows malicious mockery.

BERNARDO
It was about to speak, when the cock crew.

230 **HORATIO**
And then it started like a guilty thing
Upon a fearful summons. I have heard,
The cock, that is the trumpet to the morn,
Doth with his lofty and shrill-sounding throat
235 Awake the god of day; and, at his warning,
Whether in sea or fire, in earth or air,
The extravagant and erring spirit hies
To his confine; and of the truth herein
This present object made probation.

240 **MARCELLUS**
It faded on the crowing of the cock.
Some say that ever 'gainst that season comes
Wherein our Saviour's birth is celebrated,
The bird of dawning singeth all night long;
245 And then, they say, no spirit dares stir abroad;
The nights are wholesome; then no planets strike,
No fairy takes, nor witch hath power to charm,
So hallowed and so gracious is the time.

HORATIO
250 So have I heard and do in part believe it.
But, look, the morn, in russet mantle clad,
Walks o'er the dew of yon high eastward hill.
Break we our watch up and by my advice,
Let us impart what we have seen tonight
255 Unto young Hamlet; for upon my life,
This spirit, dumb to us, will speak to him.
Do you consent we shall acquaint him with it,
As needful in our loves, fitting our duty?

MARCELLUS
260 Let's do't, I pray; and I this morning know
Where we shall find him most conveniently.

Exeunt

---

vain useless
malicious mockery mere imitation of injury

crew (archaic) crowed

started suddenly moved
upon a fearful summons answering to a frightening call to appear before a court
morn (literary) morning
lofty high sounding
god of day Phoebus Apollo in Greek mythology
at his warning warning spirits and ghosts to avoid the sunlight
sea, fire, earth, air considered at the time the four elements
extravagant and erring wandering beyond the proper limits
hies (archaiac) hurries
confine proper home
present object recent sight
made probation gave proof
ever 'gainst just before
bird of dawning the cock
singeth (archaic) sings
stir abroad move beyond its confinement
wholesome healthy – night air was usually considered unhealthy
to strike (here) to cause destruction, according to astrology
no fairy takes no supernatural being has the power to cause s.th. evil to happen
witch Hexe • **to charm** verzaubern
hallowed heilig
in russet mantel clad clothed in a reddish-brown coat
by my advice I suggest
to impart s.th. unto s.o. (archaic) to inform s.o. about s.th.
dumb silent
to consent to agree
to acquaint s.o. with s.th. to tell s.o. about s.th.
do't do it • **I pray** I urge
conveniently easily

Summary

While the soldiers are guarding the castle at night, a ghost appears to Horatio, who then decides to inform Prince Hamlet about the apparition.

Tasks

1. The setting

a) Read the info box on stage scenery and scan Scene I for information about the setting.

Info: Stage scenery
In Elizabethan times theatres had hardly any stage setting or scenery, which is why playwrights often used language to create a vivid scenic picture of the setting in the audience's mind. Hence the term audience for the theatregoers, deriving from the Latin word *audire* meaning *to listen*. Besides, the plays were often staged in daylight, during the afternoon.

Details	Quotations/line references
time of day	
weather	
place/country	
overall situation	

b) Speculate why Shakespeare has chosen this sort of setting for the beginning of his play.
c) Make a list of the war preparations as described by Marcellus in lines 135-143.
d Challenge: Add some lines to what Marcellus says about the war preparations.

2. The ghost

a) Collect all the information about the ghost in this scene.
b) In line 133 Horatio says, "This bodes some strange eruption to our state." Speculate on what Horatio might mean by this.
c) Imagine you are a director: Explain how you would stage this scene. Would you make an actor play the ghost? What would he look like? How would he act?

3. Looking back at past events

a) Read lines 147-174 and put the paraphrases below into the correct order.
    - Enter the numbers 1 to 5 in the left column.
    - Give evidence from the text to prove your point.

	Paraphrases	Evidence
	Young Fortinbras, however, has gathered a bunch of outlaws to reclaim the lands lost by his father.	
	This is the reason why the soldiers are standing guard at the castle and why the country is preparing for war.	
	Before the war, the rival monarchs had agreed in a sealed contract to give lands that they personally possessed to the winner.	
	The late king of Denmark was waging war against old King Fortinbras of Norway, who finally died in the combat.	
	If King Hamlet had lost, all his territories would have gone to old King Fortinbras.	

b) Pair work: Write the contract that contains the agreement between old Hamlet and old Fortinbras in your own words.

4. The atmosphere

a) Group work (4): Read the beginning of the play (lines 1-41) out loud. Read the lines in the following moods:
    - angry
    - frightened
    - self-confident
b) Group work (4): In your group, discuss which is the best way to present the lines.
c) Explain how the short lines contribute to the overall atmosphere.
d) Taking the results from the previous tasks into account, describe the atmosphere in these lines. Choose the adjectives that best describe the atmosphere and explain your choice.

calm – highly charged – tense – emotional – heady – hostile – gloomy – intimate – stifling – frightening

SCENE II. A room of state in the castle.

Flourish. Enter KING CLAUDIUS, QUEEN GERTRUDE, HAMLET, POLONIUS, LAERTES, OPHELIA, VOLTIMAND, CORNELIUS, Lords, and Attendants

KING CLAUDIUS

5 Though yet of Hamlet our dear brother's death
The memory be green, and that it us befitted
To bear our hearts in grief and our whole kingdom
To be contracted in one brow of woe,
Yet so far hath discretion fought with nature
10 That we with wisest sorrow think on him,
Together with remembrance of ourselves.
Therefore our sometime sister, now our queen,
The imperial jointress to this warlike state,
Have we, as 'twere with a defeated joy,
15 With an auspicious and a dropping eye,
With mirth in funeral and with dirge in marriage,
In equal scale weighing delight and dole,
Taken to wife. Nor have we herein barred
Your better wisdoms, which have freely gone
20 With this affair along. For all, our thanks.
Now follows, that you know, young Fortinbras,
Holding a weak supposal of our worth,
Or thinking by our late dear brother's death
Our state to be disjoint and out of frame,
25 Colleaguèd with the dream of his advantage,
He hath not failed to pester us with message,
Importing the surrender of those lands
Lost by his father with all bonds of law
To our most valiant brother. So much for him.
30 Now for ourself and for this time of meeting,
Thus much the business is: we have here writ
To Norway, uncle of young Fortinbras* –
Who, impotent and bedrid scarcely hears
Of this his nephew's purpose – to suppress
35 His further gait herein, in that the levies,
The lists and full proportions are all made
Out of his subject: and we here dispatch
You, good Cornelius, and you, Voltimand,
For bearers of this greeting to old Norway,
40 Giving to you no further personal power
To business with the King, more than the scope
Of these delated articles allow.
Farewell, and let your haste commend your duty.

◉ **Questions of morality**

green (fig.) fresh, recent
it us befitted [...] in grief it is appropriate for us to be very sad
contracted drawn together
brow of woe expression of mourning
discretion rational judgement
nature natural love
That we with [...] of ourselves that feeling sorrow doesn't mean we forget ourselves
sometime former • **sister** sister-in-law
jointress joint possessor
warlike preparing for war
'twere it were • **defeated** frustrated
auspicious hopeful • **dropping** pessimistic
mirth happiness, fun
dirge song of mourning
dole sorrow • **barred** excluded
your better wisdoms your good advice

holding a weak supposal of our worth underestimating our strength

disjoint and out of frame in a chaotic state
colleaguèd linked
pester us tell us repeatedly
message demands
importing concerning
bonds of law binding agreements

writ written

impotent helpless
bedrid (archaic) bedridden, forced to stay in bed because of illness
purpose plans
further gait herein proceeding with his plans
the levies, the lists and full proportions men, money and other resources
to dispatch to send
for bearers as carriers or messengers
to business to negotiate • **scope** *Spielraum*
delated lengthy
let your haste commend your duty Let your quick departure show your loyalty

you In Shakespeare's time, "you" was equivalent to "Sie", whereas "thou" and "thee" were equivalent to "du" and "dir/dich".
suit request
speak of reason to the Dane make a reasonable request to the King of Denmark
lose your voice not have your request granted
What wouldst thou [...] thy asking What could you ask of me that I would not offer before you asked?
native to naturally connected to
instrumental serviceable

dread feared and respected
leave and favour permission and good will
whence where

bend turn
bow them to your gracious leave and pardon humbly ask you to grant permission

to wring, wrung, wrung (here) to manage to acquire
slow reluctant
laboursome petition asking again and again
sealed confirmed
hard consent agreement after all
to beseech (archaic) to ask earnestly
Take thy [...] time be thine Make the best use of your time while you can.
thy best graces [...] will your good qualities will ensure that you wisely use your time as you wish
cousin relative, kinsman
a little more than kin a bit more than just a relative
kind having friendly feelings

nighted colour black mourning clothes

vailèd lids downcast eyes

CORNELIUS and VOLTIMAND
45 In that and all things will we show our duty.
KING CLAUDIUS
We doubt it nothing. Heartily farewell.

Exeunt VOLTIMAND and CORNELIUS

And now, Laertes, what's the news with you?
50 You told us of some suit. What is't, Laertes?
You cannot speak of reason to the Dane
And lose your voice. What wouldst thou beg, Laertes,
That shall not be my offer, not thy asking?
The head is not more native to the heart,
55 The hand more instrumental to the mouth,
Than is the throne of Denmark to thy father.
What wouldst thou have, Laertes?
LAERTES
My dread lord,
60 Your leave and favour to return to France;
From whence though willingly I came to Denmark
To show my duty in your coronation,
Yet now, I must confess, that duty done,
My thoughts and wishes bend again toward France
65 And bow them to your gracious leave and pardon.
KING CLAUDIUS
Have you your father's leave? What says Polonius?
POLONIUS
He hath, my lord, wrung from me my slow leave
70 By laboursome petition, and at last
Upon his will I sealed my hard consent:
I do beseech you, give him leave to go.
KING CLAUDIUS
Take thy fair hour, Laertes, time be thine
75 And thy best graces spend it at thy will.
But now, my cousin Hamlet, and my son –
HAMLET
[*Aside*] A little more than kin*, and less than kind.
KING CLAUDIUS
80 How is it that the clouds still hang on you?
HAMLET
Not so, my lord. I am too much in the sun*.
QUEEN GERTRUDE
Good Hamlet, cast thy nighted colour off
85 And let thine eye look like a friend on Denmark.
Do not for ever with thy vailèd lids
Seek for thy noble father in the dust.
Thou knowst 'tis common all that lives must die,
Passing through nature to eternity.

◐ **Fate vs. free will**
◐ **The role(s) of women**

90 **HAMLET**
Ay, madam, it is common.

QUEEN GERTRUDE
If it be,
Why seems it so particular with thee?

95 **HAMLET**
Seems, madam? Nay it is. I know not 'seems.'
'Tis not alone my inky cloak, good-mother,
Nor customary suits of solemn black,
Nor windy suspiration of forced breath,
100 No, nor the fruitful river in the eye,
Nor the dejected behavior of the visage,
Together with all forms, moods, shapes of grief
That can denote me truly. These indeed seem,
For they are actions that a man might play,
105 But I have that within which passeth show,
These but the trappings and the suits of woe.

KING CLAUDIUS
'Tis sweet and commendable in your nature, Hamlet,   ↩ **Fate vs. free will**
To give these mourning duties to your father:
110 But you must know your father lost a father,
That father lost, lost his, and the survivor bound
In filial obligation for some term
To do obsequious sorrow: but to persever
In obstinate condolement is a course
115 Of impious stubbornness. 'Tis unmanly grief,
It shows a will most incorrect to heaven,
A heart unfortified, a mind impatient,
An understanding simple and unschooled;
For what we know must be and is as common
120 As any the most vulgar thing to sense,
Why should we in our peevish opposition
Take it to heart? Fie, 'tis a fault to heaven,
A fault against the dead, a fault to nature,
To reason most absurd, whose common theme
125 Is death of fathers, and who still hath cried,
From the first corpse* till he that died today,
"This must be so." We pray you, throw to earth
This unprevailing woe, and think of us
As of a father, for let the world take note,
130 You are the most immediate to our throne,
And with no less nobility of love
Than that which dearest father bears his son,
Do I impart toward you. For your intent
In going back to school in Wittenberg*,
135 It is most retrograde to our desire,
And we beseech you bend you to remain
Herein the cheer and comfort of our eye,
Our chiefest courtier, cousin, and our son.

---

ay [aɪ] (archaic) yes • **nature** life

particular personal

nay no
inky black • **cloak** Umhang
good-mother (ironic) stepmother
customary suits conventional clothes
windy suspiration of forced breath
    exaggerated sighs
dejected behavior depressed expression
visage (literary) face
to denote to characterize
to play to act
passeth surpasses
show mere outward signs
trappings clothing • **woe** great unhappiness

commendable worthy of praise
survivor the person who still lives after a
    family member has died
bound in filial obligation required to act
    accordingly as the son
for some term for a period of time
to do obsequious sorrow to mourn as is
    expected during funeral ceremonies
to persever to persist, to continue
obstinate condolement seemingly
    never-ending mourning
course manner of behaving
impious irreligious • **stubbornness** Sturheit
incorrect to heaven not accepting the will
    of God
unfortified not strengthened against
    misfortune
impatient not prepared to suffer
simple childish • **unschooled** unprepared
vulgar ordinary • **to sense** to our senses
peevish childish, foolish
fie expression of disapproval
fault to nature refusal to accept a natural
    law
to reason to argue • **whose** nature's
pray you ask you urgently
throw to earth bury
unprevailing useless
most immediate closest
nobility of love great love
bears his son feels toward his son
impart grant
retrograde contrary
you bend you you change your mind

chiefest main, most important

lose her prayers not achieve what she prays for

be as ourself behave as if you were king

unforced voluntary

accord agreement

sits smiling to my heart makes me happy

grace honour

jocund health joyful toast

Denmark the King

rouse drinking wine

all bruit again again loudly announce

re-speaking echoing

to thaw to melt • **to resolve** to dissolve

the Everlasting God

canon divine law • **self-slaughter** suicide

stale old, tasteless

uses business

Fie on't To hell with it.

unweeded without the weeds (*Unkraut*) having been removed

grows to seed becomes overgrown with undesirable plants

rank growing without limit

gross dense, thick

in nature as is natural

merely completely

to beteem (archaic) to allow

hang on him be so in love with him

on't about it • **frailty** weakness

ere before

wants discourse of reason does not have the ability to think

unrighteous insincere

flushing flowing tears • **gallèd** irritated

to post to hurry

dexterity haste

incestuous sheets bed where incestuous sex takes place

QUEEN GERTRUDE

140 Let not thy mother lose her prayers, Hamlet.
    I pray thee, stay with us, go not to Wittenberg.

HAMLET

    I shall in all my best obey you, madam.

KING CLAUDIUS

145 Why, 'tis a loving and a fair reply.
    Be as ourself in Denmark. [*to GERTRUDE*] Madam, come.
    This gentle and unforced accord of Hamlet
    Sits smiling to my heart, in grace whereof
    No jocund health that Denmark drinks today
150 But the great cannon to the clouds shall tell
    And the King's rouse the heavens all bruit again,
    Re-speaking earthly thunder. Come away.

Flourish. Exeunt all but HAMLET

HAMLET   ➲ The role(s) of women
155 O, that this too, too solid flesh would melt,   ➲ Questions of morality
    Thaw and resolve itself into a dew,
    Or that the Everlasting had not fixed
    His canon 'gainst self-slaughter. O God, God,
    How weary, stale, flat and unprofitable
160 Seem to me all the uses of this world!
    Fie on't! ah fie, 'tis an unweeded garden,
    That grows to seed, things rank and gross in nature
    Possess it merely. That it should come to this:
    But two months dead – nay, not so much, not two –
165 So excellent a king, that was, to this
    Hyperion* to a satyr*, so loving to my mother
    That he might not beteem the winds of heaven
    Visit her face too roughly. Heaven and earth,
    Must I remember? Why, she would hang on him
170 As if increase of appetite had grown
    By what it fed on. And yet, within a month
    (Let me not think on't – Frailty, thy name is Woman),
    A little month, or ere those shoes were old
    With which she followed my poor father's body,
175 Like Niobe*, all tears. Why she, even she –
    O God, a beast that wants discourse of reason
    Would have mourned longer – married with my uncle,
    My father's brother (but no more like my father
    Than I to Hercules*). Within a month,
180 Ere yet the salt of most unrighteous tears
    Had left the flushing in her gallèd eyes,
    She married. O most wicked speed, to post
    With such dexterity to incestuous sheets*!
    It is not, nor it cannot come to good.
185 But break, my heart, for I must hold my tongue.

Enter HORATIO, MARCELLUS, and BERNARDO

HORATIO
Hail to your lordship.
HAMLET
190 I am glad to see you well.
Horatio, or I do forget myself.*
HORATIO
The same, my lord, and your poor servant ever.
HAMLET
195 Sir, my good friend, I'll change that name with you.
And what make you from Wittenberg, Horatio? Marcellus?
MARCELLUS
My good lord.
HAMLET
200 I am very glad to see you. [*to Bernardo*] Good even, sir.
But what, in faith, make you from Wittenberg?
HORATIO
A truant disposition, good my lord.
HAMLET
205 I would not hear your enemy say so,
Nor shall you do mine ear that violence
To make it truster of your own report
Against yourself. I know you are no truant.
But what is your affair in Elsinore?
210 We'll teach you to drink deep ere you depart.
HORATIO
My lord, I came to see your father's funeral.
HAMLET
I pray thee, do not mock me, fellow student.
215 I think it was to see my mother's wedding.
HORATIO
Indeed, my lord, it followed hard upon.
HAMLET
Thrift, thrift, Horatio. The funeral baked meats
220 Did coldly furnish forth the marriage tables.
Would I had met my dearest foe in heaven
Or ever I had seen that day, Horatio.
My father, methinks I see my father.
HORATIO
225 Where, my lord?
HAMLET
In my mind's eye, Horatio.
HORATIO
I saw him once. A was a goodly king.

I'll change that name with you. You are my friend, not my servant.
what make you from Wittenberg What are you doing away from Wittenberg?

even evening
in faith in truth

truant disposition disposition to run away from school
I would not hear your enemy say so I would not let even your enemy say such a thing without objecting.
Nor shall you […] against yourself. You won't make me believe your statement, which slanders yourself.
truant person who stays away from school without permission
affair business
drink deep drink a lot of alcohol

hard upon very soon afterwards

thrift mere economy, just to save money
baked meats meat pies and pastries
coldly when cold
furnish forth the marriage tables The leftovers were used for the marriage celebration.
dearest foe most hated enemy
methinks I believe

a (archaic) he

take him for all in all If you consider him as a whole.

yesternight (archaic) last night

to season to reduce
admiration wonder, surprise
attent attentive · **to deliver** to report
upon the witness of these gentlemen based on what these gentlemen have seen
marvel miracle

waste stillness

at point completely
cap-à-pie (old French) from head to foot
stately majestically · **thrice** three times
oppressed distressed
fear-suprisèd suddenly affected by fear
truncheon [ˈtrʌntʃən] military staff, baton
distilled reduced
jelly Jelee · **act** effect
dumb speechless
dreadful full of fear · **to impart** to reveal

These hands are not more like. These hands are not more like each other than the ghost was like your father.

did address itself […] would speak start to move as though it was about to speak
even just

230 **HAMLET**
A was a man, take him for all in all,
I shall not look upon his like again.
HORATIO
My lord, I think I saw him yesternight.
235 **HAMLET**
Saw, who?
HORATIO
My lord, the King your father.
HAMLET
240 The King my father?
HORATIO
Season your admiration for awhile
With an attent ear, till I may deliver
Upon the witness of these gentlemen,
245 This marvel to you.
HAMLET
For God's love, let me hear!
HORATIO
Two nights together had these gentlemen,
250 Marcellus and Bernardo, on their watch
In the dead waste and middle of the night,
Been thus encountered. A figure like your father,
Armed at point exactly, cap-à-pie,
Appears before them, and with solemn march
255 Goes slow and stately by them. Thrice he walked
By their oppressed and fear-surprisèd eyes,
Within his truncheon's length whilst they, distilled
Almost to jelly with the act of fear
Stand dumb and speak not to him. This to me
260 In dreadful secrecy impart they did,
And I with them the third night kept the watch,
Where, as they had delivered, both in time,
Form of the thing, each word made true and good,
The apparition comes. I knew your father,
265 These hands are not more like.
HAMLET
But where was this?
MARCELLUS
My lord, upon the platform where we watched.
270 **HAMLET**
Did you not speak to it?
HORATIO
My lord, I did;
But answer made it none: yet once methought
275 It lifted up its head and did address
Itself to motion, like as it would speak;
But even then the morning cock crew loud,

And at the sound it shrunk in haste away,
And vanished from our sight.

HAMLET
280 'Tis very strange.

HORATIO
As I do live, my honoured lord, 'tis true,
And we did think it writ down in our duty
285 To let you know of it.

HAMLET
Indeed, indeed, sirs, but this troubles me.
Hold you the watch tonight?

MARCELLUS and BERNARDO
290 We do, my lord.

HAMLET
Armed, say you?

MARCELLUS and BERNARDO
Armed, my lord.

295 **HAMLET**
From top to toe?

MARCELLUS and BERNARDO
My lord, from head to foot.

HAMLET
300 Then saw you not his face?

HORATIO
O, yes, my lord; he wore his beaver up.

HAMLET
What looked he? Frowningly?

305 **HORATIO**
A countenance more in sorrow than in anger.

HAMLET
Pale or red?

HORATIO
310 Nay, very pale.

HAMLET
And fixed his eyes upon you?

HORATIO
Most constantly.

315 **HAMLET**
I would I had been there.

HORATIO
It would have much amazed you.

HAMLET
320 Very like, very like. Stayed it long?

HORATIO
While one with moderate haste might tell a hundred.

MARCELLUS and BERNARDO
Longer, longer.

---

to shrink, shrunk, shrunk away to withdraw

writ down in our duty required by our loyalty to you

beaver (here) *Visier*

frowningly with a frown

countenance face

would wish

very like very likely

to tell (archaic) to count

grizzled grey

sable silvered black with silver streaks

perchance (archaic) perhaps • **'twill** it will

to warrant to guarantee

to assume take on
to gape to open wide
bid me hold my peace asks me to be quiet
hitherto up to now
concealed not spoken about
tenable in your silence still still kept as a secret
hap (archaic) happen
give it an understanding but no tongue acknowledge it but don't tell anyone about it
requite your loves reward your affectionate behaviour
'twixt (archaic) between

your loves not merely duty

doubt suspect • **foul play** crime
Foul deeds [...] to men's eyes. Crimes will be revealed even though attempts are made to conceal them.

HORATIO
325 Not when I saw't.
HAMLET
His beard was grizzled, no?
HORATIO
330 It was, as I have seen it in his life,
A sable silvered.
HAMLET
I will watch tonight.
Perchance 'twill walk again.
335 **HORATIO**
I warrant it will.
HAMLET
If it assume my noble father's person,
I'll speak to it, though hell itself should gape
340 And bid me hold my peace. I pray you all,
If you have hitherto concealed this sight,
Let it be tenable in your silence still
And whatsoever else shall hap tonight,
Give it an understanding, but no tongue.
345 I will requite your loves. So, fare you well.
Upon the platform, 'twixt eleven and twelve
I'll visit you.
ALL THREE
Our duty to your honour.
350 **HAMLET**
Your loves, as mine to you, farewell.

Exeunt all but HAMLET

My father's spirit in arms! All is not well.
I doubt some foul play. Would the night were come.
355 Till then, sit still, my soul. Foul deeds will rise,
Though all the earth o'erwhelm them, to men's eyes.

Exit

Summary

After talking to his courtiers about his brother's death and his own wedding, the king scolds Hamlet for mourning his father's death too much. When they have left, Hamlet ponders over his mother and uncle's marriage. He is interrupted by Horatio, who discloses that he has seen the ghost of Hamlet's late father. They arrange to meet at night.

Tasks

1. Claudius

a) The summaries of Claudius' address to his courtiers have been muddled up. Link the sentences to the different parts.

Parts	Summaries
ll. 5-8	Claudius sends two messengers to Fortinbras's uncle to inform him about his nephew's demands.
ll. 9-20	Claudius reminds the courtiers of the young Norwegian prince Fortinbras, who presses the Danes to hand back the lands his late father surrendered to old King Hamlet.
ll. 21-29	Despite his grief, Claudius has married Gertrude.
ll. 30-43	Claudius mourns his brother's death.

b) This is the first time we meet the new king. Choose the adjectives from the box that best describe Claudius. Explain your choice by giving evidence from the text.

arrogant – grief-stricken – loyal – dishonest – cheerful – ambiguous – welcoming

c) Analyse the language Claudius uses when he addresses his courtiers and its effect on the audience (ll. 5-43).
d) Contrast Claudius's attitudes towards Laertes and Hamlet.

Claudius's attitude towards Laertes	Claudius's attitude towards Hamlet
• *What wouldst thou beg, Laertes, That shall not be my offer, not thy asking?* (ll. 52-53) → Claudius is willing to grant Laertes anything he asks for. • ...	• ...

2. Hamlet

a) Describe your first impression of Hamlet.

b) Choose the summary (1, 2 or 3) that best captures Hamlet's soliloquy (ll. 155-185).

Info: Soliloquy
Soliloquy is the act of talking to oneself. This can be done silently or aloud. In drama, the term describes the practice by which a character, alone on stage, utters his or her thoughts for the audience to hear. Soliloquies serve as a dramatic device to let the audience know about the character's intentions and state of mind, and also to give additional information about the action of the play. Soliloquies are often used to •   set the scene •   make the audience part of the play •   explicate the character's feelings •   clarify matters •   introduce further information.

1   Hamlet would like to kill his uncle if religion allowed it, as Claudius seems unfit to be king. He is angry with his mother, who seems to have forgotten her first husband too soon.

2   Hamlet would commit suicide if religion allowed him to do so. He mourns his father's death and cannot understand why his mother, who loved her first husband dearly, has remarried so soon.

3   Hamlet compares his state of mind to a neglected garden. Although he mourns his father's death, Hamlet can understand why his mother remarried again.

c) Analyse the language Shakespeare uses to portray Hamlet's state of mind. Use your ideas from task a), too.

SCENE III. A room in Polonius' house.

Enter LAERTES and OPHELIA, his sister

○ **The role(s) of women**

LAERTES
My necessaries are embarked. Farewell.
And sister, as the winds give benefit
5 And convoy is assistant, do not sleep,
But let me hear from you.
OPHELIA
Do you doubt that?
LAERTES
10 For Hamlet and the trifling of his favour,
Hold it a fashion and a toy in blood,
A violet* in the youth of primy nature,
Forward, not permanent, sweet, not lasting,
The perfume and suppliance of a minute,
15 No more.
OPHELIA
No more but so?
LAERTES
Think it no more.
20 For nature crescent does not grow alone
In thews and bulk, but as this temple waxes
The inward service of the mind and soul
Grows wide withal. Perhaps he loves you now,
And now no soil nor cautel doth besmirk
25 The virtue of his will; but you must fear,
His greatness weighed, his will is not his own,
For he himself is subject to his birth.
He may not, as unvalued persons do,
Carve for himself, for on his choice depends
30 The safety and health of this whole state,
And therefore must his choice be circumscribed
Unto the voice and yielding of that body
Whereof he is the head. Then if he says he loves you,
It fits your wisdom so far to believe it
35 As he in his particular act and place
May give his saying deed, which is no further
Than the main voice of Denmark goes withal.
Then weigh what loss your honour may sustain
If with too credent ear you list his songs
40 Or lose your heart, or your chaste treasure open
To his unmastered importunity.
Fear it, Ophelia, fear it, my dear sister,

necessaries are embarked luggage is on board the ship

convoy is assistant means of communication are available

For Hamlet and the trifling of his favour With regard to Hamlet and his playfully showing affection for you
Hold it a fashion consider it a passing fancy
toy in blood superficial show of passion
in the youth of primy nature in the springtime of life
forward premature
suppliance pastime

nature crescent a man's being as it grows
In thews and bulk in muscles and strength
temple body · **waxes** grows
inward service inner life
withal as well
soil impurity · **cautel** deceit
to besmirk to contaminate
the virtue of his will the sincerity of his intentions
his greatness weighed if you consider his high position as the crown prince
unvalued unimportant, ordinary
carve for himself (fig.) choose for himself as if cutting out a piece of roast
circumscribed unto limited by
voice and yielding opinion and consent
that body i.e. the state
fits your wisdom so far You would be wise to believe it only so far.
in his particular act and place in his position as prince
give his saying deed that he actually does what he says
main voice of Denmark goes withal majority opinion of Denmark will go along with
weigh consider · **sustain** have to deal with
credent trustful · **list** listen to
songs expressions of love
chaste treasure treasure of your virginity
unmastered importunity uncontrolled insistence

keep you in the rear of your affection do not allow your affection to be too obvious

chariest most cautious • **maid** young woman

prodigal wasteful • **unmask** i.e. expose

scapes (archaic) escapes

calumnious *verleumderisch*

strokes attacks • **canker** destructive worm

galls damages

infants (here) young plants • **oft** often

buttons be disclosed buds are open

blastments *Pflanzenkrankheiten*

Youth to itself [...] else near. Young people are naturally rebellious, even if there is no cause.

effect meaning • **ungracious** ungodly

puffed swollen with pride

libertine person without morals

the primrose path of dalliance treads walks along the path of pleasure, which is covered with flowers but leads to hell

recks not his own rede disregards his own advice

O fear me not. Don't worry about me.

A double blessing [...] a second leave. How wonderful it is to say good-bye to my father a second time.

for shame Shame on you.

The wind sits in the shoulder of your sail. The wind is blowing from the back into the sails.

you are stayed for you are awaited

precept rule, principle

see thou character make sure you inscribe in your memory

Give thy thoughts [...] his act. Keep your thoughts to yourself, do not act on any thought that has not been properly developed.

familiar friendly

vulgar too friendly with the common people

their adoption tried their friendship tested

grapple them grasp them, hold them

hoops *Reifen, die ein Fass zusammenhalten*

dull thy palm with entertainment make the inside of your hand insensitive because of excessive handshaking

unfledged untried

courage young, lively, superficial man

bear't bear it, carry it through

voice opinion

take each man's censure take note of everyone's opinion

costly expensive • **habit** clothing

not expressed in fancy not just in the latest fashion

rich, not gaudy expensive, but not showy

the apparel proclaims the man clothes show a man's true nature

And keep you in the rear of your affection
Out of the shot and danger of desire.
45 The chariest maid is prodigal enough
If she unmask her beauty to the moon*.
Virtue itself scapes not calumnious strokes.
The canker galls the infants of the spring
Too oft before their buttons be disclosed,
50 And in the morn and liquid dew of youth
Contagious blastments are most imminent.
Be wary then. Best safety lies in fear.
Youth to itself rebels, though none else near.

OPHELIA
55 I shall the effect of this good lesson keep
As watchman to my heart. But, good my brother,
Do not, as some ungracious pastors do
Show me the steep and thorny way to heaven
Whilst like a puffed and reckless libertine
60 Himself the primrose path of dalliance treads
And recks not his own rede.

LAERTES
O, fear me not.
I stay too long. But here my father comes.

65 *Enter POLONIUS*

A double blessing is a double grace.
Occasion smiles upon a second leave.

POLONIUS
Yet here, Laertes? Aboard, aboard, for shame!
70 The wind sits in the shoulder of your sail
And you are stayed for. There*, my blessing with thee,
And these few precepts in thy memory
See thou character. Give thy thoughts no tongue
Nor any unproportioned thought his act.
75 Be thou familiar, but by no means vulgar.
Those friends thou hast, and their adoption tried,
Grapple them to thy soul with hoops of steel,
But do not dull thy palm with entertainment
Of each new-hatched, unfledged courage. Beware
80 Of entrance to a quarrel, but being in,
Bear't that th'opposèd may beware of thee.
Give every man thy ear, but few thy voice.
Take each man's censure, but reserve thy judgment.
Costly thy habit as thy purse can buy,
85 But not expressed in fancy – rich, not gaudy;
For the apparel oft proclaims the man,
And they in France of the best rank and station

Are of all most select and generous chief in that.

Neither a borrower nor a lender be.

90 For loan oft loses both itself and friend

And borrowing dulls the edge of husbandry.

This above all, to thine ownself be true,

And it must follow, as the night the day

Thou canst not then be false to any man.

95 Farewell, my blessing season this in thee.

LAERTES

Most humbly do I take my leave, my lord.

POLONIUS

The time invites you go. Your servants tend.

100 **LAERTES**

Farewell, Ophelia, and remember well

What I have said to you.

OPHELIA

'Tis in my memory locked

105 And you yourself shall keep the key of it.

LAERTES

Farewell.

Exit

POLONIUS

110 What is't, Ophelia, he hath said to you?

OPHELIA

So please you, something touching the Lord Hamlet.

POLONIUS

Marry, well bethought.

115 'Tis told me, he hath very oft of late

Given private time to you, and you yourself

Have of your audience been most free and bounteous.

If it be so, as so 'tis put on me,

And that in way of caution, I must tell you,

120 You do not understand yourself so clearly

As it behoves my daughter and your honour.

What is between you? Give me up the truth.

OPHELIA

He hath, my lord, of late made many tenders

125 Of his affection to me.

POLONIUS

Affection, pooh! you speak like a green girl

Unsifted in such perilous circumstance.

Do you believe his "tenders" as you call them?

130 **OPHELIA**

I do not know, my lord, what I should think.

○ **The role(s) of women**

Are of all [...] chief in that. The upper classes of France are generally known for having a refined taste.

loses both itself and friend money is lost when a loan is not paid back as well as a friendship

dulls the edge makes the edge of a blade less sharp

husbandry being careful with money

my blessing season this in thee May my blessing help to make my advice more lasting and effective.

take my leave say good-bye

The time invites you. Your presence is requested.

tend await you

touching concerning

Marry by the Virgin Mary
well bethought Glad you mentioned that.
of late recently
audience attention • **free** frequent
bounteous generous
'tis put on me has been suggested to me

You do not understand yourself so clearly you don't realize the importance of the position you are in
it behoves it is fitting for
honour reputation
tenders offers

green inexperienced
unsifted inexperienced
perilous dangerous

ta'en these tenders for true pay taken these expressions of affection for the real thing

sterling real, lawful money

tender yourself more dearly offer yourself at a higher price

not to crack the wind of the poor phrase, running it thus not to overuse the word "tender" like an overworked horse that can hardly breathe anymore

tender me a fool (here) make a fool of me

to importune to address

fashion manner

fashion (here) momentary, not lasting affection

go to what nonsense

countenance support

springes traps

woodcock bird thought to be easy to catch

prodigal recklessly

lends the tongue expresses in words

blazes passionate expressions

something scanter somewhat less generous

set your entreatments [...] to parley don't allow yourself to be talked into a surrender of your chastity just because he asks to speak with you

tether rope

than may be given you than he provides

in few in brief

brokers go-betweens • **dye** colour

investments clothing

implorators dishonest lawyers

unholy suits immoral requests

breathing speaking

sanctified made holy

bawd woman who runs a house of prostitution

to beguile betrügen

This is for all to sum up

have you so slander any moment leisure waste any time

Look to't Pay attention to this.

I charge you I order you.

Come your ways. Come along.

POLONIUS
Marry, I'll teach you: think yourself a baby
That you have ta'en these tenders for true pay,
135 Which are not sterling. Tender yourself more dearly;
Or – not to crack the wind of the poor phrase,
Running it thus – you'll tender me a fool.

OPHELIA
My lord, he hath importuned me with love
140 In honourable fashion.

POLONIUS
Ay, "fashion" you may call it. Go to, go to.

OPHELIA
And hath given countenance to his speech, my lord,
145 With almost all the holy vows of heaven.

POLONIUS
Ay, springes to catch woodcocks. I do know,
When the blood burns, how prodigal the soul
Lends the tongue vows. These blazes, daughter,
150 Giving more light than heat, extinct in both
Even in their promise as it is a-making,
You must not take for fire. From this time
Be somewhat scanter of your maiden presence;
Set your entreatments at a higher rate
155 Than a command to parley. For Lord Hamlet,
Believe so much in him, that he is young
And with a larger tether may he walk
Than may be given you. In few, Ophelia,
Do not believe his vows, for they are brokers,
160 Not of that dye which their investments show,
But mere implorators of unholy suits
Breathing like sanctified and pious bawds,
The better to beguile. This is for all;
I would not, in plain terms, from this time forth
165 Have you so slander any moment leisure,
As to give words or talk with the Lord Hamlet.
Look to't, I charge you. Come your ways.

OPHELIA
I shall obey, my lord.

170 *Exeunt*

Summary

Before setting sail for France, Laertes warns his sister Ophelia against Hamlet's approaches. Their father Polonius gives his son some advice for his journey and cautions Ophelia against Hamlet's words, too.

Tasks

1. A brother's advice to his sister

Sum up Laertes' advice to Ophelia in your own words (ll.19-53).

2. A father's advice to his children

a) Check whether Polonius really gives the following pieces of advice to Laertes (ll. 71-94). Correct the ones that are wrong.

	Advice	r/w	Evidence
1	Don't say what you are thinking.		
2	Don't act before you think.		
3	Don't be too friendly to other people.		
4	Hold on to your friends, once you are sure you can trust them.		
5	Make friends quickly.		
6	Don't pick a fight.		
7	When you are in a fight, make your opponent fear you.		
8	Listen and talk to other people.		
9	Listen to other people's opinions but be careful about voicing your own.		
10	Spend as little money on clothes as possible.		
11	Never borrow money but, if necessary, lend it.		
12	Be true to yourself.		

b) Comment on Polonius' advice to his son.
c) List the pieces of advice Polonius gives his daughter (ll. 147-166).
d) Compare the advice Polonius gives his son and daughter.
e) Analyse Polonius' relationship to his two children.
f) Write down some advice parents could give their children today.

SCENE IV. The platform.

Enter HAMLET, HORATIO, and MARCELLUS

shrewdly sharply

HAMLET
The air bites shrewdly; it is very cold.
HORATIO

nipping bitter · **eager** biting
it lacks of twelve It is just before twelve.

5 It is a nipping and an eager air.
HAMLET
What hour now?
HORATIO
I think it lacks of twelve.

it is struck It has struck twelve.

10 **HAMLET**
No, it is struck.
HORATIO
Indeed? I heard it not.
It then draws near the season

season time
held his wont to walk was accustomed
  to walk

15 Wherein the spirit held his wont to walk.

two pieces of ordnance two cannons

*A flourish of trumpets, and two pieces of
ordnance shot off, within**

wake stay up late
takes his rouse drinks very much
keeps wassail gives a drinking party
swaggering upspring reels wild German-
  style dancing
drains [...] down drinks until empty
draughts large amounts
Rhenish wine from the Rhine region of
  Germany
kettledrum *Kesselpauke*
to bray out to make a loud, harsh sound
the triumph of his pledge his success in
  emptying his cup upon making a toast
native here born here
to the manner born accustomed to this
  tradition from birth
**More honoured in the breach than the
  observance.** which is more honourable
  to break than to observe
heavy-headed revel drunkenness
east and west all over Denmark
traduced and taxed of other nations
  defamed and criticized by other nations
clepe call
with swinish phrase calling us pigs
soil ruin · **addition** reputation
performed at height outstanding
pith and marrow essence
attribute reputation
vicious mole of nature natural birthmark
  that tends to vice (*Laster*)

What does this mean, my lord?
HAMLET
20 The King doth wake tonight and takes his rouse,
Keeps wassail and the swaggering upspring reels,
And, as he drains his draughts of Rhenish down
The kettledrum and trumpet thus bray out
The triumph of his pledge.
25 **HORATIO**
Is it a custom?
HAMLET
Ay, marry, is't.
But to my mind, though I am native here
30 And to the manner born, it is a custom
More honoured in the breach than the observance.
This heavy-headed revel east and west
Makes us traduced and taxed of other nations,
They clepe us drunkards, and with swinish phrase
35 Soil our addition; and indeed it takes
From our achievements, though performed at height,
The pith and marrow of our attribute.
So, oft it chances in particular men
That for some vicious mole of nature in them,
40 As, in their birth wherein they are not guilty,
Since nature cannot choose his origin,

By the o'ergrowth of some complexion,
Oft breaking down the pales and forts of reason,
Or by some habit that too much o'erleavens
45 The form of plausive manners, that these men,
Carrying, I say, the stamp of one defect,
Being Nature's livery, or Fortune's star,
His virtues else, be they as pure as grace,
As infinite as man may undergo,
50 Shall in the general censure take corruption
From that particular fault: the dram of evil
Doth all the noble substance of a doubt
To his own scandal.

HORATIO
55 Look, my lord, it comes!

Enter GHOST

HAMLET
Angels and ministers of grace defend us!
Be thou a spirit of health or goblin damned,
60 Bring with thee airs from heaven or blasts from hell,
Be thy intents wicked or charitable,
Thou comest in such a questionable shape
That I will speak to thee. I'll call thee Hamlet,
King, father, royal Dane. O, answer me!
65 Let me not burst in ignorance, but tell
Why thy canonized bones, hearsèd in death,
Have burst their cerements? Why the sepulchre,
Wherein we saw thee quietly interred,
Hath oped his ponderous and marble jaws,
70 To cast thee up again. What may this mean,
That thou, dead corpse, again in complete steel
Revisits thus the glimpses of the moon,
Making night hideous, and we fools of nature
So horridly to shake our disposition
75 With thoughts beyond the reaches of our souls?
Say, why is this? Wherefore? What should we do?

GHOST beckons HAMLET

HORATIO
It beckons you to go away with it,
80 As if it some impartment did desire
To you alone.
MARCELLUS
Look, with what courteous action
It waves you to a more removed ground:
85 But do not go with it.

---

o'ergrowth of some complexion overdevelopment of some natural character trait
pales and forts fences and fortifications
that too much o'erleavens […] manners overdoes a pleasing manner
stamp mark
Being nature's livery or fortune's star being inherited by birth or because of the influence of chance
His virtues else his other qualities
may undergo can support
to take corruption to be damaged
the dram of evil […] his own scandal Even a small amount of s.th. evil can bring down a person and shame him.

ministers of grace agents of God
of health with good intentions
goblin demon
airs gentle breezes
blasts violent, unhealthy winds
intents (archaic) intentions • **wicked** evil
charitable wishing to do good deeds
questionable inviting questions
burst in ignorance despair because of not knowing what you are
canonized properly buried with the required rites
hearsèd in death placed in a coffin
burst shot out of
cerements grave clothes
sepulchre tomb, grave
to inter to bury
oped (archaic) opened
ponderous heavy • **marble** Marmor
cast thee up throw you up
complete steel in full armour
glimpses of the moon the earth lit up by the weak light of the moon
hideous awful to see
fools of nature weak creatures limited by nature
disposition state of being in control of your feelings
to beckon s.o. to give a signal with your hand that s.o. should follow you

impartment communication

courteous *höflich*
more removed ground somewhere further away

what should be the fear What is there to
  fear?
I do […] pin's fee. I do not consider my life
  to be worth as little as a pin.
Being a thing immortal as itself My soul is
  as immortal (*unsterblich*) as the ghost.
to tempt s.o. *jdn. in Versuchung führen*
flood sea
summit top
beetles o'er projects over

toys of desperation desperate thoughts
  that might even lead to suicide
motive cause
fathom 1 fathom = 1.8 m
to roar to make a loud, deep sound

Be ruled Calm down

petty even the most insignificant
hardy strong
the Nemean lion terrible lion killed by
  Hercules in one of his twelve labours
unhand me take your hands off me
lets hinders

waxes becomes increasingly

HORATIO
No, by no means.
HAMLET
It will not speak. Then I will follow it.
90 **HORATIO**
Do not, my lord.
HAMLET
Why, what should be the fear?
I do not set my life in a pin's fee.
95 And for my soul, what can it do to that,
Being a thing immortal as itself?
It waves me forth again. I'll follow it.
HORATIO
What if it tempt you toward the flood, my lord,
100 Or to the dreadful summit of the cliff
That beetles o'er his base into the sea,
And there assume some other horrible form,
Which might deprive your sovereignty of reason
And draw you into madness? Think of it:
105 The very place puts toys of desperation,
Without more motive, into every brain
That looks so many fathoms to the sea
And hears it roar beneath.
HAMLET
110 It waves me still.
[*to* GHOST]
Go on. I'll follow thee.
MARCELLUS
You shall not go, my lord.
115 **HAMLET**
Hold off your hands.
HORATIO
Be ruled; you shall not go.
HAMLET
120 My fate cries out,   ⊙ **Fate vs.**
And makes each petty artery in this body   **free will**
As hardy as the Nemean lion's nerve.
Still am I called. Unhand me, gentlemen.
By heaven, I'll make a ghost of him that lets me!
125 I say, away! Go on! I'll follow thee.

Exeunt GHOST and HAMLET

HORATIO
He waxes desperate with imagination.
MARCELLUS
130 Let's follow. 'Tis not fit thus to obey him.

HORATIO
Have after. To what issue will this come?

MARCELLUS
Something is rotten in the state of Denmark.

135 **HORATIO**
Heaven will direct it.

MARCELLUS
Nay, let's follow him.

Exeunt

have after Let's go after him.
issue outcome

Heaven will direct it. It's in the hands of God.

Summary

Hamlet, Horatio and Marcellus are waiting for the ghost to appear on their midnight watch. When the ghost finally comes, Hamlet follows him despite his friends' objections.

Tasks

1. Hamlet meets the ghost

a) Describe the picture and explain how it relates to the scene you have just read.
b) Add speech bubbles to the characters shown in the picture.

c) Read the info box about ghosts in the Elizabethan age and speculate about the function of the ghost in *Hamlet*.

Info: Ghosts in the Elizabethan age

The Elizabethans were very much interested in the supernatural in general and ghosts in particular. In a country that had moved away from Catholicism towards Protestantism, the belief in ghosts was greatly affected by this religious climate. Thus, there were many different views on the supernatural. According to Catholic belief, souls were sent to Heaven, Hell or Purgatory. To Catholics, ghosts would be the souls of the deceased, who had been sent to Purgatory in order to suffer for their sins before they would be allowed to enter Heaven.

Ghosts were also believed to be the souls of dead people who had died under violent circumstances. The Elizabethan era was a violent time characterized by a lot of executions and premature deaths of all kinds.

Apart from that, ghosts were said to be criminals or people who had committed suicide, revisiting the earth to make compacts with the living. They were often seen as demons sent by the devil to seduce people into committing crimes.

Additionally, ghosts served a social function reminding people to be morally good, attend church services and honour their ancestors' wishes.

---

2. "Something is rotten in the state of Denmark"

Explain what Marcellus means by this statement (l. 134).

SCENE V. Another part of the platform.

Enter GHOST and HAMLET

HAMLET
Where wilt thou lead me? Speak! I'll go no further.
GHOST
5 Mark me.

> **Mark me.** Pay attention to me.

HAMLET
I will.
GHOST
My hour is almost come,
10 When I to sulphurous and tormenting flames
Must render up myself.

> **sulphurous and tormenting flames** the Catholic purgatory (*Fegefeuer*) before going to heaven
> **render up myself** appear

HAMLET
Alas, poor ghost!
GHOST
15 Pity me not, but lend thy serious hearing
To what I shall unfold.

> **lend thy serious hearing** listen attentively
> **to unfold** to narrate

HAMLET
Speak. I am bound to hear.

> **bound** ready

GHOST
20 So art thou to revenge when thou shalt hear.
HAMLET
What?
GHOST
I am thy father's spirit,
25 Doomed for a certain term to walk the night
And for the day confined to fast in fires
Till the foul crimes done in my days of nature
Are burnt and purged away. But that I am forbid
To tell the secrets of my prison-house.
30 I could a tale unfold whose lightest word
Would harrow up thy soul, freeze thy young blood.
Make thy two eyes like stars start from their spheres*,
Thy knotted and combined locks to part
And each particular hair to stand on end
35 Like quills upon the fretful porpentine.
But this eternal blazon must not be
To ears of flesh and blood. List, list, O, list!
If thou didst ever thy dear father love –
HAMLET
40 O God!
GHOST
Revenge his foul and most unnatural murder.

> ↻ **Fate vs. free will**
> ↻ **Questions of morality**

> **doomed** condemned
> **confined** forced to remain somewhere
> **to fast** *Buße tun* · **foul crimes** sins
> **days of nature** while alive
> **to purge away** to completely remove
> **forbid** (archaic) forbidden
> **prison-house** where I must stay while in purgatory
> **lightest** least offensive
> **to harrow up** to uproot, to tear up
> **start from** suddenly leave
> **sphere** socket (*Augenhöhle*)
> **knotted and combined locks** hair that is combed and wound together
> **to part** to separate
> **quill** *Stachel* · **fretful** angry
> **porpentine** porcupine (*Stachelschwein*)
> **eternal blazon** mysteries of what happens after death
> **must not [...] and blood** are not to be heard by the living
> **list** listen

> **unnatural** contrary to the love that close family members usually have for each other

HAMLET
Murder!

45 **GHOST**
Murder most foul, as in the best it is.
But this most foul, strange and unnatural.

HAMLET
Haste me to know it, that I, with wings as swift
50 As meditation or the thoughts of love
May sweep to my revenge.

GHOST
I find thee apt,
And duller shouldst thou be than the fat weed
55 That roots itself in ease on Lethe wharf*,
Wouldst thou not stir in this. Now, Hamlet, hear.
'Tis given out that, sleeping in my orchard,
A serpent stung me. So the whole ear of Denmark
Is by a forgèd process of my death
60 Rankly abused. But know, thou noble youth,
The serpent that did sting thy father's life
Now wears his crown.

HAMLET
O my prophetic soul!
65 My uncle?

GHOST
Ay, that incestuous, that adulterate beast,
With witchcraft of his wit, with traitorous gifts –
O wicked wit and gifts that have the power
70 So to seduce! – won to his shameful lust
The will of my most seeming-virtuous Queen.
O Hamlet, what a falling off was there!
From me, whose love was of that dignity
That it went hand in hand even with the vow
75 I made to her in marriage, and to decline
Upon a wretch whose natural gifts were poor
To those of mine.
But virtue, as it never will be moved,
Though lewdness court it in a shape of heaven,
80 So lust, though to a radiant angel linked,
Will sate itself in a celestial bed
And prey on garbage.
But soft, methinks I scent the morning air,
Brief let me be. Sleeping within my orchard,
85 My custom always of the afternoon,
Upon my secure hour thy uncle stole,
With juice of cursed hebenon in a vial
And in the porches of my ears did pour
The leperous distilment whose effect

as in the best it is even at best

haste me to know it tell me quickly
meditation thought
sweep to my revenge take quick action to execute my revenge
apt responsive
duller even more inactive
shouldst thou be you would have to be
the fat weed [...] Lethe wharf a plant that grows excessively on the banks of the river Lethe
to stir (here) to take action
'Tis given out It has been rumoured
orchard garden
serpent poisonous snake
to sting, stung, stung (here) to bite with poison
the whole ear of Denmark everyone in Denmark
forgèd process false account
rankly abused deceived
O my prophetic soul! Deep down in my soul I knew it.
incestuous practising incest
adulterate corrupt, adulterous (*ehebrecherisch*)
witchcraft using the black magic of a witch
wit intellect
traitorous being like a traitor (*Verräter*)
gifts qualities • **to seduce** *verführen*
lust strong sexual desire
virtuous *tugendhaft*
falling off lowering of moral standards
wretch miserable person
to compared to • **moved** made unstable
lewdness *Lüsternheit*
to court to try to win s.o. over
shape of heaven having the shape of an angel
radiant glowing, shining
to sate itself to greedily satisfy itself though still unsatisfied afterwards
celestial heavenly
to prey on to harm s.o. weak
to scent to smell
upon my secure hour at a moment free from care
stole quietly crept in
hebenon some kind of poisonous plant
vial ['faɪəl] small glass container
porches of my ears openings of my ears

⊃ Fate vs. free will
⊃ The role(s) of women
⊃ Questions of morality

90 Holds such an enmity with blood of man
    That swift as quicksilver it courses through
    The natural gates and alleys of the body
    And with a sudden vigour doth posset
    And curd, like eager droppings into milk,
95 The thin and wholesome blood. So did it mine
    And a most instant tetter barked about
    Most lazar-like*, with vile and loathsome crust
    All my smooth body.
    Thus was I sleeping by a brother's hand
100 Of life, of crown, of queen, at once dispatched,
    Cut off even in the blossoms of my sin,
    Unhouseled, disappointed, unaneled,
    No reckoning made, but sent to my account
    With all my imperfections on my head.
105 O, horrible, O, horrible, most horrible!
    If thou hast nature in thee, bear it not,
    Let not the royal bed of Denmark be
    A couch for luxury and damnèd incest.
    But, howsoever thou pursuest this act,
110 Taint not thy mind, nor let thy soul contrive
    Against thy mother aught. Leave her to heaven
    And to those thorns that in her bosom lodge
    To prick and sting her. Fare thee well at once.
    The glow-worm shows the matin to be near,
115 And 'gins to pale his uneffectual fire:
    Adieu, adieu! Hamlet, remember me.

Exit

HAMLET   ❷ Fate vs.
    O all you host of heaven! O earth! What else?   free will
120 And shall I couple hell? O, fie! Hold, hold, my heart,
    And you, my sinews, grow not instant old,   ❷ Questions
    But bear me stiffly up. Remember thee!   of morality
    Ay, thou poor ghost, while memory holds a seat
    In this distracted globe. Remember thee?
125 Yea, from the table of my memory
    I'll wipe away all trivial fond records,
    All saws of books, all forms, all pressures past
    That youth and observation copied there,
    And thy commandment all alone shall live
130 Within the book and volume of my brain
    Unmixed with baser matter. Yes, by heaven!
    O most pernicious woman!
    O villain, villain, smiling, damnèd villain!
    My tables – meet it is I set it down
135 That one may smile and smile and be a villain.

leperous causing the symptoms of leprosy (*Lepra*)

holds such an enmity with blood of man has such a negative effect on a person's blood

posset (archaic) cause the blood to clot (*gerinnen*)

to curd to cause to thicken

eager droppings into milk sour drops such as wine that curdle (*gerinnen lassen*) milk

wholesome good for your health

tetter *Ausschlag*

barked about covered like the bark (*Rinde*) of a tree

vile and loathsome disgusting and offensive

dispatched taken away, deprived

Cut off [...] my sin killed when I was still full of sin

unhouseled without having taken the sacrament of the Eucharist (*Abendmahl*)

disappointed without a deathbed confession

unaneled *ohne letzte Salbung*

no reckoning made without having considered my good and bad deeds and repented my sins

sent to my account [...] head without having been forgiven for my sins, and in such a state to appear at the Last Judgement

nature natural feelings of a son for his father

to bear to tolerate

howsoever thou [...] act however you proceed to act

to taint to corrupt, spoil

to contrive [...] aught to plan a punishment

lodge are fixed

matin morning

'gins begins • **to pale** to become less bright

uneffectual weak as compared to the fire in purgatory

host of heaven angels

couple hell include hell

fie expression of disgust

sinew muscle • **instant** immediately

stiffly strongly • **distracted** confused

globe head, world, or even the Globe Theatre and its audience

table wax tablet or slate (*Schiefertafel*)

fond foolish

saws wise sayings • **forms** general ideas

pressures past past impressions

commandment command

volume large book • **baser** less valuable

pernicious evil, malicious

villain evil person • **tables** notebooks

meet fitting, appropriate

At least I'm sure it may be so in Denmark.
[*Writing*]

word motto

So, uncle, there you are. Now to my word.
It is 'Adieu, adieu, remember me.'
140 I have sworn't.

MARCELLUS and HORATIO
[Within] My lord, my lord!

MARCELLUS
[Within] Lord Hamlet!

145 **HORATIO**

to secure to safeguard, protect

[Within] Heaven secure him!

HAMLET
So be it!

HORATIO

Illo, ho, ho Where are you?

150 [Within] Illo, ho, ho, my lord!

HAMLET
Illo, ho, ho, boy! Come, bird, come.*

Enter HORATIO and MARCELLUS

MARCELLUS
155 How is't, my noble lord?

HORATIO
What news, my lord?

HAMLET
O, wonderful!

160 **HORATIO**
Good my lord, tell it.

HAMLET

reveal tell others

No, you'll reveal it.

HORATIO
165 Not I, my lord, by heaven.

MARCELLUS
Nor I, my lord.

HAMLET
How say you, then, would heart of man once think it?

be secret keep a secret

170 But you'll be secret?

HORATIO and MARCELLUS
Ay, by heaven, my lord.

HAMLET

to dwell to live
but he's who is not
arrant knave absolute rogue (*Schurke*)

There's never a villain dwelling in all Denmark
175 But he's an arrant knave.

HORATIO
There needs no ghost, my lord, come from the grave
To tell us this.

HAMLET

180 Why, right, you are in the right;
And so without more circumstance at all
I hold it fit that we shake hands and part.
You as your business and desire shall point you –
For every man has business and desire,
185 Such as it is – and for mine own poor part,
Look you, I'll go pray.

HORATIO

These are but wild and whirling words, my lord.

HAMLET

190 I'm sorry they offend you, heartily,
Yes, faith heartily.

HORATIO

There's no offence, my lord.

HAMLET

195 Yes, by Saint Patrick, but there is, Horatio,
And much offence too. Touching this vision here
It is an honest ghost, that let me tell you.
For your desire to know what is between us,
O'ermaster it as you may. And now, good friends,
200 As you are friends, scholars and soldiers,
Give me one poor request.

HORATIO

What is't, my lord? We will.

HAMLET

205 Never make known what you have seen tonight.

HORATIO and MARCELLUS

My lord, we will not.

HAMLET

Nay, but swear't.

210 **HORATIO**

In faith,
My lord, not I.

MARCELLUS

Nor I, my lord, in faith.

215 **HAMLET**

Upon my sword.

MARCELLUS

We have sworn, my lord, already.

HAMLET

220 Indeed, upon my sword, indeed.

GHOST

[*Beneath*] Swear.

HAMLET

Ah, ha, boy! Say'st thou so? Art thou there, truepenny?
225 Come on, you hear this fellow in the cellarage.
Consent to swear.

circumstance further discussion

poor insignificant

whirling crazy

faith indeed sincerely

Saint Patrick the saint who is the keeper of purgatory
vision way of looking at s.th.

o'ermaster it deal with it

in faith sincerely
not I I won't

truepenny honest person
cellarage cellars
to consent to agree

Hic et ubique (Latin) here and everywhere
shift our ground change our position
hither here

Mole *Maulwurf*
i' in
pioneer miner or soldier who digs trenches
remove move away

as a stranger give it welcome just like you
  would welcome a stranger in your house
  without asking any questions according
  to the rules of hospitality, don't question
  the events that have just occurred
your philosophy the rational world that we
  normally believe in
so help you mercy as you hope to obtain
  God's mercy
some'er somewhere • **bear myself** behave
perchance perhaps • **meet** appropriate
to put an antic disposition on to assume
  the behaviour of a madman
encumbered folded
doubtful ambiguous
list wish • **giving out** hints
to note to make it obvious
aught something
So grace [...] help you As you hope for
  grace and mercy to help you when you
  need them most.

perturbèd restless, troubled
commend offer

friending friendship

HORATIO
Propose the oath, my lord.
HAMLET
230 Never to speak of this that you have seen,
Swear by my sword.
GHOST
[*Beneath*] Swear.
HAMLET
235 *Hic et ubique*? Then we'll shift our ground.
Come hither, gentlemen, and lay your hands
Again upon my sword. Swear by my sword
Never to speak of this that you have heard,
GHOST
240 [*Beneath*] Swear by his sword.
HAMLET
Well said, old mole! Canst work i' the earth so fast?
A worthy pioneer! Once more remove, good friends.
HORATIO
245 O day and night, but this is wondrous strange!
HAMLET
And therefore as a stranger give it welcome.
There are more things in heaven and earth, Horatio,   ❍ **Fate vs.**
Than are dreamt of in your philosophy. But come,   **free will**
250 Here, as before, never, so help you mercy,
How strange or odd some'er I bear myself,
As I perchance hereafter shall think meet
To put an antic disposition on,
That you, at such times seeing me, never shall,
255 With arms encumbered thus, or this headshake,
Or by pronouncing of some doubtful phrase,
As "Well, well, we know," or "We could, an if we would,"
Or "If we list to speak," or "There be, an if they might,"
Or such ambiguous giving out, to note
260 That you know aught of me. This not to do,
So grace and mercy at your most need help you, swear.
GHOST
[*Beneath*] Swear.

They swear

265 **HAMLET**
Rest, rest, perturbèd spirit. So, gentlemen,
With all my love I do commend me to you,
And what so poor a man as Hamlet is
May do, to express his love and friending to you,
270 God willing, shall not lack. Let us go in together

And still your fingers on your lips, I pray.
The time is out of joint. O cursèd spite
That ever I was born to set it right!
Nay, come, let's go together*.

275 *Exeunt*

still always
fingers on your lips i.e. as a sign of keeping
a secret
The time is out of joint. The times are in a
state of chaos.
spite misfortune

Summary

The ghost of the old King Hamlet discloses the details of his death to Hamlet and asks him to avenge him. Hamlet does not tell his friends about the details but makes them swear not to tell anybody about his encounter with the ghost.

Tasks

1. The ghost

a) Describe how the king really died and what the ghost asks Hamlet to do.
b) Dramatic reading: While one student is reading out the report of old Hamlet's death, the other students act out the lines.
c) Reconsider your answers from Scene IV, task 1c) and explain the function of the ghost in the play so far. Give examples from the scenes you have read to prove your point.

2. Hamlet's reaction

a) Reread Hamlet's reaction to his father's news (ll. 119-140). Pick an adjective from the box below that best describes Hamlet's reaction.

> overwhelmed – shocked – distressed – traumatized – disgusted – dumbfounded – bewildered – shaken – outraged – agitated – appalled

b) Identify the following stylistic devices in Hamlet's speech and explain their effects on the audience.

> repetition – apostrophe – anaphora – alliteration – rhetorical question

c) Use your findings from tasks a) and b) to write an analysis of Hamlet's speech.

3. Comic relief

Identify elements of comic relief in the scene and explain its function.

Info: Comic relief
Comic relief is the use of comic characters, witty remarks or funny scenes at a serious or tragic moment in a play. It relieves the dramatic tension and adds variety to the scene but can also counterpoint or enhance the seriousness of the situation.

4. Beginning madness?

Hamlet suggests that he might soon behave strangely (ll. 251-253). Speculate on what he might intend to do and why.

Looking back at Act I

1. Function of the scenes

a) Identify the main theme of each scene and explain its function. The first one has been done for you.

Scene	What happens?	What is the function of the scene?
I	*apparition of ghost during night watch*	*setting the scene and atmosphere*
II		
III		
IV		
V		

b) Discuss what the most interesting situation in this act is.

2. A nation in chaos

Marcellus and Hamlet have already hinted at the disorder Denmark is in (Scene IV, l. 134; Scene V, l. 272). What did the Elizabethans think about disordered states? Read the speech bubbles on the next page to find out what the Elizabethans believed in. Explain how this relates to the situation in *Hamlet*.

Most people believed that everything, from the lowest grain of sand to the highest angel, had its proper position in the scheme of things. This concept was called "the great chain of being". When things were in their proper place, harmony was the result; when order was violated, the entire structure was shaken.

Marriage, for example, was often arranged to bring wealth or prestige to the family, with little regard for the feelings of the bride. In fact, women were still relatively powerless under the law.

The Elizabethan world picture

Any break in the chain, such as the killing or abdication of a king or a marriage across social spheres, was believed to result in chaos.

Many Elizabethans were convinced that analogous relations existed in the universe and the political world. They believed, for example, that what the sun is to the heavens, the king is to the state. When something went wrong in the heavens, rulers worried.

The paired concepts of macrocosm and microcosm rests upon the idea that there is a corresponding similarity in pattern, nature, or structure between human beings and the universe. The concept of microcosm/macrocosm views man as a smaller representation of the universe and the universe as an anthropomorphic existence.

As God's chosen representative on Earth, the King was the supreme upholder of order on Earth. If his position was violated, it would destroy the perfect order of the universe and bring strife and chaos to the world. Any act of treason or treachery against the King was considered to be a mortal sin against God.

3. Court news

Choose: You are a reporter writing for the court. Write a court circular, which is the official record of past royal engagements.

OR

Present a one-minute presentation of Act I.

ACT II

SCENE I. A room in POLONIUS' house.

Enter POLONIUS and REYNALDO

POLONIUS
Give him this money and these notes, Reynaldo.
REYNALDO
5 I will, my lord.
POLONIUS
You shall do marvellous wisely, good Reynaldo,
Before you visit him, to make inquire
Of his behavior.
10 **REYNALDO**
My lord, I did intend it.
POLONIUS
Marry, well said very well said. Look you, sir,
Inquire me first what Danskers are in Paris;
15 And how, and who, what means, and where they keep,
What company, at what expense; and finding
By this encompassment and drift of question
That they do know my son, come you more nearer
Than your particular demands will touch it:
20 Take you, as 'twere, some distant knowledge of him,
As thus, "I know his father and his friends,
And in part him." Do you mark this, Reynaldo?
REYNALDO
Ay, very well, my lord.
25 **POLONIUS**
"And in part him, but," you may say, "not well,
But, if 't be he I mean, he's very wild,
Addicted so and so," and there put on him
What forgeries you please. Marry, none so rank
30 As may dishonour him – take heed of that –
But sir, such wanton, wild and usual slips
As are companions noted and most known
To youth and liberty.
REYNALDO
35 As gaming, my lord?
POLONIUS
Ay, or drinking, fencing, swearing,
quarrelling, drabbing – you may go so far.
REYNALDO
40 My lord, that would dishonour him.
POLONIUS
Faith, no, as you may season it in the charge
You must not put another scandal on him,

---

him Laertes • **notes** messages

marvellous very

Marry by the Virgin Mary
inquire me find out for me • **Danskers** Danes
what means what their financial situation is
keep live
by this encompassment [...] question by this roundabout and indirect manner of asking
more nearer closer to the truth
than [...] will touch it than direct questions will achieve
take pretend • **'twere** it were
some distant knowledge of him i.e. you know him only casually
as thus for example by saying
in part slightly
Do you mark this? Have you paid close attention to this?
if 't be he I mean if it is the one I'm thinking of
addicted spending too much time with all sorts of pastimes
put on him attribute to him
forgeries made-up stories • **rank** offensive
take heed of that be careful about that
wanton unrestrained
usual slips common flaws
companions accompanying characteristics
noted notorious
liberty not being restricted by the parents
gaming gambling
fencing *Fechten* • **swearing** *Fluchen*
drabbing whoring

season it in the charge make the accusation seem less serious

open to incontinency inclined to too much sex

breathe his faults so quaintly subtly hint at his faults

taints of liberty faults resulting from freedom of action

fiery easily aroused

a savageness [...] assault a wildness that results in attacks against everyone without thinking first unreclaimed untamed, wild

wherefore why

I would know that. I would like to know.

drift intention

fetch of wit clever strategy

laying these slight sullies on my son spreading around these mild criticisms about my son

As 'twere a thing a little soiled with the working as if it were somewhat dirtied by the influence of society

your party in converse your partner in the conversation

him you would sound he who you would like to sound out (*bei jdm. vorfühlen*)

prominate crimes aforementioned faults

you breathe of you hint of

closes with you in this consequence becomes confidential and speaks as follows

addition form of address or title

a he

by the mass My God!

o'ertook in's rouse overcome with drunkenness while carousing (partying)

falling out quarrelling

videlicet (Latin) That is to say.

brothel house of prostitution

bait *Köder* · **takes** catches · **carp** *Karpfen*

we of [...] reach we who are wise and able to analyse a complex situation

windlasses (here) clever tricks as when hunting an animal

assays of bias indirect attempts

That he is open to incontinency.

45 That's not my meaning – but breathe his faults so quaintly
That they may seem the taints of liberty,
The flash and outbreak of a fiery mind,
A savageness in unreclaimèd blood,
Of general assault.

50 **REYNALDO**
But, my good lord –
POLONIUS
Wherefore should you do this?
REYNALDO
55 Ay, my lord,
I would know that.
POLONIUS
Marry, sir, here's my drift –
And I believe, it is a fetch of wit –
60 You laying these slight sullies on my son,
As 'twere a thing a little soiled with the working,
Mark you, your party in converse, him you would sound,
Having ever seen in the prenominate crimes
The youth you breathe of guilty, be assured
65 He closes with you in this consequence:
"Good sir," or so, or "friend," or "gentleman,"
According to the phrase or the addition
Of man and country.
REYNALDO
70 Very good, my lord.
POLONIUS
And then, sir, does a this, a does –
What was I about to say? By the mass, I was about to say
something. Where did I leave?
75 **REYNALDO**
At "closes in the consequence," at "friend or so," and
"gentleman."
POLONIUS
At "closes in the consequence," ay, marry.
80 He closes thus: "I know the gentleman;
I saw him yesterday, or th' other day,
Or then, or then, with such, or such, and as you say,
There was a gaming, there o'ertook in's rouse;
There falling out at tennis," or perchance,
85 "I saw him enter such a house of sale,"
Videlicet, a brothel, or so forth. See you now
Your bait of falsehood takes this carp of truth,
And thus do we of wisdom and of reach,
With windlasses and with assays of bias,
90 By indirections find directions out:

So by my former lecture and advice,

Shall you my son. You have me, have you not?

REYNALDO

My lord, I have.

95 **POLONIUS**

God be wi' you, fare you well.

REYNALDO

Good my lord!

POLONIUS

100 Observe his inclination in yourself.

REYNALDO

I shall, my lord.

POLONIUS

And let him ply his music.

105 **REYNALDO**

Well, my lord.

POLONIUS

Farewell!

Exit REYNALDO

110 *Enter OPHELIA*

How now, Ophelia! what's the matter?

OPHELIA

O, my lord, my lord, I have been so affrighted.

POLONIUS

115 With what, i' the name of God?

OPHELIA

My lord, as I was sewing in my closet

Lord Hamlet, with his doublet all unbraced,

No hat upon his head, his stockings fouled,

120 Ungartered, and down-gyvèd to his ankle,

Pale as his shirt, his knees knocking each other,

And with a look so piteous in purport

As if he had been loosèd out of hell

To speak of horrors, he comes before me.

125 **POLONIUS**

Mad for thy love?

OPHELIA

My lord, I do not know;

But truly, I do fear it.

130 **POLONIUS**

What said he?

OPHELIA

He took me by the wrist and held me hard,

Then goes he to the length of all his arm;

135 And with his other hand thus o'er his brow,

He falls to such perusal of my face

---

former preceeding · **lecture** instructions

have me have understood me

Observe [...] yourself. Observe his habits closely.

ply work at

⊙ **The roles(s) of women**

affrighted frightened

with what by what · **i'** in

to sew *nähen* · **closet** private room

doublet jacket · **unbraced** not fastened

stocking *Strumpf* · **fouled** unwashed

ungartered without a garter (band) at the knee to hold up the stocking

down-gyvèd fallen down

in purport in expression

loosèd released

hard tightly

brow forehead

falls begins · **perusal** detailed examination

thrice three times	As he would draw it. Long stayed he so.
to wave up and down to move up and down	At last, a little shaking of mine arm
profound deep	And thrice his head thus waving up and down,
to shatter to break into pieces · **bulk** body	140 He raised a sigh so piteous and profound

As he would draw it. Long stayed he so.
At last, a little shaking of mine arm
And thrice his head thus waving up and down,
140 He raised a sigh so piteous and profound
As it did seem to shatter all his bulk
And end his being. That done, he lets me go
And with his head over his shoulder turned,
He seemed to find his way without his eyes
145 For out o' doors he went without their help,
And to the last bended their light on me.

POLONIUS
Come, go with me. I will go seek the King.
This is the very ecstasy of love,
150 Whose violent property fordoes itself
And leads the will to desperate undertakings
As oft as any passion under heaven
That does afflict our natures. I am sorry.
What, have you given him any hard words of late?

155 **OPHELIA**
No, my good lord, but, as you did command,
I did repel his letters and denied
His access to me.

POLONIUS
160 That hath made him mad.
I am sorry that with better heed and judgment
I had not quoted him. I feared he did but trifle,
And meant to wreck thee. But be shrew my jealousy.
By heaven, it is as proper to our age
165 To cast beyond ourselves in our opinions
As it is common for the younger sort
To lack discretion. Come, go we to the King:
This must be known, which being kept close, might move
More grief to hide than hate to utter love.

170 *Exeunt*

Glossary (left margin):

bended their light on me focused their attention on me

ecstasy madness
violent property violent quality
fordoes damages

passion (here) violent state of feeling
to afflict to affect in a harmful way

to repel (here) to refuse to accept

heed attention
quoted observed
did but trifle just played around with you
to wreck thee to ruin you by seduction
be shrew my jealousy shame on me for my suspicions
proper to our age characteristic of our old age
cast beyond [...] opinions go too far in our assumptions
known made known · **close** secret
might move [...] utter love it might lead to more ill feelings to keep this love secret than to make it known

Summary

Polonius sends his servant to Paris to spy on his son's behaviour. Ophelia tells her father that Hamlet visited her and behaved strangely towards her.

Tasks

1. Polonius's questioning technique

a) Choose the guiding principle from below that best captures Polonius's approach to find out about Laertes's behaviour in Paris.
   1 Direct questions will always bring out the truth.
   2 Using dishonouring remarks will produce the most reliable information.
   3 Indirect ways of questioning will provide better information than direct approaches.

b) Describe Polonius's plan for Reynaldo in detail.

Info: Telling name
A **telling name** is a literary device used in works of fiction to hint at certain character traits of a character. Thus, the quality of a character or the character's typical behaviour may be described. The servant's name Reynaldo (Reynard) means "the fox". A fox called Reynard (in German: Reineke Fuchs) is the protagonist of many medieval fables.

c) Pair work: Act out the dialogue between Polonius and Reynaldo (ll.1–109).
d) Pair work: With your partner, discuss how Polonius and Reynaldo come across. Polonius: foolish or serious? Reynaldo: experienced or puzzled? Try out several ways of presenting the two characters. Consider the information from the box above.
e) Comment on Polonius's approach. Bear in mind his position within the royal court.

2. Hamlet's madness

a) Group work: List the details about Hamlet's outer appearance and behaviour as described in this scene. Write them in the box below.

b) Imagine you are Claudius, Gertrude, Polonius and Ophelia: find explanations for Hamlet's appearance and behaviour. Write your explanations in the speech bubbles below.

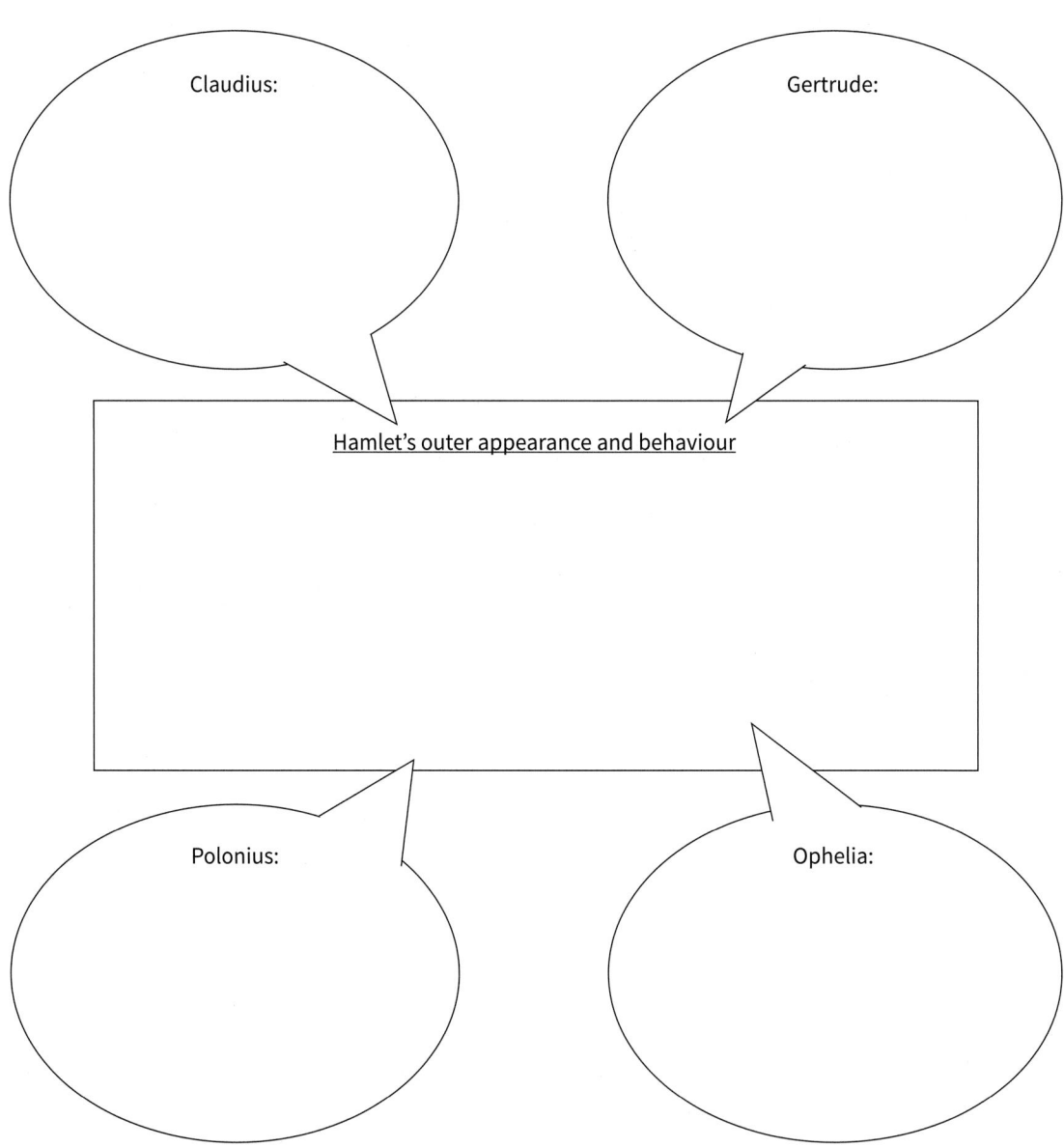

Claudius:

Gertrude:

Hamlet's outer appearance and behaviour

Polonius:

Ophelia:

SCENE II. A room in the castle.

Flourish. Enter KING CLAUDIUS, QUEEN GERTRUDE,
ROSENCRANTZ, GUILDENSTERN, and Attendants

KING CLAUDIUS

Welcome, dear Rosencrantz and Guildenstern.   ● **Questions**
                                                                  of morality
5 Moreover that we much did long to see you   **moreover** in addition to the fact that

The need we have to use you did provoke

Our hasty sending. Something have you heard

Of Hamlet's transformation – so call it,   **so call it** so we may call it

Sith nor the exterior nor the inward man   **sith nor** since neither

10 Resembles that it was. What it should be,

More than his father's death, that thus hath put him   **put him [...] himself** made his behaviour

So much from the understanding of himself,   so confused

I cannot dream of. I entreat you both,   **to entreat s.o.** to earnestly request s.o.

That, being of so young days brought up with him,   **of** from

15 And sith so neighboured to his youth and havior,   **sith** because
                                                                neighboured to [...] havior familiar with
That you vouchsafe your rest here in our court   his youthful behaviour
                                                                vouchsafe your rest agree to remain
Some little time, so by your companies   **companies** the company of each of you

To draw him on to pleasures, and to gather,   **to draw him on** to encourage him to partici-
                                                                   pate in
So much as from occasion you may glean,   **glean** pick up

20 Whether aught, to us unknown, afflicts him thus,   **aught** anything
                                                                to afflict to influence in a bad way
That opened lies within our remedy.   **opened** revealed
                                                                lies within our remedy we can cure or heal
QUEEN GERTRUDE   **adheres** feels close friendship

Good gentlemen, he hath much talked of you;

And sure I am two men there are not living   **gentry** courtesy

25 To whom he more adheres. If it will please you   **expend** spend

To show us so much gentry and good will

As to expend your time with us awhile

For the supply and profit of our hope,

Your visitation shall receive such thanks

30 As fits a king's remembrance.   **as fits [...] remembrance** as the king thinks
                                                                   an appropriate reward for this service
ROSENCRANTZ   would be

Both your majesties

Might by the sovereign power you have of us   **sovereign** royal

Put your dread pleasures more into command   **dread** causing great respect

35 Than to entreaty.   **entreaty** request

GUILDENSTERN

But we both obey,

And here give up ourselves in the full bent   **in the full bent** completely

To lay our service freely at your feet,

40 To be commanded.

KING CLAUDIUS

Thanks, Rosencrantz and gentle Guildenstern.

QUEEN GERTRUDE
Thanks, Guildenstern and gentle Rosencrantz:
45 And I beseech you instantly to visit
My too much changèd son. Go, some of you,
And bring these gentlemen where Hamlet is.
GUILDENSTERN
Heavens make our presence and our practises
50 Pleasant and helpful to him!
QUEEN GERTRUDE
Ay, amen!

Exeunt ROSENCRANTZ, GUILDENSTERN, and some Attendants

Enter POLONIUS

55 **POLONIUS**
Th' ambassadors from Norway, my good lord,
Are joyfully returned.
KING CLAUDIUS
Thou still hast been the father of good news.
60 **POLONIUS**
Have I, my lord? I assure my good liege,
I hold my duty, as I hold my soul,
Both to my God and to my gracious King.
And I do think, or else this brain of mine
65 Hunts not the trail of policy so sure
As it hath used to do, that I have found
The very cause of Hamlet's lunacy.
KING CLAUDIUS
O, speak of that, that do I long to hear.
70 **POLONIUS**
Give first admittance to the ambassadors.
My news shall be the fruit to that great feast.
KING CLAUDIUS
Thyself do grace to them, and bring them in.

75 *Exit POLONIUS*

[*To Queen Gertrude*]
He tells me, my dear Gertrude, he hath found
The head and source of all your son's distemper.
QUEEN GERTRUDE
80 I doubt it is no other but the main –
His father's death, and our o'erhasty marriage.

---

beseech ask earnestly

still always

liege lord
hold consider

hunts [...] so sure is not so good at investigating the problem at hand
lunacy madness

give admittance allow to enter
fruit dessert

Thyself do grace to them Give them a courtly welcome

head origin · **distemper** illness

main major cause

KING CLAUDIUS
Well, we shall sift him.

Re-enter POLONIUS, with VOLTIMAND and CORNELIUS

85 Welcome, my good friends!
Say, Voltimand, what from our brother Norway?
VOLTIMAND
Most fair return of greetings and desires.
Upon our first he sent out to suppress
90 His nephew's levies, which to him appeared
To be a preparation 'gainst the Polack;
But, better looked into, he truly found
It was against your highness; whereat grieved,
That so his sickness, age and impotence
95 Was falsely borne in hand, sends out arrests
On Fortinbras, which he in brief obeys,
Receives rebuke from Norway, and in fine,
Makes vow before his uncle never more
To give the assay of arms against your majesty.
100 Whereon old Norway, overcome with joy,
Gives him three thousand crowns in annual fee,
And his commission to employ those soldiers,
So levied as before, against the Polack,
With an entreaty herein further shown,

105 *Giving a paper*

That it might please you to give quiet pass
Through your dominions for this enterprise,
On such regards of safety and allowance
As therein are set down.
110 **KING CLAUDIUS**
It likes us well,
And at our more considered time we'll read,
Answer, and think upon this business.
Meantime we thank you for your well-took labour:
115 Go to your rest; at night we'll feast together:
Most welcome home.

Exeunt VOLTIMAND and CORNELIUS with Attendants

POLONIUS
This business is well ended.
120 My liege, and madam, to expostulate
What majesty should be, what duty is,
Why day is day, night night, and time is time,
Were nothing but to waste night, day and time.

---

sift him question Polonius carefully

brother Norway fellow king of Norway

fair courteous • **desires** good wishes
upon our first when we raised the matter at the beginning
to suppress to forbid
his nephew's levies his nephew forming an army
'gainst against • **the Polack** king of Poland
whereat whereupon
grieved greatly irritated
impotence helplessness
was falsely borne in hand was tricked with false information
sends out arrests sends out orders to stop this activity
in brief immediately
receives rebuke *wird streng zurechtge-wiesen*
in fine finally
give the assay of arms start a new military campaign
fee income
commission authorization
levied organized
with an entreaty [...] shown. as is shown in this document
quiet pass unopposed passage
dominions areas that make up your kingdom

likes pleases

expostulate make a speech about s.th.

were would be

brevity using few words • **wit** wisdom

tediousness long-windedness

limbs i.e. unnecessary additions

flourishes ornaments

for to define […] but mad? It would be madness to try to define what "mad" is.

let that go Let's forget it.

More matter with less art. More substance and fewer rhetorical tricks!

'tis true 'tis pity of course it is a pity

figure figure of speech

farewell it Let us no longer continue speaking in this way.

for this effect defective comes by cause because this effect, which is Hamlet's mental instability, does have a cause

Thus it remains, and the remainder thus. This the situation and this is the solution.

perpend consider carefully

while she is mine until she is married

Now gather, and surmise. Try to understand and draw your own conclusions.

celestial heavenly

beautified beautiful

ill bad

vile shameful

these this letter

stay wait

I will be faithful. I will be careful to read the letter accurately.

doubt truth suspect truth

ill at these numbers not good at writing these verses

art skill • **to reckon** to count

groan Stöhnen

machine body

is to him belongs to him, i.e. he is still alive

Therefore, since brevity is the soul of wit,
125 And tediousness the limbs and outward flourishes,
I will be brief: your noble son is mad.
Mad call I it, for to define true madness,
What is't but to be nothing else but mad?
But let that go.
130 **QUEEN GERTRUDE**   ↪ The roles(s)
More matter with less art.   of women
POLONIUS
Madam, I swear I use no art at all.
That he is mad, 'tis true, 'tis true 'tis pity;
135 And pity 'tis 'tis true – a foolish figure.
But farewell it, for I will use no art.
Mad let us grant him, then: and now remains
That we find out the cause of this effect,
Or rather say, the cause of this defect,
140 For this effect defective comes by cause:
Thus it remains, and the remainder thus. Perpend.
I have a daughter – have while she is mine –
Who, in her duty and obedience, mark,
Hath given me this. Now gather, and surmise.

145 [*Reads*]
"To the celestial and my soul's idol, the most
beautified Ophelia," –

That's an ill phrase, a vile phrase, "beautified" is
a vile phrase: but you shall hear. Thus:

150 [*Reads*]
"In her excellent white bosom, these, etc."
QUEEN GERTRUDE
Came this from Hamlet to her?
POLONIUS
155 Good madam, stay awhile, I will be faithful.

[*Reads*]
"Doubt thou the stars are fire,
Doubt that the sun doth move,
Doubt truth to be a liar,
160 But never doubt I love.
O dear Ophelia, I am ill at these numbers;
I have not art to reckon my groans, but that
I love thee best, O most best, believe it. Adieu.
Thine evermore most dear lady, whilst
165 this machine is to him, HAMLET."

This, in obedience, hath my daughter shown me,
And more above, hath his solicitings,
As they fell out by time, by means and place,
All given to mine ear.

170 **KING CLAUDIUS**
But how hath she
Received his love?

POLONIUS
What do you think of me?

175 **KING CLAUDIUS**
As of a man faithful and honourable.

POLONIUS
I would fain prove so. But what might you think,
When I had seen this hot love on the wing.
180 As I perceived it – I must tell you that –
Before my daughter told me, what might you,
Or my dear majesty your queen here, think,
If I had played the desk or table-book,
Or given my heart a winking, mute and dumb,
185 Or looked upon this love with idle sight.
What might you think? No, I went round to work,
And my young mistress thus I did bespeak:
"Lord Hamlet is a prince, out of thy star.
This must not be." And then I precepts gave her,
190 That she should lock herself from his resort,
Admit no messengers, receive no tokens.
Which done, she took the fruits of my advice,
And he, repulsèd – a short tale to make –
Fell into a sadness, then into a fast,
195 Thence to a watch, thence into a weakness,
Thence to a lightness, and, by this declension,
Into the madness wherein now he raves,
And all we mourn for.

KING CLAUDIUS
200 [*to Queen Gertrude*] Do you think 'tis this?

QUEEN GERTRUDE
It may be, very like.

POLONIUS
Hath there been such a time – I'd fain know that –
205 That I have positively said "'Tis so",
When it proved otherwise?

KING CLAUDIUS
Not that I know.

POLONIUS
210 [*Pointing to his head and shoulder*]
Take this from this, if this be otherwise
If circumstances lead me, I will find

---

more above in addition
solicitings pleadings
fell out happened

would fain would very much wish to

on the wing (fig.) flying high

played the desk or table-book remained silent and noted the matter privately for myself
given […] winking made my heart close its eyes to what was going on
with idle sight watching without much interest
round at full speed
my young mistress i.e. my daughter
bespeak spoke to
out of thy star not in your sphere
precepts instructions
resort visits
tokens gifts
took the fruits of my advice carried out my advice
repulsèd rejected
fast period of not eating anything
thence (archaic) then
watch sleeplessness
lightness lightheadedness
declension downward course
raves speaks in an uncontrolled manner
mourn for feel sad about

like likely

positively definitely

this from this my head from my shoulder
circumstances relevant evidence

centre centre of the earth

try test

together at a time
lobby entrance hall

loose my daughter to him let loose my
  daughter on him
arras a tapestry hanging in front of a wall
mark observe
thereon because of that
assistant for a state government minister
keep a farm and carters manage a farm
  and have men who drive carts

wretch miserable person

board him address him
presently immediately
Give me leave Excuse me.

God-a-mercy God have mercy on you. Note:
  a polite response to a greeting from a
  social inferior

fishmonger seller of fish, or a person who
  runs a brothel; note: Hamlet is pretending
  to be mad.

honest chaste, having sex only with one's
  spouse

Where truth is hid, though it were hid indeed
Within the centre.

215 **KING CLAUDIUS**
How may we try it further?
POLONIUS
You know, sometimes he walks four hours together
Here in the lobby.
220 **QUEEN GERTRUDE**
So he does indeed.
POLONIUS
At such a time I'll loose my daughter to him.
Be you and I behind an arras then;
225 Mark the encounter: if he love her not
And be not from his reason fallen thereon,
Let me be no assistant for a state,
But keep a farm and carters.
CLAUDIUS
230 We will try it.

Enter HAMLET, reading

QUEEN GERTRUDE
But, look, where sadly the poor wretch comes reading.
POLONIUS
235 Away, I do beseech you, both away.
I'll board him presently. O, give me leave.

Exeunt KING CLAUDIUS, QUEEN GERTRUDE, and Attendants

How does my good Lord Hamlet?
HAMLET
240 Well, God-a-mercy.
POLONIUS
Do you know me, my lord?
HAMLET
Excellent well, you are a fishmonger.
245 **POLONIUS**
Not I, my lord.
HAMLET
Then I would you were so honest a man.
POLONIUS
250 Honest, my lord?
HAMLET
Ay, sir. To be honest as this world goes is to be
one man picked out of ten thousand.
POLONIUS
255 That's very true, my lord.

HAMLET

For if the sun breed maggots in a dead dog, being a
god kissing carrion – Have you a daughter?

POLONIUS

260 I have, my lord.

HAMLET

Let her not walk i' the sun. Conception is a
blessing, but not as your daughter may conceive.
Friend, look to't.

265 **POLONIUS**

[*Aside*] How say you by that? Still harping on my
daughter. Yet he knew me not at first. He said I
was a fishmonger. He is far gone, far gone, and
truly in my youth I suffered much extremity for
270 love, very near this. I'll speak to him again.

What do you read, my lord?

HAMLET

Words, words, words.

POLONIUS

275 What is the matter, my lord?

HAMLET

Between who?

POLONIUS

I mean, the matter that you read, my lord.

280 **HAMLET**

Slanders, sir. For the satirical rogue says here
that old men have grey beards, that their faces are
wrinkled, their eyes purging thick amber and
plum-tree gum and that they have a plentiful lack of
285 wit, together with most weak hams. All which, sir,
though I most powerfully and potently believe, yet
I hold it not honesty to have it thus set down, for
yourself, sir, should be old as I am, if like a crab
you could go backward.

290 **POLONIUS**

[*Aside*] Though this be madness, yet there is method in't.

Will you walk out of the air, my lord?

HAMLET

Into my grave.

295 **POLONIUS**

Indeed, that is out of the air.

[*Aside*]

How pregnant sometimes his replies are. A happiness
that often madness hits on, which reason and sanity
300 could not so prosperously be delivered of. I will

---

breed produce

maggot *Made*; note: It was believed that
the rays of the sun produce maggots in
dead flesh.

god the sun god Apollo

carrion dead and rotting flesh

conception getting pregnant

blessing *Segen*

look to't Take care.

How say you by that? What do you say to
that?

harping on constantly talking about

extremity extreme emotions

matter subject of the book; note: Hamlet
interprets "What is the matter?" to mean
"What is wrong?"

slanders *Verleumdung*

rogue [rəʊg] dishonest person

to purge to cause to flow forth

amber (here) *Harz*

plum-tree gum thick liquid from the bark of
a plum tree

wit intellect

hams (here) *Oberschenkel*

potently mightily

honesty honourable • **set down** printed

method logic

out of the air from the fresh air (which was
thought to be harmful to sick people)
back inside

out of the air with no fresh air

pregnant full of meaning

happiness cleverness of expression

hits on is able to find

be delivered of be given birth to

suddenly immediately · **contrive** find

leave him, and suddenly contrive the means of
meeting between him and my daughter. – My
lord, I will take my leave of you.

HAMLET

withal with

305 You cannot, sir, take from me anything that I will
more willingly part withal – except my life, except
my life, except my life.

POLONIUS

Fare you well, my lord.

310 **HAMLET**

[*Aside*] These tedious old fools.

Enter ROSENCRANTZ and GUILDENSTERN

POLONIUS

You go to seek the Lord Hamlet? There he is.

315 **ROSENCRANTZ**

[*To POLONIUS*] God save you, sir!

Exit POLONIUS

GUILDENSTERN

My honoured lord.

> **Questions
> of morality**

320 **ROSENCRANTZ**

My most dear lord.

HAMLET

My excellent good friends. How dost thou,
Guildenstern? Ah, Rosencrantz! Good lads, how do ye both?

lad boy

325 **ROSENCRANTZ**

As the indifferent children of the earth.

indifferent ordinary

GUILDENSTERN

Happy in that we are not over-happy.
On Fortune's cap we are not the very button.

happy fortunate

Fortune the goddess Fortuna – often por-
trayed with a cap – who is said to control
a person's fate
very button the very top

330 **HAMLET**

Nor the soles of her shoe?

ROSENCRANTZ

Neither, my lord.

HAMLET

335 Then you live about her waist, or in the middle of
her favours*?

GUILDENSTERN

Faith, her privates we.

her privates we her sexual organs

HAMLET

340 In the secret parts of Fortune? O, most true, she
is a strumpet. What's the news?

secret parts sexual organs

strumpet whore; Fortuna is like a whore,
who is completely unreliable

ROSENCRANTZ

None, my lord, but that the world's grown honest.

HAMLET

345 Then is doomsday near. But your news is not true.
Let me question more in particular. What have you,
my good friends, deserved at the hands of Fortune,
that she sends you to prison hither?

> **hither** (archaic) to this place

GUILDENSTERN

350 Prison, my lord?

HAMLET

Denmark's a prison.

ROSENCRANTZ

Then is the world one.

355 **HAMLET**

A goodly one, in which there are many confines,
wards, and dungeons, Denmark being one o' the worst.

> **goodly** spacious · **confine** enclosure
> **ward** cell · **dungeon** [ˈdʌndʒən] *Kerker*

ROSENCRANTZ

We think not so, my lord.

360 **HAMLET**

Why, then, 'tis none to you, for there is nothing
either good or bad but thinking makes it so. To me
it is a prison.

> **'tis** i.e. Denmark is

ROSENCRANTZ

365 Why then, your ambition* makes it one; 'tis too
narrow for your mind.

HAMLET

O God, I could be bounded in a nutshell and count
myself a king of infinite space, were it not that I

> **bounded** confined, forced into
> **count myself** consider myself

370 have bad dreams.

GUILDENSTERN

Which dreams indeed are ambition, for the very
substance of the ambitious is merely the shadow of a dream.

> **airy** having no material substance
> **but** only
> **Then are our beggars [...] beggars'**
>   **shadows.** Beggars are real people of
>   substance and men in powerful positions
>   are mere shadows of beggars because
>   these men are filled with ambition, which
>   in the end is without meaning.

HAMLET

375 A dream itself is but a shadow.

ROSENCRANTZ

Truly, and I hold ambition of so airy and light a
quality that it is but a shadow's shadow.

HAMLET

380 Then are our beggars bodies, and our monarchs and
outstretched heroes the beggars' shadows. Shall we
to the court? For, by my fay, I cannot reason.

> **outstretched** having gone too far, or: shad-
>   ows that are elongated
> **by my fay** by my faith
> **I cannot reason.** I cannot carry out an intel-
>   lectual conversation.

ROSENCRANTZ and GUILDENSTERN

We'll wait upon you.

> **We'll wait upon you.** We'll accompany you.
> **No such matter.** Certainly not.

385 **HAMLET**

No such matter.* I will not sort you with the rest
of my servants, for, to speak to you like an honest
man, I am most dreadfully attended. But, in the
beaten way of friendship, what make you at Elsinore?

> **I will not sort [...] servants.** I won't put
>   you in the same class as my servants.
> **dreadfully attended** poorly attended by
>   my servants
> **in the beaten way of friendship** as old
>   friends

390 **ROSENCRANTZ**

To visit you, my lord, no other occasion.

> **make you** are you doing
> **occasion** reason

Beggar that [...] poor in thanks
as I am a powerless person, my thanks
aren't worth much
too dear a halfpenny not worth much
inclining desire

but to the purpose except an honest
answer
modesties sense of decency
craft ability · **to colour** to disguise

to teach to inform
to conjure to earnestly ask
consonancy harmonious friendship
by what [...] charge you withal by anything a more skillful speaker might urge
in appealing to you
even honest

of you on you
hold not off do not hesitate to tell me

So shall [...] your no feather By my telling
you what the secret is first, you cannot be
accused of telling me and the King and
Queen won't know how I found out.
mirth joy · **forgone** done without
custom of exercises sports
it goes [...] my disposition my mood is so
gloomy
goodly frame large structure
sterile promontory unwirtlicher Landvor-
sprung
canopy Baldachin
firmament sky, heavens
fretted decorated
foul rotten · **pestilent** infected with the pest
congregation gathering · **vapours** gases
piece of work masterpiece
faculty capabilities
express well made
apprehension understanding
paragon supreme example

HAMLET
Beggar that I am, I am even poor in thanks, but I
thank you, and sure, dear friends, my thanks are
395 too dear a halfpenny. Were you not sent for? Is it
your own inclining? Is it a free visitation? Come,
deal justly with me. Come, come. Nay, speak.
GUILDENSTERN
What should we say, my lord?
400 **HAMLET**
Why, anything but to the purpose. You were sent
for, and there is a kind of confession in your looks
which your modesties have not craft enough to colour.
I know the good King and Queen have sent for you.
405 **ROSENCRANTZ**
To what end, my lord?
HAMLET
That you must teach me. But let me conjure you by
the rights of our fellowship, by the consonancy of
410 our youth, by the obligation of our ever-preserved
love, and by what more dear a better proposer could
charge you withal, be even and direct with me
whether you were sent for or no.
ROSENCRANTZ
415 [*Aside to GUILDENSTERN*] What say you?
HAMLET
[*Aside*] Nay then, I have an eye of you. – If you
love me, hold not off.
GUILDENSTERN
420 My lord, we were sent for.
HAMLET
I will tell you why. So shall my anticipation
prevent your discovery and your secrecy to the King
and Queen moult no feather. I have of late – but
425 wherefore I know not – lost all my mirth, forgone all
custom of exercises and indeed it goes so heavily
with my disposition that this goodly frame, the
earth, seems to me a sterile promontory. This most
excellent canopy, the air, look you, this brave
430 o'erhanging firmament, this majestical roof fretted
with golden fire, why, it appears no other thing to
me than a foul and pestilent congregation of vapours.
What a piece of work is a man. How noble in reason,
how infinite in faculty, in form and moving how
435 express and admirable, in action how like an angel,
in apprehension how like a god – the beauty of the
world, the paragon of animals. And yet, to me
what is this quintessence of dust*? Man delights not

me – no, nor woman neither, though by your smiling
440 you seem to say so.

ROSENCRANTZ

My lord, there was no such stuff in my thoughts.

HAMLET

Why did you laugh then, when I said "Man delights not me?"

445 **ROSENCRANTZ**

To think, my lord, if you delight not in man, what
lenten entertainment the players shall receive from
you. We coted them on the way, and hither are they
coming, to offer you service.

450 **HAMLET**

He that plays the King shall be welcome; his majesty
shall have tribute of me. The Adventurous Knight*
shall use his foil and target, the Lover shall not
sigh gratis, the Humorous Man shall end his part
455 in peace, the Clown shall make those laugh whose
lungs are tickled o' the sear, and the Lady shall
say her mind freely, or the blank verse shall halt
for't. What players are they?

ROSENCRANTZ

460 Even those you were wont to take delight in, the
tragedians of the city.

HAMLET

How chances it they travel? Their residence, both
in reputation and profit was better both ways.

465 **ROSENCRANTZ**

I think their inhibition comes by the means of the
late innovation*.

HAMLET

Do they hold the same estimation they did when I was
470 in the city? Are they so followed?

ROSENCRANTZ

No, indeed, are they not.

HAMLET

How comes it? Do they grow rusty?

475 **ROSENCRANTZ**

Nay, their endeavour keeps in the wonted pace. But
there is, sir, an aerie of children, little eyases*,
that cry out on the top of question and are most
tyrannically clapped for't. These are now the
480 fashion, and so berattle the common stages – so they
call them – that many wearing rapiers are afraid of
goosequills and dare scarce come thither.

HAMLET

What, are they children? Who maintains 'em? How are
485 they escoted? Will they pursue the quality no
longer than they can sing? Will they not say

lenten entertainment very weak welcome; weak as in the time of Lent (*Fastenzeit*) when there is little or nothing to eat and little activity

players actors

coted caught up with and passed

tribute of me payment or praise from me

adventurous seeking adventures

foil and target sword and shield

sigh gratis sigh without some kind of reward

humorous eccentric

are tickled o' the sear easily provoked like the sear of a gun that activates (tickles) the hammer so that only slight pressure is needed for the trigger to shoot it

freely without using a script

the blank verse shall halt for't the use of blank verse will cause interruptions

wont accustomed • **tragedians** actors

How chances it why

they travel they are on tour

their residence usual residence in the city

inhibition inability to perform in the city

the late innovation the fashion of using boys as actors

estimation reputation

Are they so followed? Do they still attract a large audience?

aerie of children nestful of children

little eyases young hawks

cry out on the top of question yell at the top of their voices

tyrannically wildly

to berattle *heruntermachen*

common stages public theatres such as The Globe

many wearing […] come thither. Many fashionable gentlemen are afraid of the poet's satirical pen in the plays written for the boys' companies that belittle the public theatres, so they avoid the public theatre.

maintains provides for

escoted supported financially

Will they pursue […] can sing? Will they continue their acting profession only until their voices break?

grow themselves develop into
if their means are no better if there is no other source of income

to do turmoil
nation people in general
to tarre to provoke, to incite
no money bid for argument unless the poet and the player went to cuffs in the question no money was to be made if a play didn't make use of the fight between the dramatists of the boys' theatre and the public theatres for the purpose of entertainment
throwing about of brains great battle of wits
carry it away are victorious

mows grimaces

ducat gold coin
picture in little miniature painting
'Sblood by God's blood
more than natural abnormal
philosophy science

your hands Give me your hands.
the appurtenance of welcome the proper accompaniment of welcome
fashion and ceremony conventional ceremony
comply with you in this garb show the proper courtesy in this manner, i.e. by shaking hands
extent display of cordiality
entertainment warm welcome
deceived mistaken

mad north-north-west mad only at certain times
hawk *Habicht*

---

afterwards, if they should grow themselves to common players – as it is most like, if their means are no better – their writers do them wrong, to make them
490 exclaim against their own succession?
ROSENCRANTZ
Faith, there has been much to do on both sides, and the nation holds it no sin to tarre them to controversy. There was for a while no money bid
495 for argument unless the poet and the player went to cuffs in the question.
HAMLET
Is't possible?
GUILDENSTERN
500 O, there has been much throwing about of brains.
HAMLET
Do the boys carry it away?
ROSENCRANTZ
Ay, that they do, my lord, Hercules and his load too*.
505 **HAMLET**
It is not very strange; for mine uncle is King of Denmark and those that would make mows at him while my father lived, give twenty, forty, fifty, an hundred ducats apiece for his picture in little.
510 'Sblood, there is something in this more than natural, if philosophy could find it out.

Flourish of trumpets within

GUILDENSTERN
There are the players.
515 **HAMLET**
Gentlemen, you are welcome to Elsinore. Your hands, come, then. The appurtenance of welcome is fashion and ceremony. Let me comply with you in this garb, lest my extent to the players, which I tell you
520 must show fairly outward – should more appear like entertainment than yours.
[*He shakes hands with them*]
You are welcome. But my uncle-father and aunt-mother are deceived.
525 **GUILDENSTERN**
In what, my dear lord?
HAMLET
I am but mad north-north-west. When the wind is southerly I know a hawk from a handsaw.

530 *Enter POLONIUS*

POLONIUS
Well be with you, gentlemen.

HAMLET
[*Aside*] Hark you, Guildenstern, and you too – At each ear a
535 hearer. That great baby you see there is not yet out of his
swaddling-clouts.

hark listen
at each ear a hearer Each of you should stand close to me on each side.
swaddling-clouts strips of cloth to tightly cover a baby

ROSENCRANTZ
[*Softly*] Happily he's the second time come to them, for they say
an old man is twice a child.

happily perhaps

540 **HAMLET**
[*Softly*] I will prophesy he comes to tell me of the players.
Mark it. – [*aloud*] You say right, sir, o' Monday morning, 'twas
so indeed.

Mark it Observe what comes.
You say right […] so indeed. Hamlet is pretending to be in the middle of a conversation about a recent event.

POLONIUS
545 My lord, I have news to tell you.

HAMLET
My lord, I have news to tell you.
When Roscius* was an actor in Rome –

POLONIUS
550 The actors are come hither, my lord.

HAMLET
Buz, buz …

buz, buz blah, blah

POLONIUS
Upon mine honour.

Upon mine honour. Yes, indeed.

555 **HAMLET**
Then came each actor on his ass.

ass *Esel*

POLONIUS
The best actors in the world, either for tragedy,
comedy, history, pastoral, pastoral-comical,
560 historical-pastoral, tragical-historical, tragical-
comical-historical-pastoral, scene individable, or
poem unlimited. Seneca* cannot be too heavy, nor
Plautus* too light. For the law of writ and the
liberty, these are the only men.

tragedy, comedy, history […] tragical-comical-historical-pastoral Shakespeare is making fun of the dramatic theorists of his times in the way they classify drama and their insistence on unity of place and time. Shakespeare himself often wrote plays that did not adhere to the unities.
scene individable play that observes unity of place
poem unlimited play that does not observe unity of place and time
heavy serious
for the law of writ and the liberty with regard to plays that strictly follow the classical rules and plays like Shakespeare's that have much more freedom.
these are the only men these actors

565 **HAMLET**
O Jephthah*, judge of Israel, what a treasure hadst thou?

POLONIUS
What a treasure had he, my lord?

HAMLET
570 Why,
"One fair daughter and no more,
The which he lovèd passing well."*

POLONIUS
[*Aside*] Still on my daughter.

575 **HAMLET**
Am I not i' the right, old Jephthah?

passing extremely

that follows not That is not the next line.

by lot by chance · **wot** knows

as most like it was as most probable
the first row of the pious chanson the first stanza of the religious ballad
abridgement sudden interruption

valenced (fig.) has a beard
to beard me (here) to oppose me
By'r Lady By Our Lady – "Our Lady" means the Virgin Mary.
nearer to heaven has grown taller
altitude height
chopine shoe with a high platform sole
uncurrent gold a gold coin that has lost its full value
cracked within the ring a coin with a crack (*Riss*) in it – meant to indicate that a boy's voice has changed because of puberty.
We'll e'en to't We shall proceed at once.
like French falconers (*Falkner*) like bad falconers
straight straightaway
not above once only once
not the million not the masses
caviary (caviar) **to the general** (fig.) too exotic for the general public
received it perceived it
cried in the top of mine were of more authority than mine
digested arranged · **set down** presented
modesty moderation · **cunning** skill
sallets spicy or salty salads
savoury salty and spicy "obscene"
no matter [...] phrase nothing in the manner of expression
to indict to accuse
affectation artificiality
wholesome simple and clear
much more handsome than fine elegant but not showy

POLONIUS
If you call me Jephthah, my lord, I have a daughter that I love passing well.

580 **HAMLET**
Nay, that follows not.

POLONIUS
What follows, then, my lord?

HAMLET
585 Why
"As by lot, God wot,"
and then, you know
"It came to pass, as most like it was," –
the first row of the pious chanson will show you
590 more, for look, where my abridgement comes.

Enter four or five Players

You are welcome, masters, welcome, all. I am glad to see thee well. Welcome, good friends. O my old friend, thy face is valenced since I saw thee last.
595 Comest thou to beard me in Denmark? What, my young lady and mistress*. By'r Lady*, your ladyship is nearer to heaven than when I saw you last by the altitude of a chopine. Pray God your voice, like a piece of uncurrent gold, be not cracked within the
600 ring. Masters, you are all welcome. We'll e'en to't like French falconers* fly at anything we see. We'll have a speech straight. Come, give us a taste of your quality. Come, a passionate speech.

FIRST PLAYER
605 What speech, my good lord?

HAMLET
I heard thee speak me a speech once, but it was never acted, or, if it was, not above once, for the play, I remember, pleased not the million, 'twas
610 caviary to the general*. But it was, as I received it, and others, whose judgments in such matters cried in the top of mine, an excellent play, well digested in the scenes, set down with as much modesty as cunning. I remember one said there
615 were no sallets in the lines to make the matter savoury nor no matter in the phrase that might indict the author of affectation, but called it an honest method, as wholesome as sweet, and by very much more handsome than fine. One speech in it I
620 chiefly loved: 'twas Aeneas' tale to Dido*, and

thereabout of it especially, where he speaks of
Priam's slaughter. If it live in your memory, begin
at this line – let me see, let me see.
"The rugged Pyrrhus, like the Hyrcanian beast* ..."

625 'Tis not so, it begins with Pyrrhus –
"The rugged Pyrrhus, he whose sable arms,
Black as his purpose, did the night resemble
When he lay couchèd in the ominous horse,
Hath now this dread and black complexion smeared

630 With heraldry more dismal, head to foot
Now is he total gules, horridly tricked
With blood of fathers, mothers, daughters, sons,
Baked and impasted with the parching streets,
That lend a tyrannous and damnèd light

635 To their lord's murder. Roasted in wrath and fire,
And thus o'ersizèd with coagulate gore,
With eyes like carbuncles, the hellish Pyrrhus
Old grandsire* Priam seeks."
So, proceed you.

640 **POLONIUS**
'Fore God, my lord, well spoken, with good accent and
good discretion.

FIRST PLAYER
"Anon he finds him,

645 Striking too short at Greeks. His antique sword,
Rebellious to his arm, lies where it falls,
Repugnant to command. Unequal matched,
Pyrrhus at Priam drives, in rage strikes wide,
But with the whiff and wind of his fell sword

650 The unnervèd father falls. Then senseless Ilium*,
Seeming to feel this blow, with flaming top
Stoops to his base and with a hideous crash
Takes prisoner Pyrrhus' ear. For lo, his sword,
Which was declining on the milky head

655 Of reverend Priam, seemed i' the air to stick.
So as a painted tyrant, Pyrrhus stood,
And like a neutral to his will and matter,
Did nothing.
But as we often see, against some storm,

660 A silence in the heavens, the rack stand still,
The bold winds speechless and the orb below
As hush as death, anon the dreadful thunder
Doth rend the region so, after Pyrrhus' pause,
A rousèd vengeance sets him new a-work;

665 And never did the Cyclops'* hammers fall
On Mars'* armour forged for proof eterne
With less remorse than Pyrrhus' bleeding sword
Now falls on Priam.

rugged savage • **beast** *Bestie*
sable arms black armour
couchèd hidden
the ominous horse the giant wooden horse
(in which some Greek soldiers were hidden) that the Trojans allowed into their
walled city
complexion appearance
heraldry more dismal The blood smeared
on his face looked like the heraldic markings on his armour.
total gules totally red with blood
tricked decorated
baked and impasted with the parching streets The blood on Pyrrhus from
all the Trojans he killed was congealed
(*geronnen*) by the heat arising from the
burning city.
damnèd the light is like hell fire
their lord's murder the murder of Priam
o'ersizèd (oversized) (here) covered
coagulate gore congealed blood
carbuncle large, red precious stone that
glows in the dark
grandsire *Vorfahr*
'fore before
anon soon afterwards
striking too short not able to use his sword
effectively because of old age
repugnant to command Priam was unable
to pick the sword up and use it.
unequal matched not equally strong
drives points his sword
wide far from where the sword should strike
with the whiff and wind the swift movement of the sword cutting through the air
fell cruel
unnervèd without strength
stoops falls
his base its foundation
takes prisoner Pyrrhus' ear the sound
shocks him • **lo** (archaic) look
declining coming down
milky white-haired
reverend worthy of deep respect • **i'** in
like a neutral [...] matter unable to
complete his task in spite of his duty and
desire
against before • **rack** clouds
bold otherwise strong or aggressive
orb globe • **hush** quiet
rend the region tear through the sky
to rouse *erwecken*
for proof eterne remain indestructible for
all eternity
remorse pity • **bleeding** dripping with blood

out Damn you!

synod assembly, council

spokes *Speichen*

fellies round segments of the outside of a wheel connected and supported by the spokes

bowl roll · **nave** centre of the wheel

hill of heaven Mount Olympus, home of the gods

fiends devils

It shall [...] your beard. It needs to be shortened, just like your beard.

prithee (archaic) please · **say on** continue

jig lively and comical dancing and singing

tale of bawdry a dirty story

come to begin with

mobled *verhüllt*

threatening threatening to put out

bisson rheum blinding tears · **clout** cloth

late until recently

about her lank and all o'er-teemèd loins Her loins were shrunken and worn out from bearing so many children.

with tongue in venom steeped with extremely bitter words

make malicious sport act with great cruelty

mincing cutting to pieces

limbs *Gliedmaßen*

clamour loud outcry

things mortal the life of people on earth

move them cause them to feel emotions

milch wet with pity

he the First Player

turned his colour become pale

in's in his

well bestowed provided with comfortable accommodation

well used well treated

the abstract [...] of the time They summarize and record the events of the time.

you were better have it would be better for you to have

their ill report their telling me they were badly treated

according to their desert as they deserve

God's bodykins by God's dear body

after according to

Out, out, thou strumpet Fortune! All you gods,

670   In general synod take away her power,

Break all the spokes and fellies from her wheel*

And bowl the round nave down the hill of heaven

As low as to the fiends."

POLONIUS

675   This is too long.

HAMLET

It shall to the barber's with your beard.

[*To the FIRST PLAYER*] Prithee, say on. He's for a jig or a tale of bawdry, or he sleeps. Say on, come to Hecuba*.

680   **FIRST PLAYER**

"But who, O who had seen the mobled queen –"

HAMLET

"The mobled queen?"

POLONIUS

685   That's good; "mobled queen" is good.

FIRST PLAYER

"Run barefoot up and down, threatening the flames

With bisson rheum; a clout upon that head

Where late the diadem stood, and for a robe,

690   About her lank and all o'er-teemèd loins,

A blanket, in the alarm of fear caught up.

Who this had seen, with tongue in venom steeped,

'Gainst Fortune's state would treason have pronounced.

But if the gods themselves did see her then

695   When she saw Pyrrhus make malicious sport

In mincing with his sword her husband's limbs,

The instant burst of clamour that she made,

Unless things mortal move them not at all,

Would have made milch the burning eyes of heaven,

700   And passion in the gods."

POLONIUS

Look, whether he has not turned his colour and has tears in's eyes. [*To the FIRST PLAYER*] Pray you no more.

HAMLET

705   [*To the FIRST PLAYER*] 'Tis well. I'll have thee speak out the rest soon. [*To POLONIUS*] Good my lord, will you see the players well bestowed? Do you hear, let them be well used, for they are the abstract and brief chronicles of the time. After your death you were better have a bad

710   epitaph than their ill report while you live.

POLONIUS

My lord, I will use them according to their desert.

HAMLET

God's bodykins, man, much better. Use every man

715   after his desert, and who should 'scape whipping*?

Use them after your own honour and dignity. The less

○ **Fate vs. free will**

they deserve, the more merit is in your bounty.
Take them in.

POLONIUS

720 Come, sirs.

HAMLET

Follow him, friends. We'll hear a play tomorrow.

Exit POLONIUS with all the PLAYERS but the FIRST

Dost thou hear me, old friend? Can you play *The Murder of*
725 *Gonzago**?

FIRST PLAYER

Ay, my lord.

HAMLET

We'll ha't tomorrow night. You could, for a need,
730 study a speech of some dozen or sixteen lines, which
I would set down and insert in't, could you not?

FIRST PLAYER

Ay, my lord.

HAMLET

735 Very well. Follow that lord, and look you mock him
not.

Exeunt PLAYERS

My good friends, I'll leave you till night. You are welcome to
Elsinore.

740 **ROSENCRANTZ**

Good my lord!

HAMLET

Ay, so, God be wi' ye;

Exeunt ROSENCRANTZ and GUILDENSTERN

745 Now I am alone.
O, what a rogue and peasant slave am I!
Is it not monstrous that this player here,
But in a fiction, in a dream of passion,
Could force his soul so to his own conceit
750 That from her working all his visage wann'd,
Tears in his eyes, distraction in his aspect,
A broken voice, and his whole function suiting
With forms to his conceit? And all for nothing.
For Hecuba!
755 What's Hecuba to him, or he to Hecuba,
That he should weep for her? What would he do,
Had he the motive and the cue for passion

---

the more merit is in your bounty the more worthy is your generosity

ha't have it • **for a need** if necessary

study learn by heart

set down write down • **in't** in it

wi' ye with you

rogue dishonest person
peasant slave complete idiot
but only
dream of passion violent emotional outburst over an imaginary scene
force his soul so to his own conceit force his whole body and innermost feelings to fit the role
from her working as a result of the action of his soul
visage whole face • **wann'd** turned pale
distraction in his aspect intense feeling in his appearance
his whole [...] conceit his acting matches his imagination and inner thoughts
all for nothing The actor is expressing anguish about s.o. else's tragedy.
cue sign, signal

⊙ **Questions of morality**

to cleave to penetrate

general ear the ears of people in general

appal the free horrify the innocent

confound the ignorant confuse those who know nothing of such crimes

faculties of eyes and ears the sense of sight and hearing

dull slow and stupid

muddy-mettled slow, simple

to peak to spend your time doing nothing and feeling sorry for yourself

John-a-dreams dreamy man

unpregnant of my cause not able to turn my words into actions

pate top of the head, skull

plucks off pulls off

tweaks twists and pulls

Gives me the lie i' (in) the throat Calls me an outright liar

'swounds by God's wounds

I should take it. I should accept the insult.

pigeon-livered and lack gall weak and cowardly

to make oppression bitter to make the injustice I perceive strong enough to take action

ere before

region kites birds of prey *(Raubvögel)*

this slave's Claudius'

offal inner organs of a dead animal

lecherous lustful

kindless lacking natural feeling

ass (fig.) idiot • **brave** (ironic) admirable

must like a whore unpack my heart with words like a disreputable woman, he is too weak to convert strong passions and words into actions

a-cursing *fluchend* • **drab** whore

scullion male prostitute

Fie upon't (upon it)! Foh! Damn it!

about into action

cunning of the scene skillful, realistic presentation

presently immediately

malefactions crimes

With most miraculous organ with a super-natural voice

tent him to the quick probe him until he feels the pain

to blench to flinch, to start *(zucken)*

to assume to take on

out of exploiting, making use of

abuses deceives

to damn me perhaps to kill an innocent man

more relative more convincing, more conclusive

That I have? He would drown the stage with tears
And cleave the general ear with horrid speech,
760 Make mad the guilty and appal the free,
Confound the ignorant, and amaze indeed
The very faculties of eyes and ears. Yet I,
A dull and muddy-mettled rascal, peak,
Like John-a-dreams, unpregnant of my cause,
765 And can say nothing. No, not for a king,
Upon whose property and most dear life
A damned defeat was made. Am I a coward?
Who calls me villain? Breaks my pate across?
Plucks off my beard, and blows it in my face?
770 Tweaks me by the nose? Gives me the lie i' the throat,
As deep as to the lungs? Who does me this?
Ha, 'swounds, I should take it. For it cannot be
But I am pigeon-livered and lack gall*
To make oppression bitter, or ere this
775 I should have fatted all the region kites
With this slave's offal. Bloody, bawdy villain!
Remorseless, treacherous, lecherous, kindless villain!
O, vengeance!
Why, what an ass am I! This is most brave,
780 That I, the son of a dear father murderèd,
Prompted to my revenge by heaven and hell,
Must, like a whore, unpack my heart with words,
And fall a-cursing, like a very drab,
A scullion! Fie upon't! Foh!
785 About, my brain! I have heard
That guilty creatures sitting at a play
Have by the very cunning of the scene
Been struck so to the soul that presently
They have proclaimed their malefactions*;
790 For murder, though it have no tongue, will speak
With most miraculous organ. I'll have these players
Play something like the murder of my father
Before mine uncle. I'll observe his looks,
I'll tent him to the quick. If he but blench,
795 I know my course. The spirit that I have seen
May be the devil, and the devil hath power
To assume a pleasing shape. Yea, and perhaps
Out of my weakness and my melancholy,
As he is very potent with such spirits*,
800 Abuses me to damn me. I'll have grounds
More relative than this. The play's the thing
Wherein I'll catch the conscience of the King.

Exit

Summary

Claudius has sent for Rosencrantz and Guildenstern, two friends of Hamlet's, to make them spy on Hamlet.
In the meantime, the two messengers have returned from Norway with news about young Fortinbras and his uncle.
Polonius informs the king and queen about his suspicion that the reason for Hamlet's behaviour lies in his love sickness felt for Ophelia. To prove this, Polonius wants to set Ophelia on Hamlet to find out if he really is in love with her.
Hamlet meets his friends from university and makes them confess the true reason for their visit.
Finally, a troupe of actors arrive at Elsinore. Hamlet asks their leader to stage a play the following night that might evoke guilt in Claudius.

Tasks

1. A never-ending scene

a) Structure the scene and sum up the different parts in one sentence. The first one has been done for you.

Lines	Summary
ll.1–56	Claudius and Gertrude welcome Hamlet's friends Rosencrantz and Guildenstern.

2. Hamlet and Polonius

a) Hamlet enters the stage with a book, which scholars have been unable to identify. If you directed this play, what book would Hamlet be reading? Explain your choice.
b) Outline the conversation between Hamlet and Polonius.
c) Explain Polonius's statement, "Though this be madness, yet there is method in't." (l. 295).
d) Hamlet calls Polonius "old Jephthah" (l. 576). Look up the story of Jephthah and explain the reference.

3. Rosencrantz and Guildenstern

a) Describe how the two friends come across in this scene. Choose adjectives from the box to explain your impression. Give evidence from the scene to prove your point.

> insincere – submissive - trustworthy – warm-hearted – intimate – servile – funny – obedient – dishonest – frightened

b) Explain what Hamlet means when he says, "I am but mad north-north-west. When the wind is southerly, I know a hawk from a handsaw." (ll. 528 f.).

c) Analyse Hamlet's attitude towards his friends.

d) Read the info box on dramatic irony. Identify the passages within the part of the scene from lines 322 to 533 in which dramatic irony is displayed. Devise what Hamlet might be thinking at these moments and write it down as thought bubbles.

> **Info: Dramatic irony**
>
> This literary device is used when the audience knows more than the characters in the play.

e) Group work (4): Dramatic Reading: In your groups decide which speech bubbles fit best. In your group read out the dialogue. A fourth student echoes Hamlet's innermost thoughts.

4. Group work (6–8): The ambassadors

a) Act out the ambassadors' report (ll. 87-109):
   - Read the report and identify the characters referred to. Write their names on pieces of paper and tag each piece of paper onto another student, who will take the role.
   - Form a circle. Have one student read out the report slowly while the others point at the characters referred to.

b) Read the info box on deixis. Then use the information to analyse its effect on the audience.

> **Info: Deixis**
>
> Deixis [daɪksɪs] is Greek for "pointing". It describes the use of general words that refer to a specific person, time or place, such as *you*, *tomorrow* or *there*. As readers we need contextual information to fully understand who is meant or what place or what time is referred to. Shakespeare's plays are full of deictic words.

c) Extra: Write the entreaty mentioned in line 104 and present it to the class.

5. Young Fortinbras

a) Collect the information about young Fortinbras from Acts I and II.

b) Compare young Fortinbras' situation to Hamlet's.

c) Comment on the fact that Claudius does not seem concerned about letting young Fortinbras ride through his country with an army to attack Poland.

6. Hamlet's state of mind

a) Describe Hamlet's state of mind and name the reasons he gives to his friends (ll. 344-440).

b) Read the information about the concept of the body humours that the Elizabethans believed in on the next page. Discuss how an Elizabethan audience would have classified Hamlet's state of mind.

Info: Humours

The idea of the body humours influencing human behaviour stems from the Ancient Greeks and found its way through the Middle Ages to Shakespeare's time. It was believed that the human body consisted of four humours that corresponded to the elements. The prevalence of one humour in a person's body would influence this person's temperament. The table below shows the effects:

Humour	Element	Outer appearance	Temperament
blood	air	rose-tinted, pretty skin, slightly red	sanguine: enthusiastic, social, active
yellow bile	fire	greenish, yellow skin	choleric: aggressive, short-tempered
black bile	earth	black hair, dark eyes	melancholic: depressive, lazy, fearful, sickly
phlegm	water	white hair	phlegmatic: reserved, forgetful, low-spirited

---

c) Group work: Discuss how an actor should present Hamlet's lines (ll. 421-440): Is his tone reverent, bitter, sarcastic or sad? Does it change in the course of the monologue? Try several ways of presenting it. Explain your choice.
Use the space provided below for your notes.

I will tell you why. So shall my anticipation prevent your discovery, and your secrecy to the king and queen moult no feather. I have of late—but wherefore I know not—lost all my mirth, forgone all custom of exercises, and indeed it goes so heavily with my disposition that this goodly frame, the earth, seems to me a sterile promontory; this most excellent canopy, the air—look you, this brave o'erhanging firmament, this majestical roof fretted with golden fire—why, it appears no other thing to me than a foul and pestilent congregation of vapors. What a piece of work is a man! How noble in reason, how infinite in faculty! In form and moving how express and admirable! In action how like an angel, in apprehension how like a god! The beauty of the world. The paragon of animals. And yet, to me, what is this quintessence of dust? Man delights not me. No, nor woman neither, though by your smiling you seem to say so.	

d) Discuss to what extent Hamlet's state of mind mirrors the political situation in Denmark.

7. Group work: The actors

a) Research the story of Christopher Marlowe's play *Dido, Queen of Carthage* (1587). Exchange information with your group members.

b) Choose: Give a two-minute talk about Marlowe's play.

OR

Stage a two-minute version of Marlowe's play.

c) Read lines 626-638, 643–673. One student slowly reads the lines, the others echo every word to do with war, crime and fighting.

d) Analyse how Shakespeare creates atmosphere in these passages through his use of language.

8. Hamlet's soliloquy

a) Read Hamlet's soliloquy (ll. 745-802). Then check whether the statements below are right or wrong. Correct them if necessary.

	Statement	r/w	Evidence
0	An actor can feign emotions as he imagines the sufferings of a fictional character.	r	"this player here […] in a fiction […] Tears in his eyes" (ll. 746-750); "That he should weep for her?" (l. 755)
1	Hamlet cannot imagine the actor's reaction if he played Hamlet and his suffering.		
2	Hamlet is patient with his own behaviour.		
3	Hamlet imagines what a bully would do to him.		
4	He rages against Claudius.		

	Statement	r/w	Evidence
5	Hamlet rebukes himself for keeping his emotions to himself.		
6	He wants to stage his father's murder to see Claudius's reaction.		
7	Hamlet fears that the devil is trying to make him murder the king.		
8	Hamlet wonders whether he has enough evidence to prove Claudius's guilt.		

b) Outline Hamlet's line of argument.
c) Identify the accumulations (lists of items) in Hamlet's soliloquy and explain their effect on the audience.
d) Discuss the function of the soliloquy.
e) Extra: Choose: Write your own accumulation (e.g. about Hamlet's friends) and insert it at some point in the soliloquy. Present it to the class.
    OR
    Re-arrange the different sections of the soliloquy and justify your sequence.

Looking back at Act II

1. Group work (4–6): The themes

a) Identify the themes explored in Act II and show how they relate to each other. Start a mind-map.
b) Each group member picks a theme and gives a short talk on it to the group.
   • Sum up what happens in the play concerning the theme.
   • State the relevance of the theme for the play so far.
   • Show how it is connected to the other themes.
c) Add information about the themes to the mind-map as you read further.

2. Hamlet on the psychiatrist's couch

a) Read the info box on madness in Elizabethan times and analyse Hamlet's display of madness as shown in the following passages.

Info: Madness in Elizabethan plays

The Elizabethans took a great interest in mental disorder and its various forms. Thus, it is not surprising that many Elizabethan playwrights explored psychologically abnormal behaviour in the characters they created in their plays. This is also true for *Hamlet*. "Mad" was the most-used term to describe the wide range of behaviour beside the term "lunatic". The Elizabethans counted ecstatic, frenzied, senile and melancholic behaviour as varieties of madness. In Elizabethan plays, symptoms of madness included delusion, hallucinations, emotional instability, intellectual deficits, disordered speech or a dishevelled outer appearance. The characters spoke gibberish, had visions, sought revenge or suffered from illusions on stage.

If a cure had to be provided in a two-hour play, it often came in the form of herbs or syrups. In real life the cures of the day were whips, confinement, incantations, fresh air or quiet.

Some playwrights made their characters simply feign madness, but it was widely believed that strong emotions also increased the probability of crossing over from depression to insanity. The sources of these strong emotions were found in extreme biographical events such as the loss of a child, the partner or of one's property as well as external natural forces, e.g. the moon (hence the term "lunatic", from luna = moon). The bodily humours and strong emotions such as jealousy could also function as the sources of madness.

Act II, Scene II, ll. 239–307	
Act II, Scene II, ll. 421–440	
Act II, Scene II, ll. 515–529	

b) Imagine Hamlet goes to see a psychiatrist about his problem.

Choose: Pair work: Stage the interview between Hamlet and his psychiatrist, who tries to find out the reasons for Hamlet's state of mind.

OR

Write the psychiatrist's medical report about Hamlet. Include

- your name
- the address of your surgery or the name and address of your hospital
- Hamlet's name
- a diagnosis
- examination results
- a recommended treatment
- your signature at the end

The phrases in the box may help you write the report.

> … can be described as … – he shows symptoms of … – This trait becomes apparent when he … – Another significant feature is … – What is also striking about him is … – In addition to this … – Moreover/ Furthermore, … – It can be inferred/concluded that … – Summing up one might say that… – Taking everything into consideration/account …

3. A three-minute play

Group work (4): Act out Act II as a three-minute play.

a) Discuss which passages are the most important ones.

b) Act out these passages in a pantomime. The other students in your class must guess what passages you have chosen.

ACT III

SCENE I. A room in the castle.

Enter KING CLAUDIUS, QUEEN GERTRUDE, POLONIUS, OPHELIA, ROSENCRANTZ, GUILDENSTERN, and LORDS

KING CLAUDIUS
[*To ROSENCRANTZ and GUILDENSTERN*]

5 And can you, by no drift of circumstance
Get from him why he puts on this confusion,
Grating so harshly all his days of quiet
With turbulent and dangerous lunacy?

ROSENCRANTZ

10 He does confess he feels himself distracted,
But from what cause he will by no means speak.

GUILDENSTERN
Nor do we find him forward to be sounded,
But, with a crafty madness, keeps aloof

15 When we would bring him on to some confession
Of his true state.

QUEEN GERTRUDE
Did he receive you well?

ROSENCRANTZ

20 Most like a gentleman.

GUILDENSTERN
But with much forcing of his disposition.

ROSENCRANTZ
Niggard of question, but, of our demands,

25 Most free in his reply.

QUEEN GERTRUDE
Did you assay him to any pastime?

ROSENCRANTZ
Madam, it so fell out, that certain players

30 We o'erraught on the way. Of these we told him,
And there did seem in him a kind of joy
To hear of it. They are about the court,
And, as I think, they have already order
This night to play before him.

35 **POLONIUS**
'Tis most true,
And he beseeched me to entreat your majesties
To hear and see the matter.

KING CLAUDIUS

40 With all my heart, and it doth much content me
To hear him so inclined.

---

by no drift of circumstance by carefully directing the conversation
to put sth. on *etw. vortäuschen*
confusion mental confusion
grating disturbing, irritating
lunacy craziness
distracted seriously disturbed

forward willing · **sounded** questioned
crafty cunning, fake
keeps aloof keeps his distance

forcing of his disposition with a great effort to change his mood
niggard of question unwilling to start a conversation
free willing, helpful

assay encourage him
pastime hobby, entertainment
fell out happened
o'erraught overtook, went past

about in

to beseech to ask, to plead
to entreat to beg, to plead

inclined willing

Good gentlemen, give him a further edge,

And drive his purpose on to these delights.

ROSENCRANTZ

45 We shall, my lord.

Exeunt ROSENCRANTZ, GUILDENSTERN, and LORDS

KING CLAUDIUS

Sweet Gertrude, leave us too.

For we have closely sent for Hamlet hither

50 That he, as 'twere by accident, may here

Affront Ophelia.

Her father and myself, lawful espials,

Will so bestow ourselves that, seeing, unseen,

We may of their encounter frankly judge,

55 And gather by him as he is behaved.

If't be the affliction of his love or no

That thus he suffers for.

QUEEN GERTRUDE

I shall obey you.

60 And for your part, Ophelia, I do wish

That your good beauties be the happy cause

Of Hamlet's wildness; so shall I hope your virtues

Will bring him to his wonted way again,

To both your honours.

65 **OPHELIA**

Madam, I wish it may.

Exit QUEEN GERTRUDE

POLONIUS

[*TO OPHELIA*] Ophelia, walk you here.

70 [*TO KING CLAUDIUS*] Gracious, so please you,

We will bestow ourselves.

[*To OPHELIA*] Read on this book,

That show of such an exercise may colour

Your loneliness. We are oft to blame in this –

75 'Tis too much proved – that with devotion's visage

And pious action we do sugar o'er

The devil himself.

KING CLAUDIUS

O, 'tis too true.

80 [*Aside*] How smart a lash that speech doth give my conscience.

The harlot's cheek, beautied with plastering art

Is not more ugly to the thing that helps it

Than is my deed to my most painted word.

O heavy burden.

◐ The roles(s)
of women

---

give him a further edge motivate him even
    more

drive his purpose encourage his intentions

closely privately

affront meet face to face

lawful espials spies, in this case justifiable

bestow ourselves hide

gather by him as he is behaved deduce
    from his behaviour

if't (if it) **be the affliction of his love** i.e.
    if his love is the reason for his mental
    disturbance

good beauties internal and external
    beauties

wildness confusion, affliction

wonted normal, usual

to both your honours in a way that
    honours both of you

I wish it may. I hope you are right.

gracious gracious King

on this book from this (prayer) book

colour your loneliness provide an explana-
    tion for being alone

oft often • **too much** (here) too often

with devotion's visage having the
    appearance of praying

pious action pretending to be pious
    (*fromm*)

sugar o'er the devil himself make the devil
    seem to be harmless and sweet

smart painful • **lash** *Peitschenhieb*

harlot whore • **plastering art** makeup

the thing that helps it Possibly "the thing"
    is the servant who applies the makeup
    and knows how ugly the harlot really
    is, or the makeup is just as ugly as the
    harlot's cheek.

painted hypocritical • **burden** *Last*

arrass *Wandteppich*

slings weapons that are thrown
outrageous fortune completely irrational Fortuna
natural shocks diseases
to be heir to sth. *etw. erben*
consummation *Vollendung*
devoutly truly, passionately
perchance perhaps
rub object blocking the way
to shuffle sth. off *etw. abschütteln, loswerden*
coil *Wirrwarr* • **respect** consideration
makes calamity of so long life makes those afflicted by calamity willing to endure it for such a long time
the whips and scorns of time the injuries and insults we must endure in the world we live in
contumely humiliating insults
pangs of despised love being lovesick because of being rejected by the one you love
insolence arrogance
of office of bureaucrats
the spurns /That patient merit of the unworthy takes the setbacks that a patient and deserving person has to endure from unworthy people
his quietus make die
bare bodkin a dagger • **fardels** burdens
to grunt *stöhnen* • **bourn** border
native hue healthy colour
to sickly over *mit einer kränklichen Färbung überziehen*
cast colour
of great pitch and moment of large scale and importance
with this regard because of this consideration
turn awry go wrong
lose the name of action stop, not continue
soft you now Wait a moment.
nymph (poetic) beautiful young woman
orisons prayers

85 **POLONIUS**
I hear him coming. Let's withdraw, my lord.

KING CLAUDIUS and POLONIUS hide behind the arrass.

Enter HAMLET

HAMLET
90 To be, or not to be, that is the question.
Whether 'tis nobler in the mind to suffer
The slings and arrows of outrageous fortune,
Or to take arms against a sea of troubles,
And by opposing end them? To die, to sleep –
95 No more, and by a sleep to say we end
The heartache and the thousand natural shocks
That flesh is heir to – 'tis a consummation
Devoutly to be wished. To die, to sleep.
To sleep, perchance to dream. Ay, there's the rub,
100 For in that sleep of death what dreams may come
When we have shuffled off this mortal coil,
Must give us pause. There's the respect
That makes calamity of so long life.
For who would bear the whips and scorns of time,
105 The oppressor's wrong, the proud man's contumely,
The pangs of despised love, the law's delay,
The insolence of office and the spurns
That patient merit of the unworthy takes,
When he himself might his quietus make*
110 With a bare bodkin? Who would fardels bear,
To grunt and sweat under a weary life,
But that the dread of something after death,
The undiscovered country from whose bourn
No traveller returns, puzzles the will
115 And makes us rather bear those ills we have
Than fly to others that we know not of.
Thus conscience does make cowards of us all,
And thus the native hue of resolution
Is sicklied o'er with the pale cast of thought,
120 And enterprises of great pitch and moment
With this regard their currents turn awry,
And lose the name of action. Soft you now,
The fair Ophelia! – Nymph, in thy orisons
Be all my sins remembered.
125 **OPHELIA**
Good my lord,
How does your honour for this many a day?
HAMLET
I humbly thank you, well, well, well.

○ Fate vs. free will
○ Questions of morality

○ The roles(s) of women

OPHELIA

130 My lord, I have remembrances of yours,

That I have longèd long to redeliver;

I pray you, now receive them.

HAMLET

135 No, not I;

I never gave you aught.

OPHELIA

My honoured lord, you know right well you did,

And, with them, words of so sweet breath composed

140 As made the things more rich. Their perfume lost,

Take these again, for to the noble mind

Rich gifts wax poor when givers prove unkind.

There, my lord.

HAMLET

145 Ha, ha! Are you honest?

OPHELIA

My lord?

HAMLET

Are you fair?

150 **OPHELIA**

What means your lordship?

HAMLET

That if you be honest and fair, your honesty should

admit no discourse to your beauty*.

155 **OPHELIA**

Could beauty, my lord, have better commerce than

with honesty?

HAMLET

Ay, truly. For the power of Beauty will sooner

160 transform Honesty from what it is to a bawd than the

force of Honesty can translate Beauty into his

likeness. This was sometime a paradox, but now the

time gives it proof. I did love you once.

OPHELIA

165 In, my lord, you made me believe so.

HAMLET

You should not have believed me. For virtue cannot

so inoculate our old stock but we shall relish of

it. I loved you not.

170 **OPHELIA**

I was the more deceived.

HAMLET

Get thee to a nunnery. Why wouldst thou be a

breeder of sinners? I am myself indifferent honest

175 but yet I could accuse me of such things that it

were better my mother had not borne me. I am very

proud, revengeful, ambitious, with more offences at

remembrances gifts

aught anything

Their perfume lost The sweetness of your words are gone because of your unkindness.
wax become

honest chaste (*keusch*)

fair beautiful

your honesty should admit no discourse to your beauty your chastity should allow no dishonest dealings with your beauty
commerce associations, relationships

bawd pimp, whore
his likeness its likeness, i.e. honesty
sometime once
now the time gives it proof This paradox has been shown to be accurate.

to inoculate (here) to improve
our old stock refers to the fruit tree in the garden of Eden, symbolizes original sin
to relish of sth to taste of sth
nunnery *Nonnenkloster* – this is a *double entendre* as in Shakespeare's time "nunnery" was also the slang word for "whorehouse"
breeder of sinners a woman who gives birth to sinners
indifferent honest of average honesty
offences awful qualities

at my beck that I can call on
than I have thoughts [...] them in than I can think of

arrant complete • **knave** dishonest man

in's in his

plague curse
dowry wedding gift
calumny slander, horrible lies

if thou wilt needs if you must

monster i.e. cuckold (*Gehörnter*) i.e. man who has been deceived by his unfaithful wife
you women in general

your paintings your use of makeup
to jig to dance
to amble to walk in a slow and relaxed way
to lisp to speak in an affected way
make [...] your ignorance use ignorance as an excuse for foolish or immoral behaviour
I'll no more on't. I'll have no more of it.
keep stay

o'erthrown overthrown, destroyed
courtier *Höfling*
expectancy hope for the future
rose (fig.) symbol of youth and beauty
state country of Denmark
The glass of fashion and the mould of form the very image of fashion and the highest example of good behaviour
observed of all observers closely watched by others
deject miserable
music vows promises like music to her ears
sovereign reason reason that should dominate a person's mind
jangled sounded unpleasant
out of tune unpleasant to hear
harsh awful to listen to
That unmatched [...] blown youth that perfect image of youth in full bloom
blasted with ecstasy destroyed by madness

my beck than I have thoughts to put them in,
imagination to give them shape, or time to act them
180 in. What should such fellows as I do crawling
between earth and heaven? We are arrant knaves all.
Believe none of us. Go thy ways to a nunnery.
Where's your father?
OPHELIA
185 At home, my lord.
HAMLET
Let the doors be shut upon him that he may
play the fool nowhere but in's own house. Farewell.
OPHELIA
190 [*Aside*] O help him, you sweet heavens!
HAMLET
If thou dost marry, I'll give thee this plague for
thy dowry: be thou as chaste as ice, as pure as
snow, thou shalt not escape calumny. Get thee to a
195 nunnery, go, farewell. Or if thou wilt needs
marry, marry a fool, for wise men know well enough
what monsters you make of them. To a nunnery, go,
and quickly too. Farewell.
OPHELIA
200 O heavenly powers, restore him.
HAMLET
I have heard of your paintings* too, well enough. God
has given you one face, and you make yourselves
another. You jig, you amble, and you lisp, and
205 nickname God's creatures, and make your wantonness
your ignorance. Go to, I'll no more on't. It hath
made me mad. I say we will have no more marriages.
Those that are married already – all but one – shall
live. The rest shall keep as they are. To a
210 nunnery, go.

Exit

OPHELIA
O, what a noble mind is here o'erthrown!
The courtier's, soldier's, scholar's, eye, tongue, sword,
215 The expectancy and rose of the fair state,
The glass of fashion and the mould of form,
The observed of all observers, quite, quite down!
And I, of ladies most deject and wretched,
That sucked the honey of his music vows,
220 Now see that noble and most sovereign reason
Like sweet bells jangled, out of tune and harsh –
That unmatched form and feature of blown youth
Blasted with ecstasy. O woe is me,
To have seen what I have seen, see what I see.

225 *KING CLAUDIUS and POLONIUS step forward from
behind the arras.*

KING CLAUDIUS
Love? His affections do not that way tend,
Nor what he spake, though it lacked form a little,
230 Was not like madness. There's something in his soul
O'er which his melancholy sits on brood,
And I do doubt the hatch and the disclose
Will be some danger; which for to prevent,
I have in quick determination
235 Thus set it down. He shall with speed to England,
For the demand of our neglected tribute*.
Haply the seas and countries different
With variable objects shall expel
This something-settled matter in his heart
240 Whereon his brain's still beating puts him thus
From fashion of himself. What think you on't?
POLONIUS
It shall do well. But yet do I believe
The origin and commencement of his grief
245 Sprung from neglected love. How now, Ophelia?
You need not tell us what Lord Hamlet said –
We heard it all. My lord, do as you please,
But, if you hold it fit, after the play
Let his Queen-mother all alone entreat him
250 To show his grief. Let her be round with him
And I'll be placed, so please you, in the ear
Of all their conference. If she find him not,
To England send him, or confine him where
Your wisdom best shall think.
255 **KING CLAUDIUS**
It shall be so.
Madness in great ones must not unwatched go.

Exeunt

affections emotions
spake (archaic) spoke

o'er over
sits on brood like a hen brooding (sitting)
on her eggs
do doubt feel anxious that
the hatch (fig.) the chicks
disclose disclosure, bringing into public
view
set it down concluded, decided
haply perhaps
with variable objects different sights
expel get rid of
something-settled somewhat obsessive
his brain's still beating the constant ham-
mering in his head
puts him [...] fashion of himself causing
him not to be his usual self
on't of it • **grief** troubled state of mind

hold it consider it
entreat ask, beg
grief what is bothering him
round open, honest
in the ear within earshot
conference discussion
if she find him not if she doesn't find out
what is the matter with him
confine him lock him up

Summary

Rosencrantz and Guildenstern inform the king and queen about their meeting with Hamlet and report on the actors' arrival.

Claudius discloses his plan to Gertrude that he and Polonius have prepared to eavesdrop on an arranged conversation between Hamlet and Ophelia.

After Hamlet has contemplated the problems of living or dying, he comes across Ophelia. They talk.

Claudius senses danger and plans to send Hamlet to England.

Tasks

1. Rosencrantz and Guildenstern

a) The king asked Rosencrantz and Guildenstern to talk to Hamlet. This is what they tell the king and queen about their meeting with him. Tick the correct statements and give evidence from the text.

	Statement	Evidence	√
1	Hamlet says that he is mad.		
2	Hamlet has confessed the reasons for his melancholy to his friends.		
3	Hamlet is unwilling to answer questions about his true state of mind.		
4	He welcomed his friends without respect.		
5	Hamlet only pretends to be mad.		
6	Hamlet has asked a troupe of actors to stage a play.		

b) Turn back to Act II, Scene II and read lines 318–542 again. Examine whether Hamlet's friends have given the king and queen a thorough and true account of their meeting with Hamlet.

c) Discuss how your impression of Hamlet's friends has changed.

2. Claudius' conscience

a) Shakespeare uses an aside to disclose Claudius' conscience. Read lines 80-84 again and paraphrase Claudius' aside.

Info: Aside
This dramatic device is like a soliloquy, but with other characters present on stage.

b) Explain the function of the simile Claudius uses.

c) Speculate about Shakespeare's reasons for making Claudius reveal his state of mind at this point of the play.

3. To be or not to be

a) Match the paraphrases on the right (A–F) to the passages (1–6) on the left.

	Original text			Paraphrase
1	To be, or not to be? That is the question. Whether 'tis nobler in the mind to suffer The slings and arrows of outrageous fortune, Or to take arms against a sea of troubles, And, by opposing, end them?		A	The only obstacle is that we do not know what dreams may come in death's sleep, an uncertainty that makes us endure the sufferings for so long.
2	To die, to sleep – No more – and by a sleep to say we end The heartache and the thousand natural shocks That flesh is heir to – 'tis a consummation Devoutly to be wished!		B	Who would bear the hurts, the injustices, the humiliations, when he could commit suicide with a small dagger?
3	To die, to sleep. To sleep, perchance to dream – ay, there's the rub, For in that sleep of death what dreams may come When we have shuffled off this mortal coil, Must give us pause. There's the respect That makes calamity of so long life.		C	Consequently, our conscience makes us cowards and our thinking hinders us to act with determination and so any formerly great and important project loses its greatness.
4	For who would bear the whips and scorns of time, Th' oppressor's wrong, the proud man's contumely, The pangs of despised love, the law's delay, The insolence of office, and the spurns That patient merit of th' unworthy takes, When he himself might his quietus make With a bare bodkin?		D	Is it better to be alive and endure the sufferings or to fight against the injustices and end them?
5	Who would fardels bear, To grunt and sweat under a weary life, But that the dread of something after death, The undiscovered country from whose bourn No traveller returns, puzzles the will And makes us rather bear those ills we have Than fly to others that we know not of?		E	Dying is sleeping, a sleep that ends all the troubles. Such an ending can only be wished for.
6	Thus conscience does make cowards of us all, And thus the native hue of resolution Is sicklied o'er with the pale cast of thought, And enterprises of great pith and moment With this regard their currents turn awry, And lose the name of action.		F	Who would bear the burdens and lead an exhausting life unless he was afraid of something dreadful after death, an unknown place from which no one returns and which makes us rather put up with the problems that we know than run into the problems we do not know.

b) Outline Hamlet's ideas in two to three sentences.

c) There has been much discussion about how to deliver Hamlet's soliloquy. Watch a video and explain what the actors argue about. Go to www.westermann.de/webcode and enter the webcode to access the video.
Webcode DSW-73068-01

d) Pair work: Imagine you are directing a Hamlet movie. How would you film this soliloquy? Think about …
- the setting
- the music
- the atmosphere
- Hamlet's tone of voice, gestures, facial expressions and in what way he might move around.

Present your ideas to the class.

e) Extra: Film your version of these famous lines.

f) Extra: Write a modern version of the soliloquy.

4. Hamlet and Ophelia

a) Describe how Hamlet treats Ophelia.

b) Think-pair-share:
- Think of possible reasons why Hamlet treats Ophelia in this way. Write them down in the grid below.
- Pair: Exchange your ideas with a partner's. Evaluate your partner's choices in the grid below. Give evidence from the text to prove your point.
- Share the most likely reasons in class.

Possible reason	most likely ++	+	o	–	least likely ––

c) Pair work: You are going to read out Hamlet and Ophelia's conversation (ll. 123-210). Sit facing one another while reading. Partner A takes Hamlet's role, Partner B Ophelia's.
Before you start, decide on how to understand the reference to the "nunnery" in line 173: a convent to protect Ophelia's chastity or a brothel?

d) Pair work: How do Hamlet and Ophelia feel after their meeting? Partner A takes Hamlet's role again, partner B Ophelia's.
- Write down some thoughts in the bubbles provided on page 89.
- Present your ideas in front of the class, now sitting with your backs turned to each other.

Hamlet

Ophelia

5. Claudius and Polonius – the eavesdroppers

a) Explain Claudius' reaction to Hamlet and Ophelia's conversation.
b) Describe Polonius' plan.

trippingly lightly	
mouth it speak the lines too slowly	
I had as lief I'd prefer	
town-crier person who makes announce- ments for the town – he must speak very loudly.	
saw the air [...] **hand** gesticulate wildly	
use all gently be moderate with all your gestures	
torrent, tempest, whirlwind wildness, exaggeration	
beget get • **temperance** moderation	
robustious noisy, loud	
periwig-pated wearing a wig	
a passion a passionate speech	
to tatters to ragged pieces • **rags** *Fetzen*	
split the ears be too loud	
groundlings the audience members closest to the stage	
are capable are able to appreciate	
inexplicable dumb-shows meaningless pantomime	
o'erdoing (outdoing) being even worse than	
pray please • **I warrant** I will	
tame mild, spiritless	
discretion judgement, good sense	
tutor director • **observance** guiding rule	
o'erstep overstep, go beyond	
from opposed to • **playing** acting	
at the first in ancient times	
this overdone [...] **tardy off** if this is exaggerated or poorly acted	
the judicious the educated	
grieve feel great sadness	
the censure [...] **theatre of others.** The judgement of one educated person is more important than that of the mass of other unsophisticated audience members.	
not to speak it profanely I apologize for seeming to be disrespectful to God in the following remarks.	
Christians ordinary human beings	
gait manner of walking • **pagan** *Heide*	
to strut to walk in a pompous manner	
to bellow to shout in a loud, deep voice	
journeyman craftsman who works for another tradesman, and may also not be very good at his job	
abominably badly	
indifferently to a certain degree	
with us in our company of actors	

SCENE II. A hall in the castle.

Enter HAMLET and two or three of the PLAYERS

HAMLET
Speak the speech, I pray you, as I pronounced it to
you, trippingly on the tongue. But if you mouth it,
5   as many of your players do, I had as lief the
town-crier spoke my lines. Nor do not saw the air
too much with your hand, thus, but use all gently;
for in the very torrent, tempest and, as I may say,
the whirlwind of passion, you must acquire and beget
10   a temperance that may give it smoothness. O, it
offends me to the soul to hear a robustious
periwig-pated fellow tear a passion to tatters, to
very rags, to split the ears of the groundlings*, who
for the most part are capable of nothing but
15   inexplicable dumb-shows* and noise. I would have such
a fellow whipped for o'erdoing Termagant*. It
out-Herods Herod*. Pray you avoid it.
FIRST PLAYER
I warrant your honour.
20   **HAMLET**
Be not too tame neither, but let your own discretion
be your tutor. Suit the action to the word, the
word to the action, with this special observance – that
you o'erstep not the modesty of nature. For anything
25   so overdone is from the purpose of playing, whose end,
both at the first and now, was and is to hold as 'twere,
the mirror up to Nature, to show Virtue her own feature,
scorn her own image, and the very age and body of
the time his form and pressure. Now this overdone,
30   or come tardy off, though it makes the unskilful
laugh, cannot but make the judicious grieve, the
censure of the which one must in your allowance
o'erweigh a whole theatre of others. O, there be
players that I have seen play, and heard others
35   praise, and that highly, not to speak it profanely,
that neither having the accent of Christians nor
the gait of Christian, pagan, nor man, have so
strutted and bellowed that I have thought some of
Nature's journeymen had made men and not made them
40   well, they imitated humanity so abominably.
FIRST PLAYER
I hope we have reformed that indifferently with us,
sir.

HAMLET

45 O, reform it altogether. And let those that play
your clowns speak no more than is set down for them.
For there be of them that will themselves laugh, to
set on some quantity of barren spectators to laugh
too, though, in the meantime, some necessary
50 question of the play be then to be considered.
That's villainous, and shows a most pitiful ambition
in the fool that uses it. Go, make you ready.

Exeunt PLAYERS

Enter POLONIUS, ROSENCRANTZ, and GUILDENSTERN

55 [*To POLONIUS*] How now my lord, will the King hear this
piece of work?

POLONIUS
And the Queen too, and that presently.
HAMLET
60 Bid the players make haste.

Exit POLONIUS

Will you two help to hasten them?
ROSENCRANTZ and GUILDENSTERN
We will, my lord.

65 *Exeunt ROSENCRANTZ and GUILDENSTERN*

Enter HORATIO

HAMLET
What ho, Horatio!
HORATIO
70 Here, sweet lord, at your service.
HAMLET
Horatio, thou art e'en as just a man
As e'er my conversation coped withal.
HORATIO
75 O, my dear lord –
HAMLET
Nay, do not think I flatter,
For what advancement may I hope from thee
That no revenue hast but thy good spirits,
80 To feed and clothe thee? Why should the poor be flattered?
No, let the candied tongue lick absurd pomp,

for there be of them there are some of them
set on encourage
barren brainless, stupid

villainous vulgar, very unpleasant

presently immediately

bid ask • **make haste** hurry

sweet lord dear lord

e'en even, indeed • **just** honourable
e'er [...] withal as I ever encountered in my dealings with men

to flatter schmeicheln
advancement advantage, benefit, political power
revenue source of income
let the candied tongue [...] pomp let a person use sweet words, like a dog which licks the hand of its master, to flatter a very wealthy man

crook [...] hinges of the knee kneel
where [...] fawning so that personal profit
  will result from fawning (bootlicking,
  kissing ass)
was mistress of her choice became capable of choosing for herself
could of men distinguish could determine
  the quality of men
her election [...] herself She has identified
  you as one of her own.
as one [...] suffers nothing stoically
buffets Schicksalsschläge
ta'en taken • **blest** blessed (gesegnet)
blood passion • **judgment** reason
commingled mixed
pipe musical instrument, flute
to sound [...] she please to play whatever
  she wants
core innermost part, centre
something rather
act scene • **afoot** in action, ongoing
even [...] thy soul with the utmost attention that your soul can bear
occulted hidden
itself unkennel reveal itself
one speech one sentence
damned ghost ghost from hell not heaven
foul filthy, stinking
Vulcan's stithy (smithy) the dark, hell-like
  workplace of Vulcan, the blacksmith god
give him heedful note observe him closely
to rivet to fix, focus • **join** share
in censure of his seeming to discuss what
  can be said of his reaction

steal aught the whilst this play is playing
  manages to hide his guilty conscience
  during the play
scape detecting escape detection
I will pay the theft I will pay for it, I'll take
  the blame

idle doing nothing or mad

how fares how is • **cousin** close relative
i' faith by God
of the chameleon's dish i.e., of the air – Cha-
  meleons were believed to live in the air
promise-crammed filled with promises
capon overfed castrated chicken, (fig.) idiot
I have nothing with this answer. This
  means nothing to me.
These words are not mine. Your answer is
  completely irrelevant to what I have said.

And crook the pregnant hinges of the knee
Where thrift may follow fawning. Dost thou hear?
Since my dear soul was mistress of her choice
85 And could of men distinguish, her election
Hath sealed thee for herself. For thou hast been
As one in suffering all that suffers nothing,
A man that Fortune's buffets and rewards
Hast ta'en with equal thanks. And blest are those
90 Whose blood and judgment are so well commingled
That they are not a pipe for Fortune's finger
To sound what stop she please. Give me that man
That is not passion's slave, and I will wear him
In my heart's core, ay, in my heart of heart,
95 As I do thee. Something too much of this.
There is a play tonight before the King.
One scene of it comes near the circumstance
Which I have told thee of my father's death.
I prithee when thou seest that act afoot,
100 Even with the very comment of thy soul
Observe mine uncle. If his occulted guilt
Do not itself unkennel in one speech,
It is a damned ghost that we have seen
And my imaginations are as foul
105 As Vulcan's stithy. Give him heedful note,
For I mine eyes will rivet to his face
And after we will both our judgments join
In censure of his seeming.
HORATIO
110 Well, my lord.
If he steal aught the whilst this play is playing
And scape detecting I will pay the theft.

*Danish march. A flourish. Enter KING CLAUDIUS, QUEEN GER-
TRUDE, POLONIUS, OPHELIA, ROSENCRANTZ, GUILDEN-*
115 *STERN, and others, with the King's Guard carrying torches.*

HAMLET
[*To HORATIO*] They are coming to the play. I must be idle.
Get you a place.

KING CLAUDIUS
120 How fares our cousin Hamlet?
HAMLET
Excellent, i' faith, of the chameleon's dish. I eat
the air, promise-crammed*. You cannot feed capons so.*
KING CLAUDIUS
125 I have nothing with this answer, Hamlet. These words
are not mine.

HAMLET
No, nor mine now.
[*To POLONIUS*]
130 My lord, you played once i' the university, you say?
POLONIUS
That did I, my lord, and was accounted a good actor.
HAMLET
What did you enact?
135 **POLONIUS**
I did enact Julius Caesar. I was killed i' the
Capitol*. Brutus killed me.
HAMLET
It was a brute part of him to kill so capital a calf
140 there. Be the players ready?
ROSENCRANTZ
Ay, my lord, they stay upon your patience.
QUEEN GERTRUDE
Come hither, my dear Hamlet, sit by me.
145 **HAMLET**
No, good mother, here's metal more attractive*.

He sits by OPHELIA.

POLONIUS
[*To KING CLAUDIUS*] O, ho! Do you mark that?
150 **HAMLET**
Lady, shall I lie in your lap?
OPHELIA
No, my lord.
HAMLET
155 I mean, my head upon your lap?
OPHELIA
Ay, my lord.
HAMLET
Do you think I meant country matters?
160 **OPHELIA**
I think nothing, my lord.
HAMLET
That's a fair thought to lie between maids' legs.
OPHELIA
165 What is, my lord?
HAMLET
Nothing.
OPHELIA
You are merry, my lord.
170 **HAMLET**
Who, I?

---

nor mine now Completely irrelevant to me, too.

i' in, at

accounted considered

brute part brutal act, "brute" being a pun on "Brutus," and "part" a pun because it also means "role"
capital excellent, a pun on the word "Capitol"
calf (here) fool, simpleton
stay upon your patience are waiting for you to tell them to begin
hither hierher

➲ The roles(s) of women

metal more attractive (fig., humorous) a magnet that has the force of attraction – "attractive" is a pun.

mark notice

lie in your lap (Schoß) There is a sexual meaning implied here: "have sex with you".

country matters a rather vulgar pun as "country" is a pun on "cunt" (vulgar for "vagina")

merry in good spirits

only unrivaled
jig-maker comical actor Hamlet seems to
be comparing himself to a clown provid-
ing superficial entertainment.
within's within these

let the devil wear black, for [...] sables
The devil can have my mourning clothes
and I'll wear luxurious sables (fur) if I
consider that my father has been dead
so long.
die having died
by'r Lady by our Lady, the Virgin Mary
build churches then have chapels built
where people can pray for his soul
else shall he suffer [...] not thinking on or
endure not being thought of
the hobby-horse a dancing man with the
figure of a horse tied around his waist
epitaph (here) refrain or catchphrase
(*Schlagwort*)
hautboy musical instrument, oboe
dumb-show actors using pantomime to
summarize or anticipate the plot of a play
makes show of protestation unto him
shows that she loves him
declines leans • **him** himself
bank of flowers raised bed of flowers
anon soon
makes passionate action shows intense
grief
mutes silent actors
lament with her share her sorrow
to woo to seek the love of a woman with the
intention of marrying her
loath reluctant • **awhile** for a while

marry By the Virgin Mary!
miching malhecho dirty trick
mischief bad trouble
belike perhaps • **show** dumb-show
imports represents, signifies • **argument** plot
Prologue introduction

keep counsel keep a secret

OPHELIA
Ay, my lord.

HAMLET
175 O God, your only jig-maker. What should a man do but be merry? For, look you, how cheerfully my mother looks, and my
father died within's two hours.

OPHELIA
Nay, 'tis twice two months, my lord.

HAMLET
180 So long? Nay then, let the devil wear black, for I'll have a suit
of sables. O heavens, die two months ago, and not forgotten yet.
Then there's hope a great man's memory may outlive his life
half a year. But, by'r Lady, he must build churches then, or else
shall he suffer not thinking on, with the hobby-horse, whose
185 epitaph is "For O, for O, the hobby-horse is forgot."

Hautboys play. The dumb-show enters.

*Enter a King and a Queen very lovingly, the Queen
embracing him, and he her. She kneels, and makes
190 show of protestation unto him. He takes her up, and
declines his head upon her neck. He lays him down upon
a bank of flowers. She, seeing him asleep, leaves him.
Anon comes in a fellow, takes off his crown, kisses it,
and pours poison in the King's ears, and exit. The Queen
195 returns, finds the King dead, and makes passionate action.
The Poisoner, with some two or three Mutes, comes in
again, seeming to lament with her. The dead body is
carried away. The Poisoner woos the Queen with gifts.
She seems loath and unwilling awhile, but in the end
accepts his love.*

200 *Exeunt the PLAYERS*

OPHELIA
What means this, my lord?

HAMLET
205 Marry, this is miching malhecho. It means mischief.

OPHELIA
Belike this show imports the argument of the play.

Enter a PLAYER as the Prologue

HAMLET
210 We shall know by this fellow. The players cannot
keep counsel, they'll tell all.

OPHELIA
Will he tell us what this show meant?

HAMLET

215 Ay, or any show that you'll show him. Be not you
ashamed to show, he'll not shame to tell you what it means.

OPHELIA

You are naught, you are naught. I'll mark the play.

PLAYER as the Prologue

220 *For us, and for our tragedy,*
Here stooping to your clemency,
We beg your hearing patiently.

Exit

HAMLET

225 Is this a prologue, or the posy of a ring?

OPHELIA

'Tis brief, my lord.

HAMLET

As woman's love.

Enter two PLAYERS, KING and QUEEN

230

PLAYER KING

Full thirty times hath Phoebus' cart gone round
Neptune's salt wash and Tellus' orbèd ground,
And thirty dozen moons with borrowed sheen
235 *About the world have times twelve thirties been,*
Since love our hearts and Hymen did our hands
Unite commutual in most sacred bands.

PLAYER QUEEN

So many journeys may the sun and moon
240 *Make us again count o'er ere love be done!*
But, woe is me, you are so sick of late,
So far from cheer and from your former state,
That I distrust you. Yet, though I distrust,
Discomfort you, my lord, it nothing must.
245 *For women's fear and love holds quantity,*
In neither aught, or in extremity.
Now, what my love is, proof hath made you know
And as my love is sized, my fear is so.
Where love is great, the littlest doubts are fear.
250 *Where little fears grow great, great love grows there.*

PLAYER KING

'Faith, I must leave thee, love, and shortly too.
My operant powers their functions leave to do.
And thou shalt live in this fair world behind,
Honoured, beloved and haply one as kind
255 *For husband shalt thou* –*

Ay, or [...] not shame (not be ashamed)

to tell you what is means. Hamlet is again
being very vulgar, implying some kind of
sexual act.

naught bad, naughty, indecent

mark pay close attention to

stooping to your clemency bowing in
order to acquire your generosity

posy of a ring short inscription inside a ring

Phoebus' cart i.e. the sun – Phoebus, the
god of the sun

Neptune's salt wash i.e. the sea – Neptune,
the god of the sea

Tellus orbèd ground i.e. the earth –Tellus,
the goddess of the earth

borrowed sheen light reflected from the sun

times twelve thirties 30 years

Hymen god of marriage

commutual together

most sacred bands (bonds), i.e. marriage

count o'er count

ere love be done before our love comes to
an end, e.g. by death

woe is me I am very upset.

distrust you fear for you

discomfort you [...] nothing must you
need not worry

holds quantity are in equal proportions

neither aught [...] in extremity either fear
and love are completely absent or both
are extreme

proof hath made you know experience
has shown you

my love [...] sized, my fear so my anxiety
is as great as my love

where love is great [...] fear with great
love anxiety becomes no more than
insignificant doubts

Where [...] great love grows there. At the
same time as minor feelings of anxiety
become great so does love.

operant powers the ability to think and my
senses

leave to do no longer work

behind after my death • **haply** perhaps

Confound the rest! Don't say the next word.
treason *Verrat*
accurst cursed
None wed [...] killed the first. Let no woman wed a second husband unless she has killed the first one.
wormwood a bitter plant

instances reasons, motives • **move** lead to
base respects of thrift immoral considerations of financial or personal advantage

determine decide on
purpose is but a slave to memory Purposes are easily forgotten.
of violent birth but poor validity strong at the beginning but not long-lasting
mellow overripe, soft
Most necessary [...] debt. It is better to forget our obligations.

The violence of [...] destroy. Extreme grief or joy when converted to action destroys itself.
on slender accident for the most insignificant reason
aye ever • **prove** resolve, answer
lead is stronger than
down out of favour • **mark** notice
favorite flies favourite supporters desert him
poor advanced [...] enemies those who have not been able to advance their careers shall go over to your enemies
hitherto up to now
Love on Fortune tend Love depends on Fortune.
who not needs who is rich • **in want** poor
hollow (fig.) superficial • **try** tests
seasons him converts him to
devices plans • **still** always
overthrown are not fulfilled
none of our own not under our control
die thy thoughts What you once thought will later not be valid.
sport recreation • **repose** rest
lock from me be made not available to me
desperation *Verzweiflung*
anchor's cheer the food of an anchorite (hermit) [*Eremit*]
scope prospect for the future

PLAYER QUEEN
O, confound the rest!
Such love must needs be treason in my breast.
260 *In second husband let me be accurst;*
None wed the second but who killed the first.

HAMLET
[*Aside*] Wormwood, wormwood*.

PLAYER QUEEN
265 *The instances that second marriage move*
Are base respects of thrift, but none of love.
A second time I kill my husband dead,
When second husband kisses me in bed.

PLAYER KING
270 *I do believe you think what now you speak.*
But what we do determine oft we break.
Purpose is but the slave to memory,
Of violent birth but poor validity,
Which now like fruit unripe sticks on the tree
275 *But fall unshaken when they mellow be.*
Most necessary 'tis that we forget
To pay ourselves what to ourselves is debt.
What to ourselves in passion we propose,
The passion ending doth the purpose lose.
280 *The violence of either grief or joy*
Their own enactures with themselves destroy.
Where joy most revels, grief doth most lament;
Grief joys, joy grieves, on slender accident.
This world is not for aye, nor 'tis not strange
285 *That even our loves should with our fortunes change,*
For 'tis a question left us yet to prove,
Whether love lead fortune, or else fortune love.
The great man down, you mark his favourite flies,
The poor advanced makes friends of enemies.
290 *And hitherto doth Love on Fortune tend.*
For who not needs shall never lack a friend,
And who in want a hollow friend doth try
Directly seasons him his enemy.
But orderly to end where I begun,
295 *Our wills and fates do so contrary run*
That our devices still are overthrown.
Our thoughts are ours, their ends none of our own.
So think thou wilt no second husband wed
But die thy thoughts when thy first lord is dead.

300 **PLAYER QUEEN**
Nor earth to me give food, nor heaven light,
Sport and repose lock from me day and night.
To desperation turn my trust and hope.
An anchor's cheer in prison be my scope!

↪ The roles(s) of women

↪ Fate vs. free will
↪ The roles(s) of women

↪ The roles(s) of women

305 *Each opposite that blanks the face of joy*
Meet what I would have well and it destroy.
Both here and hence pursue me lasting strife,
If, once a widow, ever I be wife!

HAMLET

310 If she should break it now!

PLAYER KING

'Tis deeply sworn. Sweet, leave me here awhile;
My spirits grow dull, and fain I would beguile
The tedious day with sleep.

Sleeps

315

PLAYER QUEEN

Sleep rock thy brain,
And never come mischance between us twain.

Exit

320 **HAMLET**

Madam, how like you this play?

QUEEN GERTRUDE

The lady doth protest too much, methinks.

HAMLET

325 O, but she'll keep her word.

KING CLAUDIUS

Have you heard the argument? Is there no offence in't?

HAMLET

No, no, they do but jest. Poison in jest. No offence

330 i' the world.

KING CLAUDIUS

What do you call the play?

HAMLET

The Mousetrap. Marry, how tropically. This play is the image

335 of a murder done in Vienna*. Gonzago is the Duke's name, his
wife, Baptista. You shall see anon. 'Tis a knavish piece of work.
But what o' that? Your majesty and we that have free souls,
it touches us not. Let the galled jade wince, our withers are
unwrung.

Enter PLAYER LUCIANUS

340

This is one Lucianus, nephew to the King.

OPHELIA

You are as good as a chorus, my lord.

HAMLET

345 I could interpret between you and your love if I
could see the puppets dallying.

---

each opposite opposing forces
blanks the face of joy removes expressions
 of joy in the face
Meet […] it destroy. Anything that I desire
 to have, destroy it.
hence from now on
pursue me lasting strife make sure I have
 no peace but constant conflicts
break it break her vow
sworn declared like an oath (*Eid*)
fain willingly • **beguile** (fig.) charm
tedious tiring, boring

rock to move back and forth sideways like
 a baby's bed
mischance unhappiness
twain (archaic) two

The lady […] too much the lady is over-
 compensating, she is pretending
methinks (archaic) I think
argument plot
offence in't something that may offend
 (*beleidigen*) me
to jest to joke
Poison in jest. Nobody is really poisoned;
 it's just a play.
No offence i' the world. Nothing at all
 offensive.
mousetrap *Mäusefalle*
Marry by the Virgin Mary
tropically figuratively, like a trope
image precise representation
knavish wicked
free innocent
galled jade wince overworked horse kick
 out .i.e. Let the guilty person suffer.
withers highest part of a horse behind the
 neck
unwrung not sore, i.e. We are not affected.

chorus The chorus explained the forthcom-
 ing action. In a puppet show a chorus or
 "interpreter" announced the names of
 the characters and spoke the dialogue.
interpret provide the dialogue
love lover • **to dally** have sex

keen very sarcastic, witty – Note: Hamlet interprets "keen" to mean "eager for sex."

It would cost [...] take off my edge. You will have to groan (*stöhnen*) when you lose your virginity after satisfying my sexual desire.

Still better and worse wittier but more obscene

mistake Don't "take their husbands for better or worse" as in the marriage vow, but rather cheat on them by "taking" other men.

pox Pox on you! May you get syphilis!
damnable grimacing · **croaking** *krächzend*
raven *Rabe* · **bellow** shout angrily
apt skillful · **fit** ready for use
time agreeing the time right
confederate season time on my side
else no creature seeing since there is no-one else to observe me
rank foul, smelly
Hecate goddess of witchcraft · **ban** curse
thrice blasted repeated three times
dire property awful qualities
wholesome healthy · **usurp** destroy
estate position, property
extant exists, has survived · **choice** excellent

with false fire guns fired only with black powder and no bullet (*Geschoss*)

Give o'er (over) **the play.** Stop the play.

stricken fatally wounded
hart male deer · **ungalled** not wounded
watch stay awake
runs the world away That's the way the world is.

OPHELIA
You are keen, my lord, you are keen.
HAMLET
350 It would cost you a groaning to take off my edge.
OPHELIA
Still better and worse.
HAMLET
So you mistake your husbands.
355 [*To LUCANIUS*] Begin, murderer. Pox, leave thy damnable faces, and begin. Come, "the croaking raven doth bellow for revenge"*.
LUCIANUS
Thoughts black, hands apt, drugs fit, and time agreeing,
Confederate season else no creature seeing.
360 *Thou mixture rank, of midnight weeds collected*,*
With Hecate's ban thrice blasted, thrice infected,
Thy natural magic and dire property
On wholesome life usurp immediately.

He pours the poison into the sleeper's ears.

365 **HAMLET**
He poisons him i' the garden for his estate. His name's Gonzago. The story is extant, and written in choice Italian. You shall see anon how the murderer gets the love of Gonzago's wife.

CLAUDIUS rises

370

OPHELIA
The King rises.
HAMLET
What, frighted with false fire?
375 **QUEEN GERTRUDE**
[*To CLAUDIUS*] How fares my lord?
POLONIUS
Give o'er the play.
KING CLAUDIUS
380 Give me some light. Away.
COURTIERS
Lights, lights, lights!

Exeunt all but HAMLET and HORATIO

HAMLET
385   Why, let the stricken deer go weep*.
The hart ungallèd play.
For some must watch, while some must sleep.
So runs the world away.*

Would not this, sir, and a forest of feathers, if the rest of my for-
.390 tunes turn Turk with me, with two Provincial roses on my razed
shoes, get me a fellowship in a cry of players, sir?

HORATIO

Half a share.

HAMLET

395 A whole one, I.
> For thou dost know, O Damon dear,
> This realm dismantled was
> Of Jove himself, and now reigns here
> A very, very – pajock.

400 **HORATIO**

You might have rhymed.

HAMLET

O good Horatio, I'll take the Ghost's word for a thousand pound.
Didst perceive?

405 **HORATIO**

Very well, my lord.

HAMLET

Upon the talk of the poisoning?

HORATIO

I did very well note him.

410 *Enter ROSENCRANTZ and GUILDENSTERN*

HAMLET

Ah, ha! Come, some music! Come, the recorders.
> For if the King like not the comedy,
415 > Why then, belike, he likes it not, perdy.
Come, some music.

GUILDENSTERN

Good my lord, vouchsafe me a word with you.

HAMLET

420 Sir, a whole history.

GUILDENSTERN

The King, sir –

HAMLET

Ay, sir, what of him?

425 **GUILDENSTERN**

Is in his retirement marvellous distempered.

HAMLET

With drink, sir?

GUILDENSTERN

430 No, my lord, rather with choler.

HAMLET

Your wisdom should show itself more richer to signify this to
his doctor, for, for me to put him to his purgation* would perhaps plunge him into far more choler.

---

this this playlet just shown, produced by me and having the desired effect

forest of feathers feathers, as often worn by actors at the time

turn Turk with me go from bad to worse

Provincial roses ribbons with a rose-like pattern

razed with fashionable openings

fellowship partnership in an acting company

cry pack, as a pack of dogs, wolves

Damon an allusion to the legendary friend-ship of Damon and Pythias

realm kingdom • **dismantled** stripped, stolen

of Jove (Jupiter) belonging to Jove, i.e. King Hamlet

pajock a made-up word – perhaps: fool, idiot

You might [...] rhymed. "Ass" would par-tially rhyme with "was."

for a thousand pound as something com-pletely reliable

Didst perceive? Did you notice how the King reacted?

note him observe him

recorder *Blockflöte*

comedy (ironic) a comedy because it successfully had the desired effect of upsetting the King

belike perhaps

perdy corruption of "par dieu," i.e. indeed, assuredly

vouchsafe (formal) be so kind as to allow me

whole history (ironic) story, narrative

in his retirement withdrawn to his private chamber

marvellous marvellously, very

distempered upset, annoyed – also: drunk

choler anger

more richer more useful

signify tell, communicate

put him to his purgation treat/cure him

plunge him into (fig.) cause him to fall into

frame coherent form

start not don't jump away like a startled horse

from my affair from what I want to discuss

tame calm, subdued as a horse might be

pronounce proceed with what you want to say

in affliction of spirit greatly agitated

You are welcome. You are welcome to tell me that. Note: not a logical remark

courtesy courtly behaviour

breed type, kind

wholesome sane • **do** accomplish

commandment task given to me

pardon permission to leave

wit mind • **diseased** sick

command have for the asking

as you say, my mother i.e. It is my mother who is doing the commanding.

but to the matter Let's get to the point.

amazement great surprise

admiration bewilderment, confusion

sequel consequence

at the heels coming closely after

impart tell me

closet small, private room • **ere** before

we the royal "we"

were [...] our mother As if she were a super mother.

trade business

us object form of the royal "we"

by these pickers and stealers by my hands

distemper mental disorder

freely of your own free will • **bar** shut

your own liberty (1) your freedom from your mental disorder (2) your freedom, i.e. not being thrown into prison

deny refuse to speak about

griefs what disturbs you

lack advancement no possibility of acquiring a higher position

you have the voice [...] Denmark the King has said you will be the next king

435 **GUILDENSTERN**

Good my lord, put your discourse into some frame and start not so wildly from my affair.

HAMLET

I am tame, sir. Pronounce.

440 **GUILDENSTERN**

The Queen, your mother, in most great affliction of spirit, hath sent me to you.

HAMLET

You are welcome.

445 **GUILDENSTERN**

Nay, good my lord, this courtesy is not of the right breed. If it shall please you to make me a wholesome answer, I will do your mother's commandment. If not, your pardon and my return shall be the end of my business.

450 **HAMLET**

Sir, I cannot.

GUILDENSTERN

What, my lord?

HAMLET

455 Make you a wholesome answer. My wit's diseased. But, sir, such answer as I can make, you shall command, or rather, as you say, my mother. Therefore no more, but to the matter. My mother, you say?

ROSENCRANTZ

460 Then thus she says. Your behavior hath struck her into amazement and admiration.

HAMLET

O wonderful son that can so astonish a mother! But is there no sequel at the heels of this mother's admiration? Impart.

465 **ROSENCRANTZ**

She desires to speak with you in her closet, ere you go to bed.

HAMLET

We shall obey, were she ten times our mother. Have you any further trade with us?

470 **ROSENCRANTZ**

My lord, you once did love me.

HAMLET

So I do still, by these pickers and stealers*.

ROSENCRANTZ

475 Good my lord, what is your cause of distemper? You do freely bar the door upon your own liberty, if you deny your griefs to your friend.

HAMLET

Sir, I lack advancement.

480 **ROSENCRANTZ**

How can that be, when you have the voice of the King himself for your succession in Denmark?

HAMLET

Ay, but sir, "While the grass grows," the proverb is something musty.

485 *Enter the one with a recorder*

O, the recorder. Let me see one.
[*To ROSENCRANTZ and GUILDENSTERN*] To withdraw with you, why do you go about to recover the wind of me as if you
490 would drive me into a toil*?

GUILDENSTERN

O, my lord, if my duty be too bold, my love is too unmannerly.

HAMLET

I do not well understand that. Will you play upon this pipe?

495 **GUILDENSTERN**

My lord, I cannot.

HAMLET

I pray you.

GUILDENSTERN

500 Believe me, I cannot.

HAMLET

I do beseech you.

GUILDENSTERN

I know no touch of it, my lord.

505 **HAMLET**

'Tis as easy as lying. Govern these ventages with your fingers and thumb, give it breath with your mouth, and it will discourse most eloquent music. Look you, these are the stops.

GUILDENSTERN

510 But these cannot I command to any utterance of harmony. I have not the skill.

HAMLET

Why, look you now, how unworthy a thing you make of me. You would play upon me, you would seem to know my stops,
515 you would pluck out the heart of my mystery, you would sound me from my lowest note to the top of my compass. And there is much music, excellent voice, in this little organ. Yet cannot you make it speak. 'Sblood, do you think I am easier to be played on than a pipe? Call me what instrument you will, though you can fret me, yet you cannot play upon me.

520 *Enter POLONIUS*

God bless you, sir.

POLONIUS

My lord, the Queen would speak with you, and presently.

525 **HAMLET**

Do you see yonder cloud that's almost in shape of a camel?

While the grass grows, the horse starves.
i.e. Don't wait too long for what you think is the best opportunity before you take action. It might be too late.
proverb *Spruch* • **something** somewhat
musty *abgedroschen*

go about conspire
recover the wind of me [...] toil get me into a toil (net) as if I were an animal being hunted
if my duty be too bold [...] too umannerly. If I seem too aggressive in questioning you, it is because it is my duty and my love for you that makes me forget my manners.
pipe recorder

I pray you. I beg of you to do so.

beseech ask, beg

I know no touch of it I have no idea how to play it.

lying either *lügen* or *liegen*
govern cover • **ventage** finger hole, stop
discourse produce

utterance sound

pluck out pull out
heart of my mystery most personal secrets
sound me explore my depths
top of my compass upper limit of my notes
organ recorder
speak make music
'Sblood By God's blood on the cross!
pipe recorder
fret (1) irritate, (2) add frets (*Griffleisten*) to the fingerboard of a stringed instrument

and presently immediately

yonder above and far away

by th' (the) mass according to the size and shape

It is backed like it has the back of

whale *Wal*

by and by immediately
they fool me They go along with my foolishness.
to the top of my bent to an extent that is hardly bearable

POLONIUS
By th' mass, and 'tis like a camel indeed.
HAMLET
530 Methinks it is like a weasel.
POLONIUS
It is backed like a weasel.
HAMLET
Or like a whale?
535 **POLONIUS**
Very like a whale.
HAMLET
Then I will come to my mother by and by.
[*Aside*] They fool me to the top of my bent.
540 [*To POLONIUS*] I will come by and by.
POLONIUS
I will say so.
HAMLET
"By and by" is easily said.

Exit POLONIUS

545 Leave me, friends.

Exeunt all but HAMLET

very witching time best time for witches to be active
churchyard *Friedhof* · yawn *gähnen*
contagion poison, disease

quake shudder · soft Let's be quiet.
nature natural love for a mother

firm bosom (fig.) determined heart
not unnatural not physically
speak daggers (*Dolche*) hurt her with words

in this be hypocrites my words will be cruel but my actions will not
How […] somever however
she be shent she be put to shame
To give them seals to actually give my words the seal (*Siegel*) of approval, i.e. to act on my words
never my soul consent My soul would never agree to that.

'Tis now the very witching time of night,
When churchyards yawn and hell itself breathes out
550 Contagion to this world. Now could I drink hot blood*,
And do such bitter business as the day
Would quake to look on. Soft, now to my mother.
O heart, lose not thy nature. Let not ever
The soul of Nero* enter this firm bosom.
555 Let me be cruel, not unnatural.
I will speak daggers to her, but use none.
My tongue and soul in this be hypocrites.
How in my words somever she be shent
To give them seals never my soul consent.

Exit

Summary

Hamlet instructs the players in their way of acting. Hamlet confides his ruse to Horatio, whom he calls his true friend.

The visitors arrive to watch the play. After a brief exchange of words between Hamlet and his uncle, as well as with Ophelia, a dumb show begins.

When Claudius abruptly leaves the play with his entourage, Hamlet and Horatio feel convinced that the ghost has spoken the truth.

Later, Rosencrantz and Guildenstern are instructed by Gertrude to call on Hamlet, who then indicates to his friends how they have treated him.

Tasks

1. Instructing the players

a) Pair work: Explain to your partner what qualities you consider important for a good actor.

b) Read the pieces of advice below and tick (√) the ones Hamlet really gives. Correct the wrong ones and give evidence from the text.

	Piece of advice	Evidence	√
1	Exaggerate the words as does the town-crier.		
2	Use moderate hand gestures.		
3	Be passionate when showing emotions to impress the groundlings.		
4	Let your good sense guide you in your acting.		
5	Fit the action to the word and the word to the action.		
6	Act naturally.		
7	Entertain the uneducated and mock the prudent.		

c) State in your own words what Hamlet says about the purpose of playing.

"For anything so overdone is from the purpose of playing, whose end, both at the first and now, was and is to hold, as 'twere, the mirror up to nature, to show virtue her own feature, scorn her own image, and the very age and body of the time his form and pressure." (ll. 24-29)

d) In class, discuss the importance of plays for society. Consider:
- raising important issues
- mirroring society's problems
- entertaining

2. The play-within-the play

a) Summarize the main contents of the play-within-the play.
b) Group work (6): What are the characters thinking while they are watching the play? Each student puts her-/ himself into a character's shoes and writes down what his or her character is thinking. Exchange your ideas.

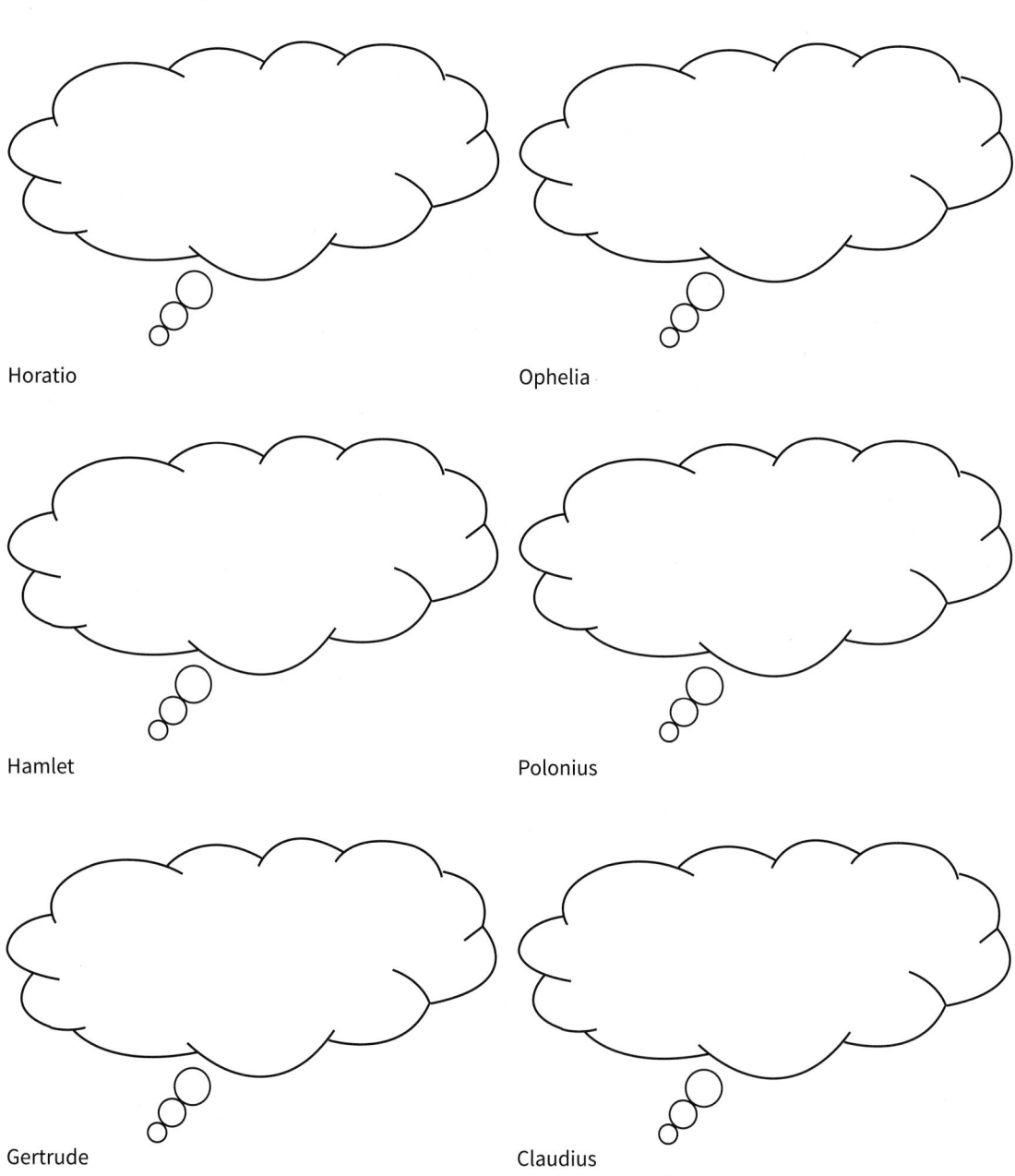

Horatio

Ophelia

Hamlet

Polonius

Gertrude

Claudius

c) When Claudius asks Hamlet about the play's name (l. 330), Hamlet invents a new name – "The Mousetrap" – for his altered version of "The Murder of Gonzago". Explain why Hamlet has changed the title of the play and what the new title implies.

d) Read the info box on the play-within-a-play and analyse the function of the play-within-a-play in *Hamlet*.

> ### Info: The play-within-a-play
>
> The play-within-a-play is a dramatic convention very popular in Shakespeare's time: a character of a story becomes the narrator of a second story.
>
> As the first professional theatre had only been established some years before in 1567, Elizabethan authors liked to explore the new technical possibilities of the theatre and the nature of entertainment. Besides, the question of the kind of truth that can be told through plays was a focus of the playwrights' interest. As it was widely believed at the time that the theatre had a real impact on its audience, the performance of a crime was believed to force the criminal spectator to admit his or her guilt.
>
> Thus, it is not surprising that a play such as *Hamlet* that evolves around the themes of performance, deception, authenticity, and reality makes use of this literary device. As it also keeps the audience at a distance from the actual crime, it also questions the reliability and the motives of the storyteller.
>
> In general, the inset story or play may have various functions. It may simply offer entertainment, provide an example of what is told in the outer story, have symbolic or psychological significance to the characters of the outer story, or reveal the truth about something that has happened in the outer story. Finally, it may also deflect the audience's attention from a plot twist.

3. Claudius' reaction

a) Assess Claudius' reaction and tick the adjective that best describes his state of mind: Is he
   ☐ terrified   ☐ confused   ☐ upset   ☐ agitated?

b) Explain your choice.

c) Imagine you are a journalist who attended the play and witnessed Claudius' reaction. Write an article for the gossip column of your newspaper.

4. Rosencrantz and Guildenstern

a) State the purpose of the two men's call on Hamlet.

b) Explain the symbolic meaning of the recorder.

c) Analyse Hamlet's attitude towards his two friends by looking at the language Hamlet uses.

5. Hamlet and Gertrude

a) Decide which summary best sums up Hamlet's soliloquy at the end of the scene.
   1 Hamlet wants to use witchcraft to avenge his father's death.
   2 Although Hamlet feels revengeful, he does not intend to harm his mother, but merely chide her.
   3 Hamlet will hide his true feelings towards his mother by using witchcraft.

b) Examine Hamlet's choice of words.

c) Hamlet contemplates his conversation with his mother. Anticipate their conversation and jot down some ideas of what they might be saying to each other.

SCENE III. A room in the castle.

Enter KING CLAUDIUS, ROSENCRANTZ, and GUILDENSTERN

KING CLAUDIUS

him his behaviour	I like him not, nor stands it safe with us
range to have free play	To let his madness range. Therefore prepare you.
commission official written order	5 I your commission will forthwith dispatch
forthwith at once • **dispatch** prepare	And he to England shall along with you.
terms of our estate the responsibilities I have as King	The terms of our estate may not endure
endure *ertragen* • **hazard** danger	Hazard so dangerous as doth hourly grow
out of his lunacies resulting from his craziness	Out of his lunacies.

10 **GUILDENSTERN**

ourselves provide take careful precautions	We will ourselves provide.
fear duty, concern, care	Most holy and religious fear it is
bodies subjects	To keep those many many bodies safe
live and feed upon are overly dependent on	That live and feed upon your majesty.

15 **ROSENCRANTZ**   ➲ **Fate vs. free will**

single and peculiar life private individuals	The single and peculiar life is bound
bound obliged	With all the strength and armour of the mind
armour *Harnisch*	To keep itself from noyance; but much more
noyance harm	That spirit upon whose weal depends and rests
spirit i.e. the King • **weal** welfare	20 The lives of many. The cease of majesty
cease of majesty the death of a king	Dies not alone, but like a gulf doth draw
gulf whirlpool • **draw** pull in	What's near it with it. It is a massy wheel,
massy massive • **wheel** i.e. wheel of fortune	Fixed on the summit of the highest mount,
summit very top • **mount** hill or mountain	To whose huge spokes ten thousand lesser things
spoke *Speiche*	25 Are mortised and adjoined, which, when it falls,
mortised fastened securely	Each small annexment, petty consequence,
adjoined connected • **annexment** addition	Attends the boisterous ruin. Never alone
petty consequence insignificant thing connected with it	Did the King sigh, but with a general groan.
attends accompanies	**KING CLAUDIUS**
boisterous ruin tumultuous downfall	30 Arm you, I pray you, to this speedy voyage,
sigh *seufzen*	For we will fetters put upon this fear,
but with a general groan The whole kingdom would also commiserate with the King.	Which now goes too free-footed.
arm you prepare yourself	**ROSENCRANTZ, GUILDENSTERN**
fetters chains	We will haste us.
free-footed (fig.) is able to walk about freely	
haste go quickly	

35 *Exeunt ROSENCRANTZ and GUILDENSTERN*

Enter POLONIUS

POLONIUS

arras wall hanging, tapestry	My lord, he's going to his mother's closet.
convey myself secretly place myself	Behind the arras I'll convey myself
process proceedings	40 To hear the process. I'll warrant she'll tax him home.
I'll warrant I am certain	And, as you said, and wisely was it said,
she'll tax him home criticize him severely for his crazy behaviour	

'Tis meet that some more audience than a mother,
Since nature makes them partial, should o'erhear
The speech, of vantage. Fare you well, my liege.
45 I'll call upon you ere you go to bed,
And tell you what I know.
KING CLAUDIUS
Thanks, dear my lord.

Exit POLONIUS

50 O, my offence is rank it smells to heaven.
It hath the primal eldest curse upon't –
A brother's murder. Pray can I not,
Though inclination be as sharp as will,
My stronger guilt defeats my strong intent,
55 And, like a man to double business bound,
I stand in pause where I shall first begin,
And both neglect. What if this cursèd hand
Were thicker than itself with brother's blood,
Is there not rain enough in the sweet heavens
60 To wash it white as snow? Whereto serves mercy
But to confront the visage of offence?
And what's in prayer but this twofold force,
To be forestallèd ere we come to fall,
Or pardoned being down? Then I'll look up.
65 My fault is past. But O, what form of prayer
Can serve my turn? "Forgive me my foul murder?"
That cannot be, since I am still possessed
Of those effects for which I did the murder –
My crown, mine own ambition and my queen.
70 May one be pardoned and retain the offence?
In the corrupted currents of this world
Offence's gilded hand* may shove by justice,
And oft 'tis seen the wicked prize itself
Buys out the law. But 'tis not so above.
75 There is no shuffling, there the action lies
In his true nature, and we ourselves compelled
Even to the teeth and forehead of our faults
To give in evidence. What then? What rests?
Try what repentance can. What can it not?
80 Yet what can it when one cannot repent?
O wretched state. O bosom black as death.
O limèd soul, that struggling to be free,
Art more engaged. Help, angels! Make assay.
Bow, stubborn knees; and heart with strings of steel*,
85 Be soft as sinews of the new-born babe.
All may be well.

**◉ Questions
of morality**

meet advisable
nature makes them partial the natural
bond of mother and child makes mothers
biased
o'erhear listen secretly
of vantage from the secret hiding place

offence crime • **rank** stinking
primal eldest curse upon't original sin, the
first murder when Cain killed Abel
inclination [...] will my desire to pray is as
strong as my determination to do so
double business bound obliged to deal with
two conflicting tasks at the same time
stand in pause [...] begin am undecided
where to begin
cursèd *verflucht*
thicker than itself with a heavy layer of
blood
Whereto [...] offence? What is the function
of mercy if it can't confront the face of
crime?
what's in prayer what's the use of prayer
twofold force two earnest requests to God
in the Lord's Prayer
forstallèd prevented • **fall** sin
being down having sinned
turn return to grace • **foul** wicked

effects advantages, benefit

retain the offence continue to enjoy what I
have achieved in spite of my crime
corrupted currents corrupt ways of doing
things
gilded golden • **shove by** thrust, push aside
buys out buys off, manipulates
shuffling trickery
the action lies [...] in his true nature wicked deeds are revealed for what they are
we ourselves compelled [...] evidence we
are forced to face our sins
What rests? What remains for me to do?
repentance *Buße* • **repent** *Buße tun*
wretched miserable • **state** *Zustand*
limèd trapped as a bird caught on a twig
covered with lime, a sticky substance
art is • **engaged** entrapped, (*verwickelt*)
make assay make an effort
to bow *beugen* • **stubborn** *stur*
heart with strings of steel His crime has
changed his heartstrings to steel.

He kneels.

Enter HAMLET behind him

HAMLET

pat conveniently	90 Now might I do it pat, now he is praying.

90 Now might I do it pat, now he is praying.
And now I'll do't.

draws pulls out

He draws his sword.

And so he goes to heaven,
And so am I revenged. That would be scanned.
95 A villain kills my father, and for that,
I, his sole son, do this same villain send
To heaven.
O, this is hire and salary, not revenge.
He took my father grossly, full of bread,
100 With all his crimes broad blown, as flush as May;
And how his audit stands who knows save heaven?
But in our circumstance and course of thought
'Tis heavy with him.
 And am I then revenged
105 To take him in the purging of his soul,
When he is fit and seasoned for his passage?
No.

Sheathes his sword

Up, sword; and know thou a more horrid hent.
110 When he is drunk asleep, or in his rage,
Or in th' incestuous pleasure of his bed,
At gaming, swearing or about some act
That has no relish of salvation in't.
Then trip him that his heels may kick at heaven,
115 And that his soul may be as damned and black
As hell, whereto it goes. My mother stays.
This physic but prolongs thy sickly days.

Exit

CLAUDIUS

120 [*Rising*] My words fly up, my thoughts remain below.
Words without thoughts never to heaven go.

Exit

Glossary (left margin):

pat conveniently

draws pulls out

That would be scanned. That needs to be carefully considered.
villain criminal
sole only
hire and salary As if I had hired him to kill my father and now I am paying him for this deed.
took killed
grossly not purified by repentance
full of bread enjoying the pleasures of life
broad blown in full blossom
as flush as May as when plants grow vigorously in May
audit account (*Konto*) with God
save except for
But in our [...] thought as far as man can understand in his limited way
heavy with him The weight of his sins is heavy.
purging cleansing • **seasoned** prepared
passage journey to heaven
to sheathe *in die Scheide stecken*
hent opportunity
drunk asleep completely drunk
in his rage sexually excited
incestuous *blutschänderisch*
gaming gambling • **swearing** *Fluchen*
about some act or similar behaviour
relish hint, trace • **salvation** *Erlösung*
trip him cause him to fall
that his heels (*Fersen*) **[...] at heaven** that he can no longer walk into heaven
stays is waiting
physic medicine
to prolong to delay

Summary

Sensing impending danger, Claudius informs Rosencrantz and Guildenstern that he intends to send Hamlet and his two friends off to England under the false pretence of a diplomatic mission.
Polonius informs Claudius about his plan to eavesdrop on Gertrude and Hamlet's conversation.
Alone on stage Claudius contemplates his offence. When Hamlet sees his uncle, he considers his options of killing him.

Tasks

1. Rosencrantz's speech

a) The paraphrases of Rosenkrantz's speech in modern-day English have been jumbled up. Bring the sentences into the correct order and identify the lines in the original text.

No.	Paraphrases	Lines
	It is like a huge wheel with less important people joined to it, which is positioned on top of a mountain.	
	When the monarch sighs, his subjects groan.	
	When the monarch dies or is dethroned, everything and everyone around him tumbles, too, as if in a whirlwind.	
	Even more so must a ruler's well-being be protected, as his subjects' lives depend on it.	
	Everyone tries to avoid harm in their life by using their intelligence.	
	When the wheel falls from the mountain, everything fixed to it falls as well.	

b) Explain how Rosencrantz comes across. Does he flatter the king? Is he worried? Does he stir the King's guilty conscience? Give evidence from the text to prove your impression.

c) How does Claudius take in Rosencrantz's words? Note down some ideas and exchange them with a partner.

2. Claudius' soliloquy

a) Look up the story of Cain and Abel in the Bible (Genesis 4:11-12) and explain the reference Claudius makes.

b) Sum up Claudius' soliloquy in your own words.

c) Identify the following stylistic devices in the soliloquy and analyse their effect on the audience.

alliteration – anaphora – apostrophe – enumeration – exclamation – rhetorical question

3. Hamlet weighing his options: to kill or not to kill?

a) Describe the situation Hamlet finds Claudius in when he enters the stage.

b) List the arguments Hamlet is weighing up to decide whether or not to kill Claudius.

c) Group work (3-4): Good angel – bad angel: Act out this passage (ll. 89-118):
One student sits on a chair taking Hamlet's part. Two students step behind him and represent his conscience. Whereas the good angel brings forward arguments why Hamlet should not kill Claudius, the bad angel states reasons for why he should kill the king.

SCENE IV. The Queen's closet.

Enter QUEEN GERTRUDE and POLONIUS

○ **Questions of morality**

straight right away
Look you [...] to him. Make sure you scold (*ausschimpfen*) him very severely.
pranks jokes, tricks • **broad** outrageous
to bear with to tolerate
your grace your highness
hath screened (fig.) acted like a fire screen in front of a fireplace
heat anger
I'll silence me even here. Now I'll hide and keep silent.
round direct, to the point
warrant promise
fear me not don't doubt me
withdraw go into hiding

POLONIUS
He will come straight. Look you lay home to him.
Tell him his pranks have been too broad to bear with,
5 And that your grace hath screened and stood between
Much heat and him. I'll silence me even here.
Pray you, be round with him.
HAMLET
[*Within*] Mother, mother, mother!
10 **QUEEN GERTRUDE**
I'll warrant you. Fear me not.
Withdraw, I hear him coming.

POLONIUS hides behind the arras

Enter HAMLET

father (here): stepfather
to offend to cause s.o. pain

my father (here): Hamlet's real father

idle foolish

go come on

15 **HAMLET**
Now, mother, what's the matter?
QUEEN GERTRUDE
Hamlet, thou hast thy father much offended.
HAMLET
20 Mother, you have my father much offended.
QUEEN GERTRUDE
Come, come, you answer with an idle tongue.
HAMLET
Go, go, you question with a wicked tongue.
25 **QUEEN GERTRUDE**
Why, how now, Hamlet?
HAMLET
What's the matter now?
QUEEN GERTRUDE
30 Have you forgot me?
HAMLET
No, by the rood, not so.
You are the Queen, your husband's brother's wife,
And – would it were not so – you are my mother.
35 **QUEEN GERTRUDE**
Nay, then I'll set those to you that can speak.
HAMLET
Come, come, and sit you down. You shall not budge.
You go not till I set you up a glass
40 Where you may see the inmost part of you.

○ **The roles(s) of women**
○ **Questions of morality**

Have you forgot me? Have you forgotten who I am?

rood cross of Jesus

then [...] can speak. Then I'll send for s.o. who can confront you more forcefully.

budge move
set you up a glass place a mirror before you

QUEEN GERTRUDE
What wilt thou do? Thou wilt not murder me?
Help, help, ho!
POLONIUS
45 [*Behind the arras*] What ho! Help, help, help!
HAMLET
[*Drawing his sword*] How now, a rat? Dead for a ducat, dead.

ducat silver or gold coin

He thrusts his sword through the arras.

POLONIUS
50 [*Behind*] O, I am slain!

to slay, slew, slain to kill violently

Falls and dies

QUEEN GERTRUDE
[*To HAMLET*] O me, what hast thou done?
HAMLET
55 Nay, I know not. Is it the King?
QUEEN GERTRUDE
O, what a rash and bloody deed is this!
HAMLET
A bloody deed – almost as bad, good-mother,
60 As kill a king and marry with his brother.

good-mother stepmother

QUEEN GERTRUDE
As kill a king?
HAMLET
Ay, lady, 'twas my word.

65 *Lifts up the arras and discovers POLONIUS*

[*To POLONIUS*] Thou wretched, rash, intruding fool, farewell.
I took thee for thy better. Take thy fortune.
Thou find'st to be too busy is some danger.
[*To QUEEN GERTRUDE*]
70 Leave wringing of your hands. Peace, sit you down
And let me wring your heart. For so I shall
If it be made of penetrable stuff,
If damnèd custom have not brassed it so
That it is proof and bulwark against sense.
75 **QUEEN GERTRUDE**
What have I done, that thou darest wag thy tongue
In noise so rude against me?
HAMLET
Such an act
80 That blurs the grace and blush of modesty.
Calls virtue hypocrite, takes off the rose
From the fair forehead of an innocent love

intruding getting involved in matters that are none of your business
thy better i.e. the king
take thy fortune accept your fate
Thou [...] danger. You found out that spying on others can be dangerous.
leave stop
wringing of your hands *die Hände ringen*
wring (here) grasp
penetrable able to show feeling
stuff substance
damnèd custom damned habit, habitual vice
brassed hardened it like brass
proof and bulwark armoured and strengthened
sense natural feeling, guilt
wag (move) **thy tongue** *schelten*
blurs ruins • **grace** beauty
blush (fig.) innocence
modesty *Anstand, Bescheidenheit*
Calls virtue hypocrite turns virtue into hypocrisy
rose traditional symbol of purity

sets causes to appear • **blister** Blase
marriage-vow Eheversprechen
dicers' oaths worthless promises of gamblers
the body of contraction the marriage contract
plucks violently pulls
sweet religion [...] rhapsody of words.
  makes sweet religion just a meaningless
  jumble of words
glow blush with shame
this solidity [...] mass solid earth, a compound of the four elements
tristful visage sad face
as against the doom as if the Day of Judgement were near
thought-sick sick at the thought
that roars [...] thunders is already so very
  emotional
in the index before you have even properly
  begun
counterfeit presentment portrait
brow forehead • **Hyperion** sun god
front forehead • **Jove** the king of the gods
Mars the god of war
station manner of standing
herald Mercury the winged messenger of
  the gods
new lighted having just landed
combination combination of physical features
to set his seal to contribute his characteristic
assurance of a man the certainty of being
  a man
mildewed affected by a disease caused by
  a fungus
ear Ähre • **blasting** making diseased
wholesome healthy
leave to feed stop feeding • **batten** fatten
heyday in the blood sexual excitement
tame lahm • **humble** respectful
waits upon is subservient to
apoplexed paralysed
for madness [...] err Even a mad person
  would not make such a mistake.
nor sense to ecstasy was ne'er (never) **so
  thralled [...] in such a difference.** Nor
  was feeling ever so overpowering that
  the person was not able to differentiate
  between normal and excessive feeling.
cozened deceived
hoodman-blind blind man's bluff (a game)
sans all without anything else
but [...] could not so mope not even a
  sickly part of one of the functioning
  senses could have acted so aimlessly
rebellious hell sexual urge that overpowers
  reason
mutine mutiny, rebel against
matron mature woman
flaming easily aroused sexually

And sets a blister there*, makes marriage-vows
As false as dicers' oaths. O, such a deed
85 As from the body of contraction plucks
The very soul, and sweet religion makes
A rhapsody of words. Heaven's face doth glow,
Yea, this solidity and compound mass
With tristful visage, as against the doom,
90 Is thought-sick at the act.
QUEEN GERTRUDE
Ay me, what act,
That roars so loud and thunders in the index?
HAMLET
95 Look here upon this picture, and on this,
The counterfeit presentment of two brothers.
See, what a grace was seated on this brow –
Hyperion's curls, the front of Jove himself.
An eye like Mars, to threaten and command,
100 A station like the herald Mercury
New lighted on a heaven-kissing hill;
A combination and a form indeed
Where every god did seem to set his seal
To give the world assurance of a man.
105 This was your husband. Look you now, what follows.
Here is your husband, like a mildewed ear
Blasting his wholesome brother. Have you eyes?
Could you on this fair mountain leave to feed,
And batten on this moor? Ha, have you eyes?
110 You cannot call it love, for at your age
The heyday in the blood is tame, it's humble
And waits upon the judgment, and what judgment
Would step from this to this? Sense, sure, you have –
Else could you not have motion. But sure, that sense
115 Is apoplexed, for madness would not err
Nor sense to ecstasy was ne'er so thralled
But it reserved some quantity of choice
To serve in such a difference. What devil was't
That thus hath cozened you at hoodman-blind*?
120 Eyes without feeling, feeling without sight,
Ears without hands or eyes, smelling sans all,
Or but a sickly part of one true sense
Could not so mope. O shame, where is thy blush?
Rebellious hell,
125 If thou canst mutine in a matron's bones,
To flaming youth let virtue be as wax

And melt in her own fire. Proclaim no shame
When the compulsive ardour gives the charge,
Since frost itself as actively doth burn
130 And reason panders will.

QUEEN GERTRUDE
O Hamlet, speak no more.
Thou turn'st mine eyes into my very soul
And there I see such black and grainèd spots
135 As will not leave their tinct.

HAMLET
Nay, but to live
In the rank sweat of an enseamèd bed,
Stewed in corruption, honeying and making love
140 Over the nasty sty –

QUEEN GERTRUDE
O, speak to me no more.
These words like daggers enter in mine ears.
No more, sweet Hamlet.

145 **HAMLET**
A murderer and a villain,
A slave that is not twentieth part the tithe
Of your precedent lord, a vice of kings*,
A cutpurse of the empire and the rule,
150 That from a shelf the precious diadem stole
And put it in his pocket –

QUEEN GERTRUDE
No more.

HAMLET
155 A king of shreds and patches –

Enter GHOST

⊙ **The roles(s)
of women**

Save me, and hover o'er me with your wings,
You heavenly guards!
[*To GHOST*] What would you, gracious figure?

QUEEN GERTRUDE
160 Alas, he's mad!

HAMLET
[*To GHOST*] Do you not come your tardy son to chide,
That, lapsed in time and passion, lets go by
The important acting of your dread command? O, say!

165 **GHOST**
Do not forget. This visitation
Is but to whet thy almost blunted purpose.
But look, amazement on thy mother sits,
O, step between her and her fighting soul.
170 Conceit in weakest bodies strongest works.
Speak to her, Hamlet.

---

her youth's • **proclaim** admit
compulsive ardour unstoppable sexual urge
give the charge goes on the attack
frost [...] burn Even in middle age the
    sexual urge can be very active.
reason panders will Reason finds excuses
    for accepting lust.
grained engrained, so fixed as to be impos-
    sible to remove
will not leave their tinct The stain cannot
    be washed away.
rank awful smelling • **enseamed** greasy
stewed boiled, cooked
honeying using love-talk
sty pigsty, place where pigs are kept

tithe tenth part
precedent lord previous husband
vice *Laster*
cutpurse thief • **rule** kingdom
diadem crown

a king [...] patches dressed like a clown
    with pieces of cloth sewn together

to hover *schweben*
heavenly guards angels
what would you what do you want
gracious kind, loving

tardy delaying action • **to chide** *schelten*
lapsed in time and passion having allowed
    too much time to pass by and the motiva-
    tion to act to weaken
lets go by does not complete

to whet to sharpen
blunted purpose task that has become like
    a knife that is blunted (*stumpf geworden*)
amazement shock
step between intervene
conceit imagination

bend your eye on direct your eyes to
vacancy empty space
incorporal having no substance
air air with no physical substance
to hold discourse to talk to • **forth** before
peep linsen
in the alarm awakened by an alarm to get ready for battle
bedded lying flat on the bed
like life in excrements as if excrements (outgrowths of the body like nails and hair) had a life of their own
distemper discontent • **sprinkle** streuen
to glare anstarren
his form [...] conjoined His appearance as a ghost and the reason for appearing are united.
capable capable of responding, of feeling
lest for fear that • **piteous** arousing pity
action manner of behaving
convert transform
stern effects determined intentions
want true colour lack the bright colour of determined action
tears perchance for blood shedding tears instead of blood

HAMLET
How is it with you, lady?
QUEEN GERTRUDE
175 Alas, how is't with you,
That you do bend your eye on vacancy,
And with the incorporal air do hold discourse?
Forth at your eyes your spirits wildly peep,
And, as the sleeping soldiers in the alarm,
180 Your bedded hair like life in excrements,
Starts up, and stands on end. O gentle son,
Upon the heat and flame of thy distemper
Sprinkle cool patience. Whereon do you look?
HAMLET
185 On him, on him. Look you, how pale he glares.
His form and cause conjoined, preaching to stones,
Would make them capable.
[*To GHOST*] Do not look upon me,
Lest with this piteous action you convert
190 My stern effects. Then what I have to do
Will want true colour, tears perchance for blood.
QUEEN GERTRUDE
To whom do you speak this?
HAMLET
195 Do you see nothing there?
QUEEN GERTRUDE
Nothing at all, yet all that is, I see.
HAMLET
Nor did you nothing hear?
200 **QUEEN GERTRUDE**
No, nothing but ourselves.
HAMLET
Why, look you there. Look how it steals away.
My father, in his habit as he lived.
205 Look where he goes even now out at the portal.

steals away slips away
in his habit as he lived dressed as he usually did
portal doorway

Exit GHOST

QUEEN GERTRUDE
This the very coinage of your brain.
This bodiless creation ecstasy
210 Is very cunning in.
HAMLET
Ecstasy?
My pulse as yours doth temperately keep time,
And makes as healthful music. It is not madness
215 That I have uttered. Bring me to the test.
And I the matter will reword, which madness
Would gambol from. Mother, for love of grace,

very coinage only an invention
This bodiless creation [...] cunning in. Madness is very clever at creating this kind of hallucination.
temperately keep time keep a steady beat
makes as healthful music by the beating of my heart you can tell how healthy I am
to utter to speak
I the matter will reword Whatever you say I will be able to repeat it precisely.
madness would gambol from madness would not be able to do
grace God

◗ The roles(s) of women
◗ Questions of morality

Lay not that flattering unction to your soul
That not your trespass, but my madness speaks.
220 It will but skin and film the ulcerous place
Whilst rank corruption, mining all within,
Infects unseen. Confess yourself to heaven;
Repent what's past, avoid what is to come,
And do not spread the compost on the weeds
225 To make them ranker. Forgive me this my virtue,
For in the fatness of these pursy times
Virtue itself of Vice must pardon beg.
Yea, curb and woo for leave to do him good.
QUEEN GERTRUDE
230 O Hamlet, thou hast cleft my heart in twain.
HAMLET
O, throw away the worser part of it,
And live the purer with the other half.
Good night – but go not to mine uncle's bed.
235 Assume a virtue if you have it not.
That monster custom, who all sense doth eat,
Of habits devil, is angel yet in this,
That to the use of actions fair and good
He likewise gives a frock or livery
240 That aptly is put on. Refrain tonight,
And that shall lend a kind of easiness
To the next abstinence, the next more easy –
For use almost can change the stamp of nature –
And shame the devil, or throw him out
245 With wondrous potency. Once more, good night,
And when you are desirous to be blessed,
I'll blessing beg of you. For this same lord

Pointing to POLONIUS

I do repent but heaven hath pleased it so,
250 To punish me with this, and this with me,
That I must be their scourge and minister.
I will bestow him, and will answer well
The death I gave him. So, again, good night.
I must be cruel, only to be kind.
255 Thus bad begins and worse remains behind.
One word more, good lady.
QUEEN GERTRUDE
What shall I do?
HAMLET
260 Not this, by no means, that I bid you do –
Let the bloat King tempt you again to bed,
Pinch wanton on your cheek, call you his mouse,
And let him for a pair of reechy kisses,

Marginal icons:

○ Fate vs.
   free will
○ The roles(s)
   of women
○ Questions
   of morality

○ The roles(s)
   of women
○ Questions
   of morality

Glossary (right column):

lay not that flattering (*schmeichelnd*) **unction** (*Salbe*) **[...] soul** don't try to lessen the pain in your soul with an unction
trespass sin
skin and film cover as if with skin
ulcerous place open wound
rank absolute, complete
mining undermining · **weeds** *Unkräuter*
ranker worse, more disgusting
this my virtue *meine Moralpredigt*
fatness being excessively fat and vulgar
pursy flabby, flatulant
pardon beg ask for forgiveness
curb bow · **woo** seek affection

cleft my heart in twin split my heart in two

assume take on
monster custom habit that is hard to break
all sense doth eat consumes natural feelings and common sense
of habits devil, is angel yet even bad habits may also have good aspects
that to the use [...] fair and good when good or just deeds are involved
He i.e. monster custom
frock dress · **livery** special uniform
aptly easily
refrain hold yourself back
lend a kind of easiness make it easier
abstinence refraining from sex · **use** habit
stamp of nature natural inclination
wondrous potency wonderful power
blessing beg of you ask you to bless me

heaven hath pleased it so It was the will of God.
to punish me with this to cause me to kill Polonius
this with me That I will be punished for killing Polonius.
their scourge and minister heaven's agent to carry out punishments
bestow put away
answer well explain properly

bloat bloated, filled with alcohol, fat
tempt *in Versuchung führen*
pinch wanton on your cheeks pinch (squeeze) the skin on your cheeks to make them wantonly (*schamlos*) red
reechy filthy

paddling fingering fondly
make you to ravel all this matter out
   cause you to reveal everything
in craft as a deception
'Twere good It would be good if
sober reasonable
paddock toad
bat *Fledermaus* • **gib** tomcat
dear concernings important matters
in despite of in spite of
sense and secrecy being reasonable and
   prudent about keeping s.th. secret
unpeg remove the pegs (*Holznagel*)
ape *Menschenaffe*
try conclusions see what happens
creep *kriechen* • **down** falling down
assured certain
Be thou assured [...] said to me. You can
   be dead certain I will not reveal anything
   you have said to me.

alack alas: *leider*
concluded decided

sealed closed with a seal (*Siegel*), official
adder poisonous snake
fanged with two sharp, pointed teeth
They bear the mandate They have been
   ordered.
they must sweep my way They must
   prepare the way for me.
marshal me to knavery set a trap for me
sport game
engineer the maker of military devices
hoist blown up • **petard** bomb
and 't shall go hard It will be quite an
   explosion.
delve dig • **yard** 1 yard = 0.9114 m
their mines tunnels built under the city wall
at towards
When in one line [...] meet. When two
   clever strategies collide.
this man i.e. Polonius
set me packing force me to leave
lug drag • **guts** corpse
neighbor neighbouring
counsellor advisor
grave serious, also a pun on grave (*Grab*)
prating knave chattering, tricky fellow
to draw toward an end with you to con-
   clude our conversation

Or paddling in your neck with his damned fingers,
265 Make you to ravel all this matter out,
    That I essentially am not in madness,
    But mad in craft. 'Twere good you let him know,
    For who that's but a queen, fair, sober, wise,
    Would from a paddock, from a bat, a gib,
270 Such dear concernings hide? Who would do so?
    No, in despite of sense and secrecy,
    Unpeg the basket on the house's top.
    Let the birds fly, and, like the famous ape,
    To try conclusions, in the basket creep,
275 And break your own neck down.*
    QUEEN GERTRUDE
    Be thou assured, if words be made of breath,
    And breath of life, I have no life to breathe
    What thou hast said to me.
280 **HAMLET**
    I must to England. You know that?
    QUEEN GERTRUDE
    Alack, I had forgot.
    'Tis so concluded on.
285 **HAMLET**
    There's letters sealed, and my two schoolfellows,
    Whom I will trust as I will adders fanged,
    They bear the mandate, they must sweep my way
    And marshal me to knavery. Let it work,
290 For 'tis the sport to have the engineer
    Hoist with his own petard, and 't shall go hard
    But I will delve one yard below their mines,
    And blow them at the moon. O, 'tis most sweet
    When in one line two crafts directly meet.
295 This man shall set me packing.
    I'll lug the guts into the neighbour room.
    Mother, good night. Indeed this counsellor
    Is now most still, most secret and most grave,
    Who was in life a foolish prating knave.
300 Come, sir, to draw toward an end with you.
    Good night, mother.

Exeunt separately; HAMLET dragging in POLONIUS

Summary

While Hamlet is talking to his mother, he by mistake kills Polonius, who is hiding behind a wall tapestry. A harsh exchange of words follows between mother and son that is finally interrupted by the ghost's appearance. Hamlet leaves his mother for his mission to England.

Tasks

1. Hamlet and his mother – Part I

a) Read ll. 15-77 and describe the mother-son relationship.
b) Read the info box on stichomythia and identify examples of stichomythia in the passage encompassing the lines 15-34.

Info: Stichomythia
Stichomythia [ˌstɪkəʊˈmɪθɪə] is a dialogue of rapidly alternating lines, a device often used in a play when two characters have a vigorous exchange of words or when the emotional intensity of a scene is emphasized. Characters may take turns stating antithetical opinions, take up the other character's words or use puns on them.

c) Analyse the effect on the audience.

2. The murder

a) Describe how Hamlet kills Polonius.
b) Group work (3): Discuss Hamlet's motive for killing Polonius. Consider the following possibilities: Does he mistake Polonius for Claudius? Does he seek revenge? Is it a mere accident? Is it madness?
c) Read the info box on the use of the second-person pronouns in Shakespeare's time and identify the second-person pronouns that the characters use in the extracts (1–3) on p. 118 when they address each other.

Info: Second-person pronouns
Whereas in modern-day English the pronouns 'you' and 'your' may refer to one person or several people, in Shakespeare's time the use of the pronouns 'thee', 'thy', 'thine' and 'thou' was very common alongside 'you' and 'your', and the people were very sensitive to the different implications these pronouns had. Depending on the social context, speakers would switch from one pronoun to the other.   • 'Thou' might be friendly and familiar but could also show contempt for someone socially inferior and even express an insult.   • 'You' was used for a more formal, distant, respectful form of address.   • A character might switch from one register to the other to express a change of mood or attitude towards the other character.

1   POLONIUS
He will come straight. Look you lay home to him.
Tell him his pranks have been too broad to bear with,
And that your grace hath screened and stood between
Much heat and him. I'll silence me even here.
Pray you, be round with him.
HAMLET
(*Within*) Mother, mother, mother!
GERTRUDE
I'll warrant you. Fear me not. Withdraw, I hear him coming.

2   GERTRUDE
Have you forgot me?
HAMLET
No, by the rood, not so.
You are the queen, your husband's brother's wife,
And – would it were not so! – you are my mother.
GERTRUDE
Nay, then I'll set those to you that can speak.
HAMLET
Come, come, and sit you down. You shall not budge.
You go not till I set you up a glass
Where you may see the inmost part of you.
GERTRUDE
What wilt thou do? Thou wilt not murder me?
Help, help, ho!

3   GERTRUDE
O me, what hast thou done?
HAMLET
Nay, I know not. Is it the king?
GERTRUDE
Oh, what a rash and bloody deed is this!
HAMLET
A bloody deed? Almost as bad, good mother,
As kill a king and marry with his brother.
GERTRUDE
As kill a king?
HAMLET
Ay, lady, 'twas my word.
Thou wretched, rash, intruding fool, farewell.
I took thee for thy better. Take thy fortune.
Thou find'st to be too busy is some danger.
[*To GERTRUDE*] Leave wringing of your hands. Peace. Sit you down
And let me wring your heart.

d) Explain what feelings the use of the pronouns reveal. The words and phrases from the box below might help you.

> to show contempt/hatred/anger for sb – to scorn sb – to mock sb – to loathe sb – to abhor sth –
> to express one's aggression towards – to treat sb harshly/respectfully/leniently – to find sb guilty of sth –
> to accuse sb of sth – to chide sb for sth

e) Group work (3): Dramatic reading: Take parts as Polonius, Hamlet and Gertrude. Try to emphasise the characters' use of the second-person pronoun to express their feelings for each other. Present your dialogue to the class.

f) Extra: Write Polonius' obituary in which you look back on his life.

> **Info: Obituary**
>
> An obituary is a news article that announces a well-known person's recent death and informs the reader about this person's life and achievements. It has become a quite popular subgenre in British and American newspapers. It consists of a headline, a sub-heading, the name of the author, a main part and a concluding paragraph. An obituary does not always praise the person but may also show the mysterious and indecent sides of the person.

3. Hamlet and his mother – Part II

a) Read lines 70-140 and list Hamlet's accusations against his mother.

b) Hamlet compares his father with Claudius (ll. 94-109). Collect the information he attributes to the two brothers in a grid. What do you find striking?

The late King Hamlet	King Claudius
• "grace […] on this brow" (l. 97) → graceful • …	• …

c) Analyse the language Hamlet uses towards his mother.

d) Pair work: After their meeting Hamlet and Gertrude are brooding over their conversation. Write their inner monologues in the form of soliloquies. Partner A takes Hamlet's role, Partner B Gertrude's.

e) Extra: In lines 95-96 Hamlet refers to two pictures of his father and his uncle. Either draw these pictures or find some suitable ones on the Internet. Present them to the class.

Looking back at Act III

1. The themes

Update the mind-map you started in *Looking back at Act II*.

2. The most important moments

Group work: Divide the class into four groups. Each group works out a freeze-frame showing the most important moment in one scene. The other groups must guess what moment is shown in the freeze-frame.

3. Hamlet – a paragon of virtue?

In Scene I Ophelia pictures Hamlet as the epitome of an ideal prince (ll. 212-224).
a) List Hamlet's qualities as described by Ophelia and explain them.
- "a noble mind" (l. 213) → honest and caring
- "courtier" (l. 214) → …
- …
b) Discuss to what extent Hamlet has shown these qualities in the play so far.
c) Speculate why Shakespeare makes Ophelia paint this picture of Hamlet.

ACT IV

SCENE I. A room in the castle.

Enter KING CLAUDIUS, QUEEN GERTRUDE,
ROSENCRANTZ, and GUILDENSTERN

KING CLAUDIUS   ◓ **The roles(s)**
There's matter in these sighs, these profound heaves: **of women**
5 You must translate. 'Tis fit we understand them.
Where is your son?
QUEEN GERTRUDE
[*To ROSENCRANTZ and GUILDENSTERN*]
Bestow this place on us a little while.

10 *Exeunt ROSENCRANTZ and GUILDENSTERN*

Ah, my good lord, what have I seen tonight!
KING CLAUDIUS
What, Gertrude? How does Hamlet?
QUEEN GERTRUDE
15 Mad as the sea and wind when both contend
Which is the mightier. In his lawless fit,
Behind the arras hearing something stir,
Whips out his rapier, cries, "A rat, a rat!"
And in this brainish apprehension kills
20 The unseen good old man.
KING CLAUDIUS
O heavy deed!
It had been so with us had we been there.
His liberty is full of threats to all –
25 To you yourself, to us, to everyone.
Alas, how shall this bloody deed be answered?
It will be laid to us, whose providence
Should have kept short, restrained and out of haunt
This mad young man. But so much was our love,
30 We would not understand what was most fit,
But, like the owner of a foul disease,
To keep it from divulging, let it feed
Even on the pith of life. Where is he gone?
QUEEN GERTRUDE
35 To draw apart the body he hath killed,
O'er whom his very madness, like some ore
Among a mineral of metals base,
Shows itself pure. He weeps for what is done.*
KING CLAUDIUS
40 O Gertrude, come away!

matter s.th. of importance
profound heaves heavy breathing
fit important

Bestow this place on us Leave us alone here.

contend fight each other
lawless out of control
fit sudden, emotional activity
stir move slightly
whips out quickly pulls out
rapier long, narrow two-edged sword
brainish impulsive • **apprehension** belief

heavy dreadful

answered explained
It will be laid to us we will be made
   responsible
providence good judgement
short under strict control
restrained held back
out of haunt away from other people
fit appropriate
owner person suffering from
foul awful
divulging becoming public knowledge
feed become worse and spread
on the pith of life in the marrow (*Knochen-mark*)
draw apart drag away
ore *Goldader*
mineral mine • **base** of little value

the sun [...] touch by sunrise
hence from here • vile horrible
majesty royal power
countenance face

The sun no sooner shall the mountains touch
But we will ship him hence; and this vile deed
We must, with all our majesty and skill,
Both countenance and excuse. Ho, Guildenstern!

45 *Enter ROSENCRANTZ and GUILDENSTERN*

join you with some further aid find more
   men to help you
to slay, slew, slain to kill violently

speak fair speak courteously
haste in this Be quick about it.

Friends both, go join you with some further aid.
Hamlet in madness hath Polonius slain,
And from his mother's closet hath he dragged him.
Go seek him out, speak fair, and bring the body
50 Into the chapel. I pray you, haste in this.

Exeunt ROSENCRANTZ and GUILDENSTERN

what's untimely done what mistakes have
   been made

discord conflict, disharmony • dismay anxiety

Come, Gertrude, we'll call up our wisest friends
And let them know both what we mean to do
And what's untimely done ...
55 O, come away!
My soul is full of discord and dismay.

Exeunt

Summary

The queen informs the king about Hamlet's crime. He sends Rosencrantz and Guildenstern to find Hamlet and accompany him to England.

Tasks

1. Rosencrantz and Guildenstern

Although Rosencrantz and Guildenstern enter the stage with the King, they are sent off immediately by the Queen. Speculate on why Shakespeare has made them appear on stage in the first place.

2. Claudius

a) Describe Claudius' reaction to Gertrude's news. Does he seem surprised, worried or furious? Does he feel responsible for what has happened? Give evidence from the text.
b) As a director, describe how you would make Claudius come across in this scene.
c) After line 54, four lines have been either lost or deleted by Shakespeare. Write these lines, starting with "And what's untimely done …".

SCENE II. Another room in the castle.

Enter HAMLET

HAMLET
Safely stowed.
ROSENCRANTZ and GUILDENSTERN
5 [*Within*] Hamlet, Lord Hamlet!
HAMLET
What noise? Who calls on Hamlet? O, here they come.

Enter ROSENCRANTZ, GUILDENSTERN and OTHERS

ROSENCRANTZ
10 What have you done, my lord, with the dead body?
HAMLET
Compounded it with dust, whereto 'tis kin*.
ROSENCRANTZ
Tell us where 'tis that we may take it thence and bear it to the chapel.
15 **HAMLET**
Do not believe it.
ROSENCRANTZ
Believe what?
HAMLET
20 That I can keep your counsel and not mine own. Besides, to be demanded of a sponge – what replication should be made by the son of a king?
ROSENCRANTZ
Take you me for a sponge, my lord?
25 **HAMLET**
Ay, sir, that soaks up the King's countenance, his rewards, his authorities. But such officers do the King best service in the end. He keeps them, like an ape an apple in the corner of his jaw, first mouthed, to be last swallowed. When he needs what you have 30 gleaned, it is but squeezing you, and, sponge, you shall be dry again.
ROSENCRANTZ
I understand you not, my lord.
HAMLET
I am glad of it. A knavish speech sleeps in a foolish ear.
35 **ROSENCRANTZ**
My lord, you must tell us where the body is, and go with us to the King.
HAMLET
The body is with the King, but the King is not with the body. 40 The King is a thing –

---

safely stowed safely hidden

compounded it with dust combined it with dust, i.e. buried it

whereto 'tis kin where it (the body) will turn to dust and thus be the same as the surrounding earth.
thence from that place • **bear** carry

counsel secret, i.e. the secret that you are the agents of the King
mine own my secret where the body is
demanded questioned • **of** by
sponge *Schwamm* • **replication** answer

soaks up *aufsaugen*
countenance (here) favour
authorities delegated powers
mouthed taken into the mouth
last at last
gleaned (fig.) have found out
to squeeze *quetschen* – Note: Hamlet is implying that King Claudius will get rid of Rosencrantz and Guildenstern when they are no longer useful.
A knavish speech sleeps in a foolish ear. A sarcastic remark is not understood by s.o. who is stupid.

GUILDENSTERN
A thing, my lord?
HAMLET
Of nothing.* Bring me to him. Hide fox, and all after.

45 *Exeunt running, pursued by the OTHERS*

Hide fox, and all after a reference to a hide-
and-seek game played by children

Summary

Rosencrantz tries to pump Hamlet for information about the whereabouts of Polonius' corpse.

Tasks

1. Hamlet speaking in riddles

a) Explain what Hamlet means.

1	Compounded it with dust, whereto 'tis kin. (l. 12)	
2	ROSENCRANTZ Take you me for a sponge, my lord? HAMLET "Ay, sir, that soaks up the king's countenance, his rewards, his authorities. But such officers do the king best service in the end. […] When he needs what you have gleaned, it is but squeezing you and, sponge, you shall be dry again. (ll. 23-30)	
3	He keeps them, like an ape an apple in the corner of his jaw, first mouthed to be last swallowed. (ll. 28-29)	
4	A knavish speech sleeps in a foolish ear. (l. 34)	
5	The body is with the king, but the king is not with the body. The king is a thing – (ll. 39-40)	
6	Hide fox, and all after! (l. 44)	

b) Analyse the strategies Hamlet uses to avoid telling his friends where Polonius' corpse is hidden.
c) Examine how Hamlet's attitude towards his friends has changed.

SCENE III. Another room in the castle.

Enter KING CLAUDIUS, attended

KING CLAUDIUS
I have sent to seek him, and to find the body.
How dangerous is it that this man goes loose?
5 Yet must not we put the strong law on him.
He's loved of the distracted multitude,
Who like not in their judgment but their eyes,
And where 'tis so, the offender's scourge is weighed,
But never the offence. To bear all smooth and even,
10 This sudden sending him away must seem
Deliberate pause. Diseases desperate grown
By desperate appliance are relieved,
Or not at all.

Enter ROSENCRANTZ

15 How now, what hath befallen?
ROSENCRANTZ
Where the dead body is bestowed, my lord,
We cannot get from him.
KING CLAUDIUS
20 But where is he?
ROSENCRANTZ
Without, my lord, guarded, to know your pleasure.
KING CLAUDIUS
Bring him before us.
25 **ROSENCRANTZ**
Ho, Guildenstern! Bring in my lord.

Enter HAMLET and GUILDENSTERN

KING CLAUDIUS
Now, Hamlet, where's Polonius?
30 **HAMLET**
At supper.
KING CLAUDIUS
At supper! Where?
HAMLET
35 Not where he eats, but where he is eaten. A certain convocation
of politic worms are e'en at him. Your worm is your only emperor
for diet.* We fat all creatures else to fat us, and we fat ourselves
for maggots. Your fat king and your lean beggar is but variable
service, two dishes, but to one table. That's the end.
40 **KING CLAUDIUS**
Alas, alas!

---

goes loose can freely move about
put the strong law on him punish him to the full extent of the law
of by · **distracted** irrational
multitude the general public
Who [...] eyes who base their choices on outward appearance rather than reason
offender *Straftäter/-in* · **scourge** crime
is weighed is considered
offence the crime itself
to bear all [...] even to conduct everything carefully and fairly
deliberate pause carefully thought out
desperate critical, grave
appliance remedies · **relieved** cured

hath befallen has happened

without outside

convocation assembly
politic cunning (*schlau*)
e'en (even) just in the process of eating him
Your worm [...] for diet. Even an emperor will be food for worms.
fat fatten
maggot *Made* · **lean** *schlank*
beggar *Bettler* · **but** just
variable service various courses of a meal

HAMLET
A man may fish with the worm that hath eat of a king, and eat of the fish that hath fed of that worm.

KING CLAUDIUS
45 What dost thou mean by this?

HAMLET
Nothing but to show you how a king may go a progress through the guts of a beggar.

KING CLAUDIUS
50 Where is Polonius?

HAMLET
In heaven. Send thither to see. If your messenger find him not there, seek him i' the other place yourself. But indeed, if you find him not within this month, you shall nose him as you go 55 up the stairs into the lobby.

KING CLAUDIUS
[*To some ATTENDANTS*] Go seek him there.

HAMLET
He will stay till ye come.

60 *Exeunt ATTENDANTS*

KING CLAUDIUS
Hamlet, this deed, for thine especial safety –
Which we do tender as we dearly grieve
For that which thou hast done – must send thee hence
65 With fiery quickness. Therefore prepare thyself.
The barque is ready, and the wind at help,
The associates tend, and everything is bent
For England.

HAMLET
70 For England?

KING CLAUDIUS
Ay, Hamlet.

HAMLET
Good.

75 **KING CLAUDIUS**
So is it, if thou knewest our purposes.

HAMLET
I see a cherub that sees them. But come, for England. Farewell, dear mother.

80 **KING CLAUDIUS**
Thy loving father, Hamlet.

HAMLET
My mother. Father and mother is man and wife. Man and wife is one flesh, so, my mother. Come, for England!

85 *Exit*

---

hath eat of has eaten
fed of fed on

go a progress make an official, royal journey through a monarch's kingdom
guts digestive system

i' (in) **the other place** i.e. hell
nose smell
lobby passage or corridor often used as a waiting room

which we do tender which we feel great concern about
as as much as
dearly grieve feel great sorrow
with fiery quickness as rapidly as spreading fire
barque small sailing ship • **at help** on our side
associates companions • **tend** are waiting
bent ready

if thou knewest our purposes if only you knew what our reasons are
cherub one of the second order of angels with special heavenly knowledge
sees (here) understands

KING CLAUDIUS

[*To ROSENCRANTZ and GUILDENSTERN*]
Follow him at foot. Tempt him with speed aboard.
Delay it not. I'll have him hence tonight.

90 Away, for everything is sealed and done
That else leans on the affair. Pray you, make haste.

Exeunt ROSENCRANTZ and GUILDENSTERN

And, England, if my love thou holdest at aught –
As my great power thereof may give thee sense,

95 Since yet thy cicatrice looks raw and red
After the Danish sword*, and thy free awe
Pays homage to us – thou mayst not coldly set
Our sovereign process, which imports at full
By letters conjuring to that effect,

100 The present death of Hamlet. Do it, England,
For like the hectic in my blood he rages,
And thou must cure me. Till I know 'tis done,
However my haps, my joys were ne'er begun.

Exit

at foot at his heels, closely · **tempt** urge
with speed aboard to move as quickly as
possible even when on board the ship
everything is sealed and done all the
instructions are in a sealed document
that else leans on the affair that has to do
with the mission

England king of England
holdest at aught means anything
yet still · **cicatrice** scar · **raw** not healed
red bleeding · **after** after experiencing
thy free awe pays homage to us you show
your respect for us by the tribute you pay us
**thou mayst not coldly set our sovereign
process** You may not cooly disregard our
royal command.
which imports […] death of Hamlet
which provides full written details that
request, in effect, that Hamlet should
immediately be killed
hectic fever
rages causes great turbulence and pain
however my haps however my fortune may
have been
my joys were ne'er begun I will never have
a joyful time.

Summary

Hamlet is brought in front of the king to tell him where he has hidden Polonius' corpse. He is immediately sent off to England.

Tasks

1. Claudius' plan

a) What is Claudius' plan? Decide if the statement is right or wrong and find evidence from the text to prove your point.

	Statement	r/w	Evidence
1	Claudius has sent men to question Hamlet about the whereabouts of Polonius' corpse.		
2	Claudius sees the danger Hamlet poses.		
3	The Danish people do not care about Hamlet's fate.		
4	Claudius wants to send Hamlet to England as soon as possible.		
5	He wants the English King to look after Hamlet.		

b) Write Claudius' letter addressed to the King of England.

2. Hamlet's joking allusion

a) Read the info box and explain the ambiguity of the phrase "the diet of worms".

Info: The Diet of Worms
The Diet of Worms (1521) was an assembly (convocation) at the city of Worms, Germany, where Martin Luther defended his anti-papal views.

b) Explain what Hamlet means when he answers Claudius in lines 35-39.

3. Do it, England

Claudius wants the English monarch to kill Hamlet. Back in Shakespeare's time it might have been up to the City Council of London to decide on such matters. Imagine you are members of the City Council. Have the class form two groups, one is in favour of Hamlet's death, the other group is against it.
Carry out the discussion on whether England should kill Hamlet or not.

SCENE IV. A plain in Denmark.

Enter FORTINBRAS, a CAPTAIN, and SOLDIERS, marching

PRINCE FORTINBRAS
Go, Captain, from me greet the Danish king.
Tell him that by his licence, Fortinbras
5 Craves the conveyance of a promised march
Over his kingdom. You know the rendezvous.
If that his majesty would aught with us,
We shall express our duty in his eye,
And let him know so.
10 **CAPTAIN**
I will do't, my lord.
PRINCE FORTINBRAS
Go softly on.

Exeunt FORTINBRAS and SOLDIERS

15 *Enter HAMLET, ROSENCRANTZ, GUILDENSTERN, and OTHERS*

HAMLET
[*To CAPTAIN*] Good sir, whose powers are these?
CAPTAIN
They are of Norway, sir.
20 **HAMLET**
How purposed, sir, I pray you?
CAPTAIN
Against some part of Poland.
HAMLET
25 Who commands them, sir?
CAPTAIN
The nephew to old Norway, Fortinbras.
HAMLET
Goes it against the main of Poland, sir,
30 Or for some frontier?
CAPTAIN
Truly to speak, and with no addition,
We go to gain a little patch of ground
That hath in it no profit but the name.
35 To pay five ducats, five, I would not farm it,
Nor will it yield to Norway or the Pole
A ranker rate, should it be sold in fee.
HAMLET
Why, then the Polack never will defend it.

license permission
craves desires • **conveyance** granting
over across • **rendezvous** meeting place
would aught with us would like to have a
    conference with us
express our duty in his eye pay our
    respects to him face to face

go softly march at a leisurely pace

powers troops

how purposed For what purpose?
I pray you I ask you.

old Norway the old king of Norway

it the troops • **main** central part
for towards • **frontier** fortress at the frontier

truly to speak to tell the truth
with no addition with no exaggeration
gain acquire, get • **patch** piece
no profit but the name we are only doing it
    in the name of "conquest"
to pay five ducats […] farm it It would not
    be worth the small amount of five ducats
    to rent this land.
yield result in • **the Pole** the king of Poland
ranker rate should it be sold in fee a
    higher sum of money if sold outright as a
    freehold (land without any restrictions to
    whoever uses it)

it is already garrisoned. It already has
defending troops.
**Will not debate [...] the question of this
straw.** Will not be enough to settle this
trivial matter.
This the imposthume (abscess) **[...]
wealth and peace.** i.e., when there is a
long period of too much wealth and a
long period of peace, war will follow.
inward breaks breaks inside the body
shows no cause without why the man dies
shows no outward signs of why a man dies
humbly *ergeben*
wi' with

40 **CAPTAIN**
Yes, it is already garrisoned.
HAMLET   ○ Fate vs.
Two thousand souls and twenty thousand ducats   free will
Will not debate the question of this straw.
45 This is the imposthume of much wealth and peace,
That inward breaks, and shows no cause without
Why the man dies. I humbly thank you, sir.
CAPTAIN
God be wi' you, sir.

50 *Exit*

ROSENCRANTZ
Wilt please you go, my lord?
HAMLET
I'll be with you straight. Go a little before.

55 *Exeunt all except HAMLET*

straight right away
occasions occurrences
inform against me dishonour me
spur encourage
my dull revenge my taking little action to
carry out my revenge
chief main
market of his time that for which he sells
his time
but only · **large discourse** great wisdom
looking before and after unlike animals
able to think about the past and the future
fust become mouldy (*schimmelig*)
bestial oblivion forgetfulness more typical
of animals
craven scruple cowardly hesitation
of caused by
thinking too precisely on the event wast-
ing too much time analysing a possible
outcome
quartered divided evenly into four parts
ever always · **to do** still to do
sith since · **gross** obvious · **exhort** urge
witness look at
mass and charge size and expense
delicate fine of character · **tender** youthful
puffed inspired
makes mouths at makes faces at, laughs at
invisible event unforeseeable outcome of
his campaign
exposing [...] dare allowing his and his
armed forces' welfare to be threatened by
Fortuna, death, and danger

How all occasions do inform against me,   ○ Fate vs.
And spur my dull revenge! What is a man,   free will
If his chief good and market of his time   ○ Questions
Be but to sleep and feed? A beast, no more.   of morality
60 Sure, he that made us with such large discourse,
Looking before and after, gave us not
That capability and god-like reason
To fust in us unused. Now, whether it be
Bestial oblivion, or some craven scruple
65 Of thinking too precisely on the event –
A thought which, quartered, hath but one part wisdom
And ever three parts coward – I do not know
Why yet I live to say "This thing's to do",
Sith I have cause and will and strength and means
70 To do't. Examples gross as earth exhort me.
Witness this army of such mass and charge,
Led by a delicate and tender prince,
Whose spirit with divine ambition puffed
Makes mouths at the invisible event,
75 Exposing what is mortal and unsure
To all that fortune, death and danger dare,

Even for an eggshell. Rightly to be great
Is not to stir without great argument,
But greatly to find quarrel in a straw
80 When honour's at the stake. How stand I then,
That have a father killed, a mother stained.
Excitements of my reason and my blood,
And let all sleep? While, to my shame, I see
The imminent death of twenty thousand men,
85 That, for a fantasy and trick of fame,
Go to their graves like beds, fight for a plot
Whereon the numbers cannot try the cause,
Which is not tomb enough and continent
To hide the slain. O, from this time forth,
90 My thoughts be bloody, or be nothing worth!

Exit

eggshell s.th. worthless
stir fight
straw trivial matter
at the stake at risk
how stand I How am I to be considered?
stained (fig.) dishonoured
blood passion

imminent soon to happen
trick illusion
plot piece of land
**whereon the numbers cannot try the
    cause** There is not enough room for these
    armies to fight on to settle the dispute.
not tomb enough does not have enough
    burial ground
continent graves · **hide** bury
importunate troublesome · **distract** mad

Summary

Hamlet watches young Fortinbras' troops passing by and meditates on his own behaviour.

Tasks

1. Fortinbras

a) Sum up Fortinbras' plan.
b) Describe Fortinbras' motives for carrying out his plan as stated by the Captain Hamlet is talking to.
c) Analyse Fortinbras' character: Choose the adjectives you think fit best and give evidence from the text.

> respectful – vindictive – dutiful – domineering – prudent – irresponsible – clever – deceitful – impulsive – hot-headed

2. Hamlet

a) Tick the description that best captures Hamlet's mood in this scene.
   ☐ Hamlet admires young Fortinbras for his audaciousness and his strong will.
   ☐ Hamlet does not understand why young Fortinbras wants to fight against Poland.
   ☐ Hamlet is surprised that men will fight and kill over nothing, and yet he has failed to kill Claudius over a significant matter.
b) Write a modern version of Hamlet's thoughts in lines 56-70.
c) Analyse the language Shakespeare uses for Hamlet when he states his opinion of young Fortinbras. Use the space provided for your notes. You may start like this:

Witness this army of such mass and charge	*use of antithesis to highlight the huge under-taking carried out by so young a prince*
Led by a delicate and tender prince,	
Whose spirit with divine ambition puffed	
Makes mouths at the invisible event,	
Exposing what is mortal and unsure	
To all that fortune, death, and danger dare,	*use of alliteration …*
Even for an eggshell. Rightly to be great	
Is not to stir without great argument,	
But greatly to find quarrel in a straw	
When honor's at the stake. How stand I then,	
That have a father killed, a mother stained,	
Excitements of my reason and my blood,	
And let all sleep – while, to my shame, I see	
The imminent death of twenty thousand men,	
That for a fantasy and trick of fame	
Go to their graves like beds, fight for a plot	
Whereon the numbers cannot try the cause,	

| Which is not tomb enough and continent
To hide the slain? Oh, from this time forth,
My thoughts be bloody, or be nothing worth! | |

d) Pair work: Collect the arguments Hamlet presents for taking action. Then carry out a conversation between Hamlet, who wants to take action, and a close friend and advisor.

SCENE V. Elsinore. A room in the castle.

Enter QUEEN GERTRUDE and HORATIO

⊃ **The roles(s) of women**

QUEEN GERTRUDE
I will not speak with her.
HORATIO
5 She is importunate, indeed distract.
Her mood will needs be pitied.
QUEEN GERTRUDE
What would she have?
HORATIO
10 She speaks much of her father, says she hears
There's tricks i' the world, and hems and beats her heart,
Spurns enviously at straws, speaks things in doubt
That carry but half sense. Her speech is nothing,
Yet the unshapèd use of it doth move
15 The hearers to collection. They aim at it
And botch the words up fit to their own thoughts,
Which, as her winks, and nods, and gestures yield them,
Indeed would make one think there might be thought,
Though nothing sure, yet much unhappily.
20 **QUEEN GERTRUDE**
'Twere good she were spoken with, for she may strew
Dangerous conjectures in ill-breeding minds.
Let her come in.

HORATIO withdraws to admit OPHELIA.

25 [*Aside*] To my sick soul, as sin's true nature is,
Each toy seems prologue to some great amiss.
So full of artless jealousy is guilt,
It spills itself in fearing to be spilt.

Enter OPHELIA, playing a lute and her hair down

30 **OPHELIA**
Where is the beauteous majesty of Denmark?
QUEEN GERTRUDE
How now, Ophelia!
OPHELIA
35 [*Sings*]
How should I your true love know
From another one?
By his cockle hat and staff,
And his sandal shoon*.

---

will needs must be

What would she have? What does she want?

tricks plots • **'i** in
hems makes a "hem" sound
beats her heart beats on her chest
spurns enviously at straws reacts aggressively when confronted with trivial matters
in doubt ambiguously
carry but half sense hardly make any sense
nothing nonsense
unshapèd use of it the incoherence of what she says
move the hearers to collection causes people to find some logic in what she says
aim at it try to find a meaning in what she says
botch the words up clumsily put the words together
to wink zwinkern • **to nod** nicken
yield them give her words additional meaning
thought some intention
unhappily 1) unskilfully, 2) maliciously, or 3) close to the truth
strew dangerous conjectures spread dangerous rumours
ill-breeding minds people who like to find scandals
as sin's true nature is sin is a sickness of the soul
toy s.th. seemingly insignificant
prologue to the start of • **amiss** disaster
So full of artless jealousy [...] spilt Guilt produces such uncontrolled mistrust that it reveals itself because of the very fear of revelation.
beauteous beautiful
how now How are you?
cockle hat hat with a shell badge worn by pilgrims
staff walking stick
sandal shoon sandals

40 **QUEEN GERTRUDE**
Alas, sweet lady, what imports this song?
OPHELIA
Say you? Nay, pray you, mark.

[*Sings*]
45 He is dead and gone, lady,
He is dead and gone.
At his head a grass-green turf,
At his heels a stone.

She sighs.

50 **QUEEN GERTRUDE**
Nay, but, Ophelia –
OPHELIA
Pray you, mark.

[*Sings*]
55 White his shroud as the mountain snow –

Enter KING CLAUDIUS

QUEEN GERTRUDE
Alas, look here, my lord.
OPHELIA
60 [*Sings*]
Larded with sweet flowers
Which bewept to the grave did – not – go
With true-love showers.*
KING CLAUDIUS
65 How do you, pretty lady?
OPHELIA
Well, God 'ild you! They say the owl was a baker's daughter.*
Lord, we know what we are, but know not what we may be. God
be at your table.
70 **KING CLAUDIUS**
[*To QUEEN GERTRUDE*] Conceit upon her father.
OPHELIA
Pray you, let's have no words of this. But when they ask you
what it means, say you this:

75 [*Sings*]
Tomorrow is Saint Valentine's Day.*
All in the morning betime,
And I a maid at your window,
To be your Valentine.
80 Then up he rose, and donned his clothes,

---

what imports this song What does this
song mean?

say you Is that what you want me to say?
mark Pay close attention.

at his head a grass-green turf a layer of
earth covered with green grass above
his head
heels *Fersen* • **stone** gravestone

shroud piece of cloth used to cover a dead
body

larded decorated
Which bewept to the grave [...] showers.
who was not lamented when he went to
his grave

How do you [...] How are you doing?

God 'ild (yield) **you** God reward you.
God be at your table. a blessing said
before a meal

Conceit upon her father. Fantasies about
her dead father.

betime early

donned put on

dupped opened
maid young woman, virgin

And dupped the chamber door,
Let in the maid, that out a maid
Never departed more.
KING CLAUDIUS
85 Pretty Ophelia.
OPHELIA
Indeed, la, without an oath, I'll make an end on't.

without an oath without having to use
"God" or "Christ" in an oath
on't (on it) to it

by Gis by Jesus
alack alas: an expression of unhappiness
fie for shame It's disgusting how shameful
this behaviour is.
Young men will do't, if they come to't
Young men will have sex with a virgin if
they have the opportunity.
by Cock corruption of "by God," also a pun
on the meaning of "cock" as the vulgar
word for "penis"
quoth zitierte • **tumbled me** had sex with me
to wed to marry
ha' have • **by yonder sun** in full daylight
an if

[*Sings*]
By Gis and by Saint Charity,
90 Alack, and fie for shame!
Young men will do't, if they come to't,
By Cock, they are to blame.
Quoth she, "Before you tumbled me,
You promised me to wed."
95 He answers:
"So would I ha' done, by yonder sun,
An thou hadst not come to my bed."
KING CLAUDIUS
[*To Queen GERTRUDE*] How long hath she been thus?
100 **OPHELIA**
I hope all will be well. We must be patient, but I cannot choose
but weep, to think they should lay him i' the cold ground. My
brother shall know of it. And so I thank you for your good
counsel. Come, my coach! Good night, ladies; good night. Sweet
105 ladies, good night, good night.

Exit

counsel advice • **coach** Kutsche

KING CLAUDIUS
[*To HORATIO*] Follow her close. Give her good watch, I pray you.

Exit HORATIO

Give her good watch Watch over her
closely.

sorrows events causing grief
single spies lone soldiers sent out ahead of
the main army
author the one causing s.th.
remove removal, being sent or perhaps
killed
muddied confused
thick and unwholesome like bad blood
whispers gossip
for because of • **greenly** naively
in hugger-mugger in secrecy
to inter to bury
divided from herself [...] fair judgement
not in her right mind
pictures just a semblance of a human being
last in addition • **containing** as important
these all these crises

110 O, this is the poison of deep grief. It springs
All from her father's death. O Gertrude, Gertrude,
When sorrows come, they come not single spies
But in battalions. First, her father slain;
Next, your son gone, and he most violent author
115 Of his own just remove; the people muddied,
Thick and unwholesome in their thoughts and whispers,
For good Polonius' death – and we have done but greenly,
In hugger-mugger to inter him. Poor Ophelia
Divided from herself and her fair judgement,
120 Without the which we are pictures, or mere beasts;
Last, and as much containing as all these,
Her brother is in secret come from France,

Feeds on this wonder, keeps himself in clouds
And wants not buzzers to infect his ear
125 With pestilent speeches of his father's death –
Wherein necessity, of matter beggared,
Will nothing stick our person to arraign
In ear and ear. O my dear Gertrude, this,
Like to a murdering-piece, in many places
130 Gives me superfluous death.

A noise within

QUEEN GERTRUDE
Alack, what noise is this?
KING CLAUDIUS
135 Where is my Switzers? Let them guard the door.

Enter a MESSENGER

What is the matter?
MESSENGER   **Questions**
Save yourself, my lord!   **of morality**
140 The ocean, overpeering of his list,
Eats not the flats with more impetuous haste
Than young Laertes in a riotous head,
O'erbears your officers. The rabble call him lord.
And, as the world were now but to begin,
145 Antiquity forgot, custom not known,
The ratifiers and props of every word,
They cry, "Choose we! Laertes shall be king!"
Caps, hands, and tongues, applaud it to the clouds –
"Laertes shall be king! Laertes king!"
150 **QUEEN GERTRUDE**
How cheerfully on the false trail they cry.

Noise within

O, this is counter, you false Danish dogs!
KING CLAUDIUS
155 The doors are broke.

Enter LAERTES with FOLLOWERS

LAERTES
Where is this king? Sirs, stand you all without.
FOLLOWERS
160 No, let's come in.
LAERTES
I pray you, give me leave.

Feeds on this wonder is trying to come to grips with the extraordinary events
keeps himself in clouds does not reveal what he plans to do
wants not buzzers to infect his ears does not want to be bothered with rumours
pestilent speeches vicious talk
of matter beggared because there are no known facts
will nothing stick our person to arraign will not hesitate to accuse me of murdering Polonius
in ear and ear [this accusation] will pass from one person to another
murdering-piece small cannon that fires many small projectiles at a time
Give me superfluous death causes me to die many times over
Switzers Swiss guards

overpeering of his list rising over the boundary of its shore
eats not the flats with more impetuous haste does not overrun low-lying land at a higher speed
in a riotous head in a rebellious horde
o'erbears (overbears) overwhelms
rabble mob
as the world were now but to begin as if the civilized world were to begin now
antiquity the past
The ratifiers and props of every word the basis of every political contract
tongues cheers
on the false trail without knowing what really happened

counter improper

without outside

give me leave leave me alone

FOLLOWERS

We will, we will.

165 **LAERTES**

I thank you, keep the door.

Exeunt FOLLOWERS and MESSENGER

O thou vile king,

Give me my father!

170 **QUEEN GERTRUDE**

[*Holding him*] Calmly, good Laertes.

LAERTES

That drop of blood that's calm proclaims me bastard,

Cries cuckold to my father, brands the harlot

175 Even here, between the chaste unsmirchèd brows

Of my true mother.*

KING CLAUDIUS

What is the cause, Laertes,

That thy rebellion looks so giant-like?

180 Let him go, Gertrude. Do not fear our person.

There's such divinity doth hedge a king,

That treason can but peep to what it would,

Acts little of his will. Tell me, Laertes,

Why thou art thus incensed. Let him go, Gertrude.

185 Speak, man.

LAERTES

Where is my father?

KING CLAUDIUS

Dead.

190 **QUEEN GERTRUDE**

[*To LAERTES*] But not by him.

KING CLAUDIUS

Let him demand his fill.

LAERTES

195 How came he dead? I'll not be juggled with.

To hell allegiance, vows to the blackest devil,

Conscience and grace to the profoundest pit.

I dare damnation. To this point I stand,

That both the worlds I give to negligence,

200 Let come what comes. Only I'll be revenged

Most throughly for my father.

KING CLAUDIUS

Who shall stay you?

LAERTES

205 My will, not all the world,

And for my means, I'll husband them so well

They shall go far with little.

---

keep guard

vile wicked

cuckold husband deceived by his unfaithful wife

to brand to make a mark on the skin with a hot iron

harlot whore

chaste *treu* · **unsmirchèd** unstained

brows forehead

That drop [...] true mother. Remaining calm would make me look like I wasn't my father's son, and my father like he was deceived by an unfaithful wife, although she has been faithful and is my biological mother.

giant-like huge

fear our person fear for my person

such divinity doth hedge (protect) **a king** Claudius is invoking the principle of Divine Right, i.e that kings are representatives of God and so protected from any attacks.

That treason [...] his will. so that treason can only take a quick look at what it wants to do, but do very little

incensed very angry

demand his fill demand that he be fully informed

juggled with deceived, manipulated

allegiance loyalty · **vow** promise

grace God's grace

profoundest pit deepest part of hell

damnation being damned by God

to this point I stand I will not change my mind on this point

That both [...] negligence I don't care what happens to me in this world or the next

throughly thoroughly

stay stop

not all the world The world can't stop me.

means resources · **husband** manage

KING CLAUDIUS

Good Laertes,

210 If you desire to know the certainty

Of your dear father's death, is't writ in your revenge

That, sweepstake, you will draw both friend and foe,

Winner and loser?

LAERTES

215 None but his enemies.

KING CLAUDIUS

Will you know them then?

LAERTES

To his good friends thus wide I'll ope my arms

220 And like the kind life-rendering pelican

Repast them with my blood*.

KING CLAUDIUS

Why, now you speak

Like a good child and a true gentleman.

That I am guiltless of your father's death,

225 And am most sensibly in grief for it,

It shall as level to your judgment 'pear

As day does to your eye.

VOICES

230 [*Within*] Let her come in.

LAERTES

How now, what noise is that?

⊙ **The roles(s) of women**

Enter OPHELIA with flowers in her hand

O heat, dry up my brains, tears seven times salt

235 Burn out the sense and virtue of mine eye.

By heaven, thy madness shall be paid by weight

Till our scale turn the beam. O rose of May,

Dear maid, kind sister, sweet Ophelia,

O heavens, is't possible, a young maid's wits

240 Should be as mortal as an old man's life?

Nature is fine in love, and where 'tis fine

It sends some precious instance of itself

After the thing it loves.

OPHELIA

245 [*Sings*]

They bore him barefaced on the bier,

Hey non nony, nony, hey nony,

And in his grave rained many a tear –

Fare you well, my dove.

250 **LAERTES**

Hadst thou thy wits, and didst persuade revenge,

It could not move thus.

---

sweepstake winning everything in a game from all players

draw take

is't writ [...] winner and loser? Is it necessary that the innocent and guilty should suffer in the pursuit of revenge?

ope open

life-rendering giving nourishment

repast feed

sensibly with intense feeling

level straightforward · **'pear** appear

day daylight

tears seven times salt tears with seven times more salt

burn out destroy · **virtue** natural power

the beam horizontal bar of a balance (*Waage*) with scales hanging on each side

thy madness [...] turn the beam The scales of the balance shall be overbalanced because the weight of revenge in one scale shall be heavier than the weight of her madness in the other scale.

wits sanity

as mortal as an old man's life as fragile as an old man about to die

Nature is fine in [...] the thing it loves. Human nature is made pure by love and sends a special sample of itself to the object of its love.

to bear, bore, borne to carry

bier *Tragbahre*

dove *Taube*

persuade argue for

It could not move thus. It would not move me to act this forcefully.

becomes it is suitable
steward servant

This nothing's [...] matter. This nonsense might have some significance.

rosemary *Rosmarin*
pansy *Stiefmütterchen*

document lesson · **thoughts** depression

fennel *Fenchel* · **columbine** *Akelei*
rue *Gartenraute*
with a difference for a different reason
daisy *Gänseblümchen*
to wither *verdorren*
made a good end died well

bonny handsome
Robin name which appears in numerous love ballads, also *Rotkehlchen*
affliction madness · **passion** suffering
favour beauty

all flaxen completely white like flax
his poll his head

we cast away moan We waste our time with mourning.

OPHELIA
[*Sings*]
255 You must sing "A-down a-down",
And you "Call him a-down-a."
O, how the wheel becomes it! It is the false
steward that stole his master's daughter.

LAERTES
260 This nothing's more than matter.

OPHELIA
[*To LAERTES*] There's rosemary, that's for remembrance. Pray, love, remember. And there is pansies*, that's for thoughts.

LAERTES
265 A document in madness, thoughts and remembrance fitted.

OPHELIA
There's fennel* for you, and columbines*. There's rue* for you, and here's some for me. We may call it "herb of grace" o' Sundays. O you must wear your rue with a difference. There's a
270 daisy.* I would give you some violets*, but they withered all when my father died. They say he made a good end.
[*Sings*]
For bonny sweet Robin is all my joy.

LAERTES
275 Thought and affliction, passion, hell itself.
She turns to favour and to prettiness.

OPHELIA
[Sings]
And will he not come again,
280 And will he not come again?
No, no, he is dead.
Go to thy deathbed.
He never will come again.

His beard was as white as snow,
285 All flaxen was his poll.
He is gone, he is gone,
And we cast away moan.
God ha' mercy on his soul.
And of all Christian souls, I pray God. God be wi' you.

290 *Exeunt OPHELIA and QUEEN GERTRUDE*

LAERTES
Do you see this, O God?

KING CLAUDIUS

Laertes, I must commune with your grief,

295 Or you deny me right. Go but apart,

Make choice of whom your wisest friends you will.

And they shall hear and judge 'twixt you and me,

If by direct or by collateral hand

They find us touched, we will our kingdom give,

300 Our crown, our life, and all that we can ours,

To you in satisfaction. But if not,

Be you content to lend your patience to us,

And we shall jointly labour with your soul

To give it due content.

305 **LAERTES**

Let this be so.

His means of death, his obscure funeral –

No trophy, sword, nor hatchment o'er his bones,

No noble rite nor formal ostentation –

310 Cry to be heard, as 'twere from heaven to earth,

That I must call't in question.

KING CLAUDIUS

So you shall.

And where the offence is, let the great axe fall.

315 I pray you, go with me.

Exeunt

---

commune with share
right the right
go but apart go your separate way

'twixt (bewixt) between
by direct or by collateral hand through direct or indirect (collateral) sources
find us touched find me guilty of Polonius' death
in satisfaction as recompense

labour work
to give it due content to give your soul the peace it deserves

means of death manner of dying
obscure not open to the public
trophy memorial
hatchment tablet showing the coat of arms of the dead person
rite *Ritus* · **ostentation** ceremony
that I must [...] question so that I must demand an explanation

offence i.e. the criminal
great axe axe of execution

Summary

Horatio and Gertrude discuss Ophelia's state of mind. She seems to have gone mad while grieving for her father's death and because of Hamlet's rejection. Claudius meanwhile fears the consequences of Hamlet's murder. Laertes arrives at the castle with a gang of rebels swearing to avenge his father.

Tasks

1. Ophelia's state of mind

Instead of answering the questions the Queen asks her, Ophelia sings snatches of old ballads.
a) Group work (3–4): Read the snatches of the ballads in the scene again and identify their core messages.

Snatch	Message
How should I your true love know From another one? By his cockle hat and staff, And his sandal shoon.	
He is dead and gone, lady, He is dead and gone. At his head a grass-green turf, At his heels a stone.	
White his shroud as the mountain snow –	
Larded with sweet flowers Which bewept to the grave did – not – go With true-love showers.	
Tomorrow is Saint Valentine's Day. All in the morning betime, And I a maid at your window, To be your Valentine. Then up he rose, and donned his clothes, And dupped the chamber door, Let in the maid, that out a maid Never departed more.	
By Gis and by Saint Charity, Alack, and fie for shame! Young men will do't, if they come to't, By Cock, they are to blame. Quoth she, "Before you tumbled me, You promised me to wed." He answers: "So would I ha' done, by yonder sun, An thou hadst not come to my bed."	

Snatch	Message
They bore him barefaced on the bier, Hey non nony, nony, hey nony, And in his grave rained many a tear – Fare you well, my dove.	
And will he not come again, And will he not come again? No, no, he is dead. Go to thy deathbed. He never will come again. His beard was as white as snow, All flaxen was his poll. He is gone, he is gone, And we cast away moan. God ha' mercy on his soul.	

b) Explain how the snatches relate to the play's events.

c) Research the symbolic associations of the flowers Ophelia mentions and either draw the flower or find a picture.

Flower/herb	Symbolic association
rosemary	
pansy	
fennel	
columbine	
rue	
daisy	
violet	

d) Critics believe that Ophelia, while handing a bouquet of flowers to the King and Queen, is conveying a message to them. Using the symbolic associations from task c), interpret Ophelia's message.

e) Imagine you are a psychiatrist and Ophelia is brought to you. Analyse her state of mind using the information from tasks a)-d) and write the medical report.

2. Laertes

a) Briefly outline what Laertes intends to do.

b) Tick the adjectives that best describe the young man and give evidence from the scene to prove your point.

hot-tempered vindictive angry infuriated quick-tempered rash rabble-rousing outraged worried desperate	

c) Examine Laertes's language in lines 196-202.

d) Try several ways of speaking the lines: bombastically, worriedly, furiously, humorously and discuss the effect on the audience.

e) In class, speculate whether Laertes will be successful in his undertaking and give reasons.

SCENE VI. Another room in the castle.

Enter HORATIO and a SERVANT

HORATIO
What are they that would speak with me?

> **What [...] with me?** What persons wish to speak to me?

SERVANT
Sailors, sir. They say they have letters for you.
HORATIO
Let them come in.

Exit SERVANT

I do not know from what part of the world
I should be greeted, if not from Lord Hamlet.

Enter SAILORS

FIRST SAILOR
God bless you, sir.
HORATIO
Let Him bless thee too.
FIRST SAILOR
He shall, sir, an't please Him. There's a letter for you, sir – it comes from the ambassador that was bound for England – if your name be Horatio, as I am let to know it is.

> **an't** if it
> **bound for** heading for
> **let to know** informed

HORATIO
[*Reads*] "Horatio, when thou shalt have overlooked this, give these fellows some means to the King. They have letters for him. Ere we were two days old at sea, a pirate of very warlike appointment gave us chase. Finding ourselves too slow of sail, we put on a compelled valour and in the grapple I boarded them. On the instant they got clear of our ship, so I alone became their prisoner. They have dealt with me like thieves of mercy but they knew what they did. I am to do a good turn for them. Let the King have the letters I have sent, and repair thou to me with as much speed as thou wouldst fly death. I have words to speak in thine ear will make thee dumb. Yet are they much too light for the bore of the matter. These good fellows will bring thee where I am. Rosencrantz and Guildenstern hold their course for England. Of them I have much to tell thee. Farewell.
He that thou knowest thine,
Hamlet"

> **overlooked** looked over
> **means to** access to
> **ere** before
> **were two days old** had spent two days
> **pirate** pirate ship
> **warlike appointment** equipped for fighting a battle
> **put on a compelled valour** were forced to fight bravely
> **in the grapple** with ropes with a hook at the end thrown onto the deck of the other ship – the two ships being parallel to each other
> **got clear of our ship** were able to sail away from our ship
> **thieves of mercy** thieves showing mercy
> **turn** favour
> **repair** come
> **fly** escape from
> **dumb** speechless
> **much too light [...] of the matter** much too trivial in comparison to the importance of the matter

Come, I will give you way for these your letters,
And do't the speedier that you may direct me
To him from whom you brought them.

> **give you way** provide you with access
> **do't the speedier** take care of it as fast as possible

Exeunt

Summary

Horatio receives a letter from Hamlet.

Tasks

1. The letter

a) The modern version of Hamlet's letter addressed to Horatio is jumbled up. Bring it into the correct order by matching the modern versions (A–J) to the original lines (1–10).

	Original lines		Modern lines
1	When thou shalt have overlooked this, give these fellows some means to the King. They have letters for him.	A	We were too slow to escape so we had to fight against them with me ending up on their ship.
2	Ere we were two days old at sea, a pirate of very warlike appointment gave us chase.	B	I have such news for you that will surprise you, but it's only half the truth.
3	Finding ourselves too slow of sail, we put on a compelled valour, and in the grapple I boarded them.	C	These men will bring you to me.
4	On the instant, they got clear of our ship, so I alone became their prisoner.	D	Goodbye. Your close friend, Hamlet
5	They have dealt with me like thieves of mercy, but they knew what they did. I am to do a good turn for them.	E	Give the letters I've written to the King and come to see me as quickly as possible.
6	Let the king have the letters I have sent, and repair thou to me with as much speed as thou wouldst fly death.	F	After two days at sea we were pursued by a pirate ship equipped for battle.
7	I have words to speak in thine ear will make thee dumb, yet are they much too light for the bore of the matter.	G	Rosencrantz and Guildenstern are on their way to England. I need to tell you a lot about them.
8	These good fellows will bring thee where I am.	H	When you've read this letter, make sure that these men can see the King. They have letters for him.
9	Rosencrantz and Guildenstern hold their course for England. Of them I have much to tell thee.	I	They immediately left our ship and sailed off with me.
10	Farewell. He that thou knowest thine. Hamlet.	J	They have treated me humanely, but they knew what they were doing. They want me to do them a favour.

b) Briefly outline the contents of the letter.
c) Speculate about the contents of the other letters that are brought to the King. Jot down some ideas.
d) Read the info box on page 149 and discuss the function of the letter in this scene.

> **Info: Letters in Shakespeare's plays**
>
> Letters in Shakespeare's plays serve various functions. They may
> - interrupt the action
> - bring a different dimension of time into the play
> - advance the plot
> - create a specific atmosphere
> - raise suspense as the audience cannot read the letter
> - provide a different perspective on the themes of the play
> - bridge the gap between past and present events.

e) Choose: Group work (4–7): Act out the contents of the letter.

OR

Discuss how you would perform the reading of the letter in a film or on stage.

SCENE VII. Another room in the castle.

Enter KING CLAUDIUS and LAERTES

KING CLAUDIUS

Now must your conscience my acquaintance seal,
And you must put me in your heart for friend,
5 Sith you have heard, and with a knowing ear,
That he which hath your noble father slain
Pursued my life.

LAERTES

It well appears. But tell me
10 Why you proceeded not against these feats,
So crimeful and so capital in nature,
As by your safety, wisdom, all things else,
You mainly were stirred up.

KING CLAUDIUS   ☉ **The roles(s) of women**

15 O, for two special reasons,
Which may to you, perhaps, seem much unsinewed,
But yet to me they are strong. The Queen his mother
Lives almost by his looks, and for myself –
My virtue or my plague, be it either which –
20 She's so conjunctive to my life and soul,
That, as the star moves not but in his sphere*,
I could not but by her. The other motive,
Why to a public count I might not go,
Is the great love the general gender bear him;
25 Who, dipping all his faults in their affection,
Would, like the spring that turneth wood to stone*,
Convert his gyves to graces, so that my arrows,
Too slightly timbered for so loud a wind,
Would have reverted to my bow again,
30 And not where I had aimed them.

LAERTES

And so have I a noble father lost,
A sister driven into desperate terms,
Whose worth, if praises may go back again,
35 Stood challenger on mount of all the age
For her perfections. But my revenge will come.

KING CLAUDIUS

Break not your sleeps for that. You must not think
That we are made of stuff so flat and dull
40 That we can let our beard be shook with danger
And think it pastime. You shortly shall hear more.
I loved your father, and we love ourself.
And that, I hope, will teach you to imagine –

Enter a MESSENGER with letters

---

must your [...] seal confirm my innocence
sith since
a knowing ear an ability to quickly grasp the situation
pursued my life was out to murder me

feats deeds
capital requiring the death penalty
as by your safety taking your safety into consideration
mainly greatly • **stirred up** ready to take action

much unsinewed very weak

lives almost by his looks is happy just to have him nearby
virtue *Tugend*
be it either which whichever of the two
conjunctive closely united
I could [...] by her I could not live without her.
count indictment (*Anklage*)
general gender the common people
bear him have for him
to dip to place quickly in water
spring small river • **turneth** turns
gyves guilt, faults • **graces** positive qualities
slightly timbered with wooden shafts that are too small
loud (here) strong
reverted returned

terms circumstances
go back again recall what she was once
stood challenger [...] for her perfections i.e. It would be impossible to find a more perfect woman.

break interrupt
flat and dull unable to act
that we can let [...] danger that we would let danger insult us by pulling our beard
pastime nothing serious

45 How now? What news?

MESSENGER

Letters, my lord, from Hamlet.

This to your majesty, this to the Queen.

KING CLAUDIUS

50 From Hamlet? Who brought them?

MESSENGER

Sailors, my lord, they say. I saw them not.

They were given me by Claudio. He received them

Of him that brought them.

50 **KING CLAUDIUS**

Laertes, you shall hear them. Leave us.

Exit MESSENGER

[*Reads*]

"High and mighty. You shall know I am set naked on your king- | **naked** unarmed, without resources
60 dom. Tomorrow shall I beg leave to see your kingly eyes, when | **beg leave** humbly request
I shall, first asking your pardon, thereunto recount the occasion | **pardon** permission · **thereunto** and then
of my sudden and more strange return. | **occasion** circumstances

Hamlet"

What should this mean? Are all the rest come back?

65 Or is it some abuse, and no such thing? | **abuse** trick

LAERTES

Know you the hand? | **hand** handwriting

KING CLAUDIUS

'Tis Hamlet's character. "Naked," | **character** handwriting

70 And in a postscript here, he says "alone".

Can you advise me?

LAERTES

I'm lost in it, my lord. But let him come. | **I'm lost in it** I don't know what to think.

It warms the very sickness in my heart

75 That I shall live and tell him to his teeth,

"Thus didest thou." | **Thus didest thou.** This is what you did.

KING CLAUDIUS

If it be so, Laertes – | **Questions**
                          | **of morality**

As how should it be so? How otherwise? –

80 Will you be ruled by me? | **ruled by me** be guided by me

LAERTES

Ay, my lord, | **so you will not o'errule** (overrule) **me to a**
So you will not o'errule me to a peace. | **peace** as long as you will not prevent me
                                          | from having my revenge, which will result
                                          | in my peace of mind

KING CLAUDIUS

85 To thine own peace. If he be now returned, | **checking at his voyage** suddenly ending
As checking at his voyage, and that he means | his voyage and returning
No more to undertake it, I will work him | **work him to an exploit** get him to get
To an exploit, now ripe in my device, | involved in a plot
Under the which he shall not choose but fall, | **now ripe in my device** now worked out in
                                                | my planning
                                                | **not choose but fall** not have any choice
                                                | but to die

uncharge the practise not blame us for the circumstances

devise arrange

organ agent of Hamlet's death

It falls right. This fits my plans well.

And that in Hamlet's hearing Hamlet is aware of it

quality talent, accomplishment

your sum of parts all your talents put together

pluck such envy from him cause him to be envious

unworthiest siege lowest rank

A very riband in the cap of youth a very useful quality for young men

no less becomes is no less suited to

livery clothes

settled age middle and old age

sables and his weeds fur-lined clothing

importing signifying

graveness being serious and dignified

since before

served against took part in military action against

can well on horseback are skilled riders

gallant heroic

witchcraft seemingly magic powers

in't in his riding of horses

as as if

incorpsed [...] beast became one body, half horse, half man

topped my thought went beyond my expectations

in forgery of shapes and tricks imagining what tricks could be done with horses

upon my life I bet my life on it.

brooch jewel

gem *Edelstein*

made confession of you acknowledged you

for art [...] defence theory and practice of fencing

90   And for his death no wind of blame shall breathe,
But even his mother shall uncharge the practise
And call it accident.
LAERTES
My lord, I will be ruled.
95   The rather, if you could devise it so
That I might be the organ.
KING CLAUDIUS
It falls right.
You have been talked of since your travel much,
100   And that in Hamlet's hearing, for a quality
Wherein, they say, you shine. Your sum of parts
Did not together pluck such envy from him
As did that one, and that, in my regard,
Of the unworthiest siege.
105   **LAERTES**
What part is that, my lord?
KING CLAUDIUS
A very riband in the cap of youth,
Yet needful too. For youth no less becomes
110   The light and careless livery that it wears
Than settled age his sables and his weeds,
Importing health and graveness. Two months since,
Here was a gentleman of Normandy* –
I've seen myself, and served against, the French,
115   And they can well on horseback. But this gallant
Had witchcraft in't. He grew unto his seat,
And to such wondrous doing brought his horse,
As he had been incorpsed and demi-natured
With the brave beast. So far he topped my thought,
120   That I, in forgery of shapes and tricks,
Come short of what he did.
LAERTES
A Norman was't?
KING CLAUDIUS
125   A Norman.
LAERTES
Upon my life, Lamord.
KING CLAUDIUS
The very same.
130   **LAERTES**
I know him well. He is the brooch indeed
And gem of all the nation.
KING CLAUDIUS
He made confession of you,
135   And gave you such a masterly report
For art and exercise in your defence

And for your rapier most especially,
That he cried out, 'twould be a sight indeed,
If one could match you. The scrimers of their nation,
140 He swore, had had neither motion, guard, nor eye,
If you opposed them. Sir, this report of his
Did Hamlet so envenom with his envy
That he could nothing do but wish and beg
Your sudden coming o'er, to play with you.
145 Now, out of this –
LAERTES
What out of this, my lord?
KING CLAUDIUS
Laertes, was your father dear to you?
150 Or are you like the painting of a sorrow,
A face without a heart?
LAERTES
Why ask you this?
KING CLAUDIUS
155 Not that I think you did not love your father,
But that I know love is begun by time,
And that I see, in passages of proof,
Time qualifies the spark and fire of it.
There lives within the very flame of love
160 A kind of wick or snuff that will abate it,
And nothing is at a like goodness still,
For goodness, growing to a pleurisy,
Dies in his own too much. That we would do
We should do when we would, for this "would" changes
165 And hath abatements and delays as many
As there are tongues, are hands, are accidents;
And then this "should" is like a spendthrift sigh,
That hurts by easing. But, to the quick of the ulcer –
Hamlet comes back. What would you undertake,
170 To show yourself your father's son in deed
More than in words?
LAERTES
To cut his throat i' the church.
KING CLAUDIUS
175 No place, indeed, should murder sanctuarize.
Revenge should have no bounds. But, good Laertes,
Will you do this, keep close within your chamber.
Hamlet returned shall know you are come home.
We'll put on those shall praise your excellence
180 And set a double varnish on the fame
The Frenchman gave you, bring you in fine together,
And wager on your heads. He, being remiss,
Most generous and free from all contriving,

'twould it would
scrimers fencers
guard defensive skills
envenom poison
play fence

Questions of morality

painting of a sorrow weak version of sorrow
a face without a heart a person without feeling

time certain circumstances
in passages of proof from experiences that have put this love to the test
qualifies modifies
wick *Docht*
snuff the burned part of the wick that must be cut off to avoid the flame becoming less bright
abate make less intense
like similar
pleurisy excess
too much overabundance · **would** want to
tongues what people say
hands people who help or hinder
accidents things that happen by chance
spendthrift wasteful
hurts by easing lessens your willpower even while giving relief
quick (centre) **of the ulcer** (*Geschwür*) (fig.) main concern
i' in

should murder sanctuarize give sanctuary to a murderer
keep close within stay inside
put on those arrange that some people
set a double varnish (*Lack*) **on the fame** exaggerate your fame
in fine finally
wager bet · **remiss** careless
free from all contriving not deceitful

peruse examine
foil fencing sword tipped with a button
shuffling secretly exchanging swords
unbated with a sharp point and no button
in a pass of practice in a thrust (*Schwerthieb*) during practice
requite pay him back

anoint rub over the tip with an ointment (*Salbe*)
unction ointment • **of** from
mountebank charlatan
mortal fatal • **but** just
draws blood causes bleeding
cataplasm dressing for a wound
simple plant with medicinal properties
have virtue under the moon are most effective when collected under moonlight
the thing the wound
withal with it • **point** tip of my sword
contagion poison • **gall** scratch

weigh think about
fit us to our shape be suitable to our plan of action
our drift [...] bad performance our plan be found out because of making mistakes
'Twere better not assayed It would be better not to carry it through.
a back or second a plan B
that might hold that would be certain to succeed
this should blast in proof should be a complete failure like when a musket or cannon explodes when tested
cunnings Hamlet's and your skill at fencing
ha't have it • **motion** exertion • **dry** thirsty
as therefore • **bouts** sword thrusts
to that end for that purpose
chalice drinking cup • **nonce** occasion
venomed poisoned • **stuck** thrust

woe tragedy • **tread** walk

willow *Weide*
askant on the side of and leaning over
brook *Bach*
hoar grey, the colour of the underside of the leaves
fantastic extravagant • **garland** *Kranz*
crowflower, nettle, daisy, long purple different kinds of flowers and plants
liberal not decent • **grosser** more vulgar
cold chaste (*keusch*)

Will not peruse the foils. So that, with ease,
190 Or with a little shuffling, you may choose
A sword unbated, and in a pass of practice
Requite him for your father.
LAERTES
I will do't.
195 And, for that purpose I'll anoint my sword.
I bought an unction of a mountebank,
So mortal that, but dip a knife in it,
Where it draws blood no cataplasm so rare,
Collected from all simples that have virtue
200 Under the moon, can save the thing from death
That is but scratched withal. I'll touch my point
With this contagion, that if I gall him slightly,
It may be death.
KING CLAUDIUS
205 Let's further think of this.
Weigh what convenience both of time and means
May fit us to our shape. If this should fail,
And that our drift look through our bad performance,
'Twere better not assayed. Therefore this project
210 Should have a back or second, that might hold,
If this should blast in proof. Soft, let me see.
We'll make a solemn wager on your cunnings –
I ha't! When in your motion you are hot and dry –
As make your bouts more violent to that end –
215 And that he calls for drink, I'll have prepared him
A chalice for the nonce, whereon but sipping,
If he by chance escape your venomed stuck,
Our purpose may hold there. But stay, what noise?

Enter QUEEN GERTRUDE

220 How now, sweet queen!
QUEEN GERTRUDE   ➲ **The roles(s)**
One woe doth tread upon another's heel,   **of women**
So fast they follow. Your sister's drowned, Laertes.
LAERTES
225 Drowned! O, where?
QUEEN GERTRUDE
There is a willow grows askant a brook
That shows his hoar leaves in the glassy stream.
There with fantastic garlands did she come
260 Of crowflowers, nettles, daisies, and long purples,
That liberal shepherds give a grosser name,
But our cold maids do dead men's fingers call them.

There on the pendent boughs her coronet weeds
Clambering to hang*, an envious sliver broke,
265 When down her weedy trophies and herself
Fell in the weeping brook. Her clothes spread wide
And, mermaid-like, awhile they bore her up,
Which time she chanted snatches of old tunes,
As one incapable of her own distress,
270 Or like a creature native and endued
Unto that element. But long it could not be
Till that her garments, heavy with their drink,
Pulled the poor wretch from her melodious lay
To muddy death.
275 **LAERTES**
Alas, then, she is drowned?
QUEEN GERTRUDE
Drowned, drowned.
LAERTES
280 Too much of water hast thou, poor Ophelia,
And therefore I forbid my tears. But yet
It is our trick; nature her custom holds,
Let shame say what it will.
When these are gone,
284 The woman will be out. Adieu, my lord,
I have a speech of fire, that fain would blaze,
But that this folly drouts it.

Exit

KING CLAUDIUS
290 Let's follow, Gertrude.
How much I had to do to calm his rage.
Now fear I this will give it start again.
Therefore let's follow.

Exeunt

pendent hanging over • **boughs** branches
coronet weeds crown of wild flowers
clambering climbing up
envious malicious, wishing to do harm
sliver branch
trophies garlands
awhile for a while
bore her up kept her afloat
which time while at the same time
chanted sang • **snatches** bits
incapable unable to understand
endued naturally adapted
wretch pitiful person • **lay** song

trick normal impulse
nature human nature
her customs holds does what it must
these the tears
The woman will be out The woman in me
will be gone.
I have a speech [...] drouts it. My revenge
is like a fiercely burning fire, but this
stupid crying extinguishes it.

Summary

While the King and Laertes continue their conversation, a messenger arrives with letters for the king and queen. The king and Laertes prepare a ruse to kill Hamlet and make it look like an accident. The queen arrives announcing Ophelia's death.

Tasks

1. Pair work: Claudius and Laertes meet again

a) Write a modern version of the first part of Claudius and Laertes' conversation (ll. 1–43). You can start like this:
   King: You must agree that I am not guilty but that I am your friend …
b) Act out the conversation.
c) Discuss how Claudius comes across in this extract.

2. The letter

a) State the contents of the letter in your own words.
b) Compare the letter with your ideas from Scene VI, task 1 c). Did you guess correctly?

3. The ruse

a) Outline the ruse the King and Laertes plan.
b) Examine how Claudius persuades Laertes to take his revenge.
c) Pair work: Act out lines 77-218. Try speaking the lines conspiratorially.

4. Ophelia's death

a) Sum up Gertrude's account of Ophelia's death.
b) Imagine you are a police reporter summoned to the scene. Fill in the police report below and on page 157 based on Gertrude's account.

<table>
<tr><td colspan="2" align="center">**Police report**</td></tr>
<tr><td>Case no: _____</td><td>Date: _____</td></tr>
<tr><td colspan="2">Reporting officer: _____</td></tr>
<tr><td colspan="2">Incident: _____
_____
_____</td></tr>
</table>

Details:

1. Who was involved? _____

_____

_____

2. What happened? _____

_____

_____

_____

_____

3. Where did the incident occur?   _____

_____

4. When did the incident happen?   _____

_____

5. Why do you think the accused/victim did this?   _____

_____

_____

Actions taken:

Summary:

c) Complete the grid you started in Scene V, task 1 c), adding the flowers and herbs mentioned in Gertrude's account.

d) Analyse the language Shakespeare uses in these lines and its effect on the audience.

Looking back at Act IV

1. The themes

Update the mind-map you started in *Looking back at Act II*.

2. Taking stock

Make a list of
1   the people killed so far, and
2   the people seeking revenge for their deaths.

People killed	Avengers

3. Political activities

a)   There are some political events mentioned in Act IV. Match them to the correct scene.

an insurrection in Denmark
a war against France
England's defeat by Danish troops
the Norwegian army marching against Poland

Scene III
Scene IV
Scene V
Scene VII

b)   Write a court circular reporting on one of these events. For the text type, see *Looking back at Act I*.

4. The most crucial moments

a)   Identify the most crucial moments in Act IV.
b)   Pair work: Compare your ideas with a partner's.

ACT V

SCENE I. A churchyard.

Enter two CLOWNS/GRAVEDIGGERS with spades and pickaxes

pickaxe *Spitzhacke*

GRAVEDIGGER
Is she to be buried in Christian burial that wilfully seeks her own salvation?

5 **OTHER**
I tell thee she is, and therefore make her grave straight. The crowner hath sat on her, and finds it Christian burial.

salvation *Erlösung*
straight *immediately*
crowner (informal) coroner: official who determines the cause of death
sat on her examined her to determine the cause of death
finds it Christian burial i.e. decided it was not a suicide
in her own defence to defend herself

GRAVEDIGGER
How can that be, unless she drowned herself in her own
10 defence*?

OTHER
Why, 'tis found so.

'**tis found so** That was the decision of the coroner.

GRAVEDIGGER
It must be "se offendendo", it cannot be else. For here lies the
15 point: if I drown myself wittingly, it argues an act, and an act hath three branches: it is, to act, to do, to perform: argal, she drowned herself wittingly.*

se offendendo (Latin, law) He means "se defendendo": "killing in self-defence".
here lies the point This is the main argument.
wittingly on purpose • **argues** implies
branches aspects
argal a corruption of "ergo" (therefore)

OTHER
Nay, but hear you, Goodman Delver.

Goodman polite form of address to a working-man as a prefix to his occupation
delver digger

20 **GRAVEDIGGER**
Give me leave. Here lies the water – good. Here stands the man – good. If the man go to this water, and drown himself, it is, will he nill he, he goes. Mark you that. But if the water come to him and drown him, he drowns not himself: argal he that is not
25 guilty of his own death, shortens not his own life.

Give me leave. Permit me to go on.
will he nill he willy-nilly: whether he wants to or not

OTHER
But is this law?

GRAVEDIGGER
Ay, marry, is't: crowner's quest law.

marry by the Virgin Mary • **is't** it is
quest law laws that regulate an inquest (official investigation of the cause of death, in cases where a crime is considered possible)

30 **OTHER**
Will you ha' the truth on't? If this had not been a gentlewoman, she should have been buried out o' Christian burial.

Will you [...] on't? Do you want to know the truth?
out o' (of) without a

GRAVEDIGGER
Why, there thou sayest, and the more pity that great folk should
35 have countenance in this world to drown or hang themselves, more than their even Christian. Come, my spade. There is no ancient gentleman but gardeners, ditchers, and grave-makers. They hold up Adam's profession.

there thou sayest You speak the truth
countenance privilege
even Christian Christians who are not members of the nobility
ancient *ehrwürdig*
ditcher person who digs ditches (*Gräben*)
hold up continue with

OTHER
40 Was he a gentleman*?

GRAVEDIGGER
He was the first that ever bore arms.

to bear arms to carry weapons

OTHER
Why, he had none.

45 **GRAVEDIGGER**
What, art a heathen? How dost thou understand the Scripture? The Scripture says "Adam digged."* Could he dig without arms? I'll put another question to thee. If thou answerest me not to the purpose, confess thyself –

50 **OTHER**
Go to.

GRAVEDIGGER
What is he that builds stronger than either the mason, the shipwright, or the carpenter?

55 **OTHER**
The gallows-maker; for that frame outlives a thousand tenants.

GRAVEDIGGER
I like thy wit well, in good faith. The gallows does well. But how does it well? It does well to those that do ill. Now thou dost ill

60 to say the gallows is built stronger than the church. Argal, the gallows may do well to thee. To't again, come.

OTHER
Who builds stronger than a mason, a shipwright, or a carpenter?

GRAVEDIGGER
65 Ay, tell me that, and unyoke.

OTHER
Marry, now I can tell.

GRAVEDIGGER
To't.

70 **OTHER**
Mass, I cannot tell.

Enter HAMLET and HORATIO, at a distance

GRAVEDIGGER
Cudgel thy brains no more about it, for your dull ass will not
75 mend his pace with beating; and when you are asked this question next, say "a grave-maker", the houses that he makes last till doomsday. Go, get thee to Yaughan. Fetch me a stoup of liquor.

Exit OTHER

He digs and sings.

80 In youth, when I did love, did love,
Methought it was very sweet
To contract – O – the time, for – a – my behove.
O methought there – a – was nothing – a – meet.*

Glossary (left margin):

heathen sb who does not believe in God
Scripture Bible
confess thyself leave me alone (cf. the saying "Confess thyself and be hanged.")

Go to. Come on!

mason stonemason: person who prepares stones for building
shipwright builder of ships

gallows *Galgen* • **frame** structure
tenant (ironic) *Mieter*

wit sense of humour • **in good faith** indeed

The gallows does well. That's a good answer.
to't again Let's have another joke.

unyoke unyoke (release) your team of oxen, i.e Let's call it a day.

to't Get on with it.

mass an oath: by the mass (*Messe*)

cudgel beat with a stick • **dull** stupid
ass *Esel*
mend improve • **pace** speed
doomsday *der Jüngste Tag*
Yaughan perhaps a nearby tavern-keeper
stoup jug, pitcher, cup

methought I thought
contract shorten – Actually he wants to say "lengthen".
behove advantage
meet suitable

Enter HAMLET and HORATIO

85 **HAMLET**
Has this fellow no feeling of his business that he sings at grave-making?
HORATIO
Custom hath made it in him a property of easiness.
90 **HAMLET**
'Tis e'en so; the hand of little employment hath the daintier sense.
GRAVEDIGGER
[*Sings*]
95 But age, with his stealing steps
Hath clawed me in his clutch
And hath shipped me intil the land,
As if I had never been such.

Throws up a skull

100 **HAMLET**
That skull had a tongue in it, and could sing once. How the knave jowls it to the ground as if it were Cain's jawbone*, that did the first murder! It might be the pate of a politician which this ass now o'erreaches, one that would circumvent God,
105 might it not?
HORATIO
It might, my lord.
HAMLET
Or of a courtier, which could say "Good morrow, sweet lord.
110 How dost thou, good lord?" This might be my Lord Such-a-one, that praised my Lord Such-a-one's horse when he meant to beg it, might it not?
HORATIO
Ay, my lord.
115 **HAMLET**
Why, e'en so, and now my Lady Worm's, chapless, and knocked about the mazzard with a sexton's spade. Here's fine revolution, an we had the trick to see't. Did these bones cost no more the breeding but to play at loggats with 'em? Mine ache to think
120 on't.
GRAVEDIGGER
[Sings]
A pickaxe, and a spade, a spade,
For and a shrouding sheet.
125 O, a pit of clay for to be made
For such a guest is meet.

Throws up another skull

Custom [...] easiness. Constantly digging graves eventually became an easy thing to do.
'Tis (it is) **e'en** (even) **so** It can be seen this way.
the hand of little [...] daintier sense. The hand that does little rough work is more sensitive.
clawed me in his clutch caught me in his clasp
shipped me sent me off
intil the land toward my grave
never been such never been young

knave [neɪv] rogue, dishonest man
jowls it smashes it
pate head
politician here with the negative meaning of sb deceitful
o'erreaches gets the better of
circumvent outwit

courtier *Höfling*

to beg it to borrow it
Why, e'en (even) **so** That might be the case.
my Lady Worm perhaps the skull of a woman, now food for worms
chapless without a lower jaw
mazzard upper part of the skull
sexton caretaker of a church and its churchyard
revolution turn of Fortune's wheel
an if • **trick** ability
Did these bones [...] loggats with 'em? Was it so inexpensive and easy to bring up the person from childhood to adulthood to now use his/her bones for a game of loggats?
Loggats a game in which thick sticks (loggats) are thrown at stakes fixed in the ground.
Mine ache to think on't. I get a headache thinking about it.
for and and also
shrouding sheet cloth to cover the corpse
pit of clay i.e. grave

quiddities hairsplitting arguments
quillets subtle arguments that make fine distinctions of meaning
tenures holdings of property
tricks trickery • **suffer** permit
sconce head
tell him of his action of battery tell him that he can be arrested for battery (*Körperverletzung*)
in's in his
statues, recognizances legal documents that make land a guarantee for the payment of debts
fines agreements using legal tricks to arrange the transfer of land ownership
double vouchers using two false witnesses in a real estate deal
recoveries final outcomes of dishonest deals, i.e. profit
this i.e. death • **fine** (here) the end
recovery return • **vouch** guarantee
pair of indentures contract that is an agreement between two parties that is cut in half and given to each party
conveyances documents showing the ownership of land
box coffin • **inheritor** owner, i.e. this lawyer
jot a little bit
parchment skin of animals used for writing manuscripts
sheep and calves fools
assurance in that security in legal documents
sirrah term of address to sb of a lower class

thou liest 1. *du liegst*, 2. *du lügst*

quick living

'twill it will

HAMLET
There's another. Why may not that be the skull of a lawyer? Where be his quiddities now, his quillets, his cases, his tenures, and his tricks? Why does he suffer this rude knave now to
130 knock him about the sconce with a dirty shovel, and will not tell him of his action of battery? Hum! This fellow might be in's time a great buyer of land, with his statutes, his recognizances, his fines, his double vouchers, his recoveries. Is this the fine of his fines, and the recovery of his recoveries, to have his fine
135 pate full of fine dirt? Will his vouchers vouch him no more of his purchases, and double ones too, than the length and breadth of a pair of indentures*? The very conveyances of his lands will hardly lie in this box, and must the inheritor himself have no more, ha?
140 **HORATIO**
Not a jot more, my lord.
HAMLET
Is not parchment made of sheepskins?
HORATIO
145 Ay, my lord, and of calf-skins too.
HAMLET
They are sheep and calves which seek out assurance in that. I will speak to this fellow.
[*To the GRAVEDIGGER*] Whose grave's this, sirrah?
150 **GRAVEDIGGER**
Mine, sir.
[*Sings*]
O, a pit of clay for to be made
For such a guest is meet.
155 **HAMLET**
I think it be thine, indeed. For thou liest in't.
GRAVEDIGGER
You lie out on't, sir, and therefore it is not yours. For my part, I do not lie in't, and yet it is mine.
160 **HAMLET**
Thou dost lie in't, to be in't and say it is thine. 'Tis for the dead, not for the quick. Therefore thou liest.
GRAVEDIGGER
'Tis a quick lie, sir, 'twill away again from me to you.
165 **HAMLET**
What man dost thou dig it for?
GRAVEDIGGER
For no man, sir.
HAMLET
170 What woman, then?

GRAVEDIGGER

For none, neither.

HAMLET

Who is to be buried in't?

175 **GRAVEDIGGER**

One that was a woman, sir; but, rest her soul, she's dead.

HAMLET

How absolute the knave is! We must speak by the card, or equivocation will undo us. By the Lord, Horatio, these three

180 years I have taken a note of it. The age is grown so picked that the toe of the peasant comes so near the heel of the courtier he galls his kibe.

[*To the GRAVEDIGGER*] How long hast thou been a grave-maker?

185 **GRAVEDIGGER**

Of all the days i' the year, I came to't that day that our last King Hamlet overcame Fortinbras.

HAMLET

How long is that since?

190 **GRAVEDIGGER**

Cannot you tell that? Every fool can tell that. It was the very day that young Hamlet was born. He that is mad and sent into England.

HAMLET

195 Ay, marry. Why was he sent into England?

GRAVEDIGGER

Why, because he was mad. He shall recover his wits there; or, if he do not, it's no great matter there.

HAMLET

200 Why?

GRAVEDIGGER

'Twill not be seen in him there. There the men are as mad as he.

HAMLET

How came he mad?

205 **GRAVEDIGGER**

Very strangely, they say.

HAMLET

How strangely?

GRAVEDIGGER

210 Faith, e'en with losing his wits.

HAMLET

Upon what ground?

GRAVEDIGGER

Why, here in Denmark. I have been sexton here, man and boy,

215 thirty years.

HAMLET

How long will a man lie i' the earth ere he rot?

---

absolute precise
by the card with absolute precision, by the book
equivocation ambiguity, double meanings
the age our time
picked over-refined, attentive to detail
peasant simple farmer without his own land
galls his kibe causes an inflammation in his heel to become

Fortinbras the old Fortinbras who was slain by King Hamlet in a duel

recover his wits regain his sanity

seen noticed

faith in faith (mild oath)

ground reason – But the gravedigger interprets it to mean "land".

i' in • **ere** before • **to rot** verrotten

rotten *verfault*
pocky diseased because of small pox or syphilis
scarce hold the laying in will hardly remain intact during the burial
tanner *Gerber*

hide skin • **to tan** *gerben*
trade occupation • **sore** most awful
decayer agent of decay (*verwesen*)
whoreson son of a whore, wretched

a pestilence on him The plague on him.
for for being • **rogue** [rəʊg] *Schlingel*
A he • **flagon** large bottle
Rhenish Rhine wine

jester a man employed by a king or queen to entertain the court with jokes and humorous stories

E'en (even) **that.** Yes, that's right.

infinite limitless • **jest** sense of humour
fancy imagination • **borne** carried
abhorred horrible
My gorge rises at it. I feel like vomiting.
gibe provoking remark
gambol trick with the body
that were wont to set the table on a roar that used to cause waves of laughter from the people eating at a table
your own grinning Note: A skull without its lower jaw seems to be grinning.
chap-fallen with a dropped lower jaw, also: feeling miserable
to this favour (facial appearance) **[…] come** i.e. eventually look like dead Yorick
prithee please

o' (of) **this fashion** in this way

GRAVEDIGGER
Faith, if he be not rotten before he die – as we have many pocky
220 corpses nowadays that will scarce hold the laying in – he will last you some eight year or nine year. A tanner will last you nine year.

HAMLET
Why he more than another?

225 **GRAVEDIGGER**
Why, sir, his hide is so tanned with his trade, that he will keep out water a great while, and your water is a sore decayer of your whoreson dead body. Here's a skull now. This skull has lain in the earth three and twenty years.

230 **HAMLET**
Whose was it?

GRAVEDIGGER
A whoreson mad fellow's it was. Whose do you think it was?

HAMLET
235 Nay, I know not.

GRAVEDIGGER
A pestilence on him for a mad rogue! A poured a flagon of Rhenish on my head once.

240 *He picks up the skull.*

This same skull, sir, was Yorick's skull, the King's jester.

HAMLET
This?

GRAVEDIGGER
E'en that.

245 **HAMLET**
Let me see.

Takes the skull

Alas, poor Yorick. I knew him, Horatio, a fellow of infinite jest, of most excellent fancy. He hath borne me on his back a thou-
250 sand times. And now how abhorred in my imagination it is! My gorge rises at it. Here hung those lips that I have kissed I know not how oft. Where be your gibes now, your gambols, your songs, your flashes of merriment, that were wont to set the table on a roar? Not one now, to mock your own grinning?
255 Quite chap-fallen? Now get you to my lady's chamber and tell her, let her paint an inch thick, to this favour she must come.* Make her laugh at that. Prithee, Horatio, tell me one thing.

HORATIO
What's that, my lord?

260 **HAMLET**
Dost thou think Alexander* looked o' this fashion i' the earth?

HORATIO

E'en so.

HAMLET

265 And smelt so? Pah!

He throws down the skull.

HORATIO

E'en so, my lord.

HAMLET

270 To what base uses we may return, Horatio. Why may not imagination trace the noble dust* of Alexander till he find it stopping
a bunghole?

HORATIO

'Twere to consider too curiously to consider so.

275 **HAMLET**

No, faith, not a jot. But to follow him thither with modesty
enough, and likelihood to lead it, as thus: Alexander died,
Alexander was buried, Alexander returneth into dust, the dust
is earth. Of earth we make loam, and why of that loam whereto
280 he was converted, might they not stop a beer-barrel?
Imperious Caesar dead and turned to clay,
Might stop a hole to keep the wind away.
O, that that earth, which kept the world in awe.
Should patch a wall to expel the winter flaw.
285 But soft, but soft, awhile! Here comes the King.

*HAMLET and HORATIO stand aside. Enter KING CLAUDIUS,
QUEEN GERTRUDE, LAERTES, a coffin, with a PRIEST and
LORDS attendant*

290 The Queen, the courtiers – who is this they follow,
And with such maimèd rites? This doth betoken   ⊙ **The roles(s)**
The corpse they follow did with desperate hand   **of women**
Fordo its own life. 'Twas of some estate.
Couch we awhile, and mark.

LAERTES

295 What ceremony else?

HAMLET

[*Aside to HORATIO*] That is Laertes, a very noble youth. Mark.

LAERTES

What ceremony else?

.300 **PRIEST**

Her obsequies have been as far enlarged
As we have warranties. Her death was doubtful,
And but that great command o'ersways the order
She should in ground unsanctified have lodged
305 Till the last trumpet. For charitable prayers,

E'en so. Yes, indeed.

Pah! expression of disgust

base lowly, commonplace
trace *zurückführen* • **to stop** *stopfen*
bunghole opening of a cask (*Fass*)

'twere it would be
too curiously too cleverly
him the imagination
thither in that direction
modesty reasonable speculation
likelihood quite probably
to lead it to cause it (the imagination) to
    conclude
loam clay and sand mixed with water to
    plaster walls, etc.
barrel *Fass*
that earth Caesar when alive

expel keep out • **flaw** strong wind

coffin *Sarg*
attendant accompanying

maimèd rites not the usual elaborate
    rituals
betoken signify • **fordo** destroy
'Twas of some estate. It was sb. from the
    upper class.
couch we Let us hide. • **mark** observe
else in addition

noble of the nobility

obsequies funeral rites • **enlarged** extended
warranty authorization
great command the King's command
o'ersways (oversways) has cancelled
ground unsanctified unholy ground
have lodged have been buried
the last trumpet Judgement Day
for instead of
charitable prayers prayers to bless a dead
    person

shard piece of pottery (*Steingut*)
flint small piece of dark quartz
pebble *Kieselstein*
virgin *Jungfrau*
crant garland
maiden virgin
strewments flowers scattered on the coffin
　　or grave
the bringing home [...] burial being
　　brought to her final resting place with the
　　church bell ringing and a proper burial
profane show disrespect to
the service of the dead those having a
　　Christian burial
requiem funeral song
such rest to her pray that she rests in peace
peace-parted souls those who have had a
　　natural death
unpolluted pure
churlish rude, bad-tempered
ministering angel angel who helps the needy
liest lie • **howling** crying in hell

Shards, flints and pebbles should be thrown on her.
Yet here she is allowed her virgin crants,
Her maiden strewments and the bringing home
Of bell and burial.

310 **LAERTES**
Must there no more be done?
PRIEST
No more be done.
We should profane the service of the dead
315 To sing a requiem and such rest to her
As to peace-parted souls.
LAERTES
Lay her i' the earth:
And from her fair and unpolluted flesh
320 May violets spring. I tell thee, churlish priest,
A ministering angel shall my sister be
When thou liest howling.
HAMLET
[*To Horatio*] What, the fair Ophelia!
325 **QUEEN GERTRUDE**

sweets sweet flowers

Sweets to the sweet. Farewell.

Scattering flowers

I hoped thou shouldst have been my Hamlet's wife.

decked strewn with flowers

I thought thy bride-bed to have decked, sweet maid,
330 And not have strewed thy grave.
LAERTES

treble three times • **woe** grief, misfortune
cursèd *verflucht*
wicked (evil) **deed** i.e. killing Polonius
to deprive sb of sth to take sth away from sb
the earth i.e. the earth to fill the grave

O, treble woe
Fall ten times treble on that cursèd head,
Whose wicked deed thy most ingenious sense
335 Deprived thee of. Hold off the earth awhile,
Till I have caught her once more in mine arms*.

Leaps into the grave

quick living
flat level ground
to o'ertop (overtop) to be higher than
old ancient • **skyish** high up in the sky
head summit

Now pile your dust upon the quick and dead,
Till of this flat a mountain you have made,
340 To o'ertop old Pelion* or the skyish head
Of blue Olympus.
HAMLET
[*Advancing*] What is he whose grief

bears [...] emphasis is so intense
phrase expression
conjures puts a magic spell on
wandering stars planets
wonder-wounded struck with wonder

Bears such an emphasis, whose phrase of sorrow
345 Conjures the wandering stars, and makes them stand
Like wonder-wounded hearers? This is I,
Hamlet the Dane*.

Leaps in after Laertes

350 **LAERTES**
The devil take thy soul.

Grappling with him

to grapple to take a firm hold of sb. and struggle with this person

HAMLET
Thou pray'st not well.
I prithee take thy fingers from my throat.
355 For, though I am not splenitive and rash,

splenitive quick-tempered · **rash** impulsive

Yet have I something in me dangerous,
Which let thy wiseness fear. Hold off thy hand.

wiseness good sense

KING CLAUDIUS
[*To the LORDS*] Pluck them asunder.

pluck them asunder pull them apart

360 **QUEEN GERTRUDE**
Hamlet, Hamlet!
ALL THE LORDS
Gentlemen!
HORATIO
365 [*To HAMLET*] Good my lord, be quiet.

be quiet calm down

HAMLET and LAERTES are separated.

HAMLET
Why I will fight with him upon this theme
Until my eyelids will no longer wag.

until [...] wag (move) i.e. until I die

370 **QUEEN GERTRUDE**
O my son, what theme?
HAMLET
I loved Ophelia. Forty thousand brothers
Could not, with all their quantity of love,
375 Make up my sum. What wilt thou do for her?
KING CLAUDIUS
O, he is mad, Laertes.
QUEEN GERTRUDE
[*To LAERTES*] For love of God, forbear him.

forbear him leave him alone

380 **HAMLET**
[*To LAERTES*] 'Swounds, show me what thou'lt do.
Woo't weep, woo't fight, woo't fast, woo't tear thyself,
Woo't drink up easel, eat a crocodile?
I'll do't. Dost thou come here to whine,
385 To outface me with leaping in her grave?
Be buried quick with her, and so will I.
And if thou prate of mountains, let them throw
Millions of acres on us, till our ground,
Singeing his pate against the burning zone,

'swounds by Christ's wounds
woo't wilt thou
fast eat little or nothing, usually for religious reasons
easel vinegar (*Essig*) · **to whine** to complain
to outface to confront boldly · **with** by
quick alive
prate talk at length
our ground mound of earth burying us
singeing his pate burning its head (summit)
the burning zone the orbit in which the sun moves

390

wart *Warze* • **an** if
mouth speak pompously
rant speak bombastically
mere pure
fit moment of madness
work on him affect him
anon soon afterwards • **dove** *Taube*
couplets baby birds • **disclosed** hatched

His silence [...] drooping. He will be quiet.

use treat
ever always
Hercules Perhaps Hamlet is comparing
   Laertes to Hercules.
The cat will mew [...] day. But I will have
   my day in the end.

pray you beg of you
wait upon him look after him

Strengthen your patience Don't let Hamlet
   get you upset but remain patient.
in by thinking of • **speech** discussion
put the matter to the present push we
   will take immediate action
living monument either a monument for
   all times or Hamlet's death
proceeding plan

Make Ossa like a wart. Nay, an thou'lt mouth,
I'll rant as well as thou.

QUEEN GERTRUDE
This is mere madness,
And thus awhile the fit will work on him.
395 Anon, as patient as the female dove,
When that her golden couplets are disclosed,
His silence will sit drooping.

HAMLET
[*To LAERTES*] Hear you, sir.
400 What is the reason that you use me thus?
I loved you ever. But it is no matter.
Let Hercules himself do what he may,
The cat will mew and dog will have his day.

405 *Exit*

KING CLAUDIUS
I pray you, good Horatio, wait upon him.

Exit HORATIO

[*To LAERTES*] Strengthen your patience in our last night's speech.
We'll put the matter to the present push. –
410 Good Gertrude, set some watch over your son.
This grave shall have a living monument.
An hour of quiet shortly shall we see;
Till then in patience our proceeding be.

415 *Exeunt*

Summary

Two gravediggers talk about the suicide of the woman whose grave they are digging. Hamlet turns up at the scene, accompanied by Horatio. Watching the gravediggers, Hamlet contemplates mortality when he is interrupted by a burial procession. When he realizes that it is Ophelia's funeral, he starts a fight with Laertes.

Tasks

1. The gravediggers

a) Tick the summary that best captures the problem the gravediggers talk about and give evidence from the text.

	Summary	Evidence
	Two gravediggers talk about noble people being more privileged than the poor and having rather costly funeral processions.	
	Two gravediggers argue about whether the woman whose grave they are digging has really drowned.	
	Two gravediggers wonder why the woman who seems to have committed suicide and whose grave they are digging will be given a Christian burial.	

b) Read the info box about humour in Shakespeare's plays. Identify the humorous devices in the gravediggers' scene and analyse their functions. Use the grid on page 170.

Info: Humorous literary devices
Shakespeare frequently uses various literary devices in his plays to create a comical effect. Examples are:
• **verbal irony:** saying one thing but meaning another, the opposite
• **dramatic irony:** when the audience knows more than the characters in the play
• **a pun:** use of a word that has two or more different meanings so that its ambiguity can be used for comic effect
• **malapropism:** This term was coined in 1775, named after the fictitious character of Mrs Malaprop in R. B. Sheridan's play *The Rivals*. It means using words inappropriately, muddling up and confusing their meanings. In Shakespeare's time this technique was called catachresis [katəˈkrēsəs].
⇨ All these devices usually have the same function: to mock or to mislead other characters and to provide comic relief.

Humorous device	Example/evidence	Analysis: effect/function
verbal irony		
dramatic irony		
puns		
malapropism		

c) Pair work: Dramatic reading: Read out the dialogue between Hamlet and the gravedigger (ll. 149-246). Try different ways of emphasizing the humour in these lines.

2. Hamlet

a) Answer the questions below.
   1 What does Hamlet think about the gravedigger's singing?
   2 Who according to Hamlet can afford to be sensitive?
   3 How does Hamlet like the gravedigger digging up a skull?
   4 Who does Hamlet think the first skull belonged to?
   5 What does Hamlet think about the gravedigger's behaviour towards him?
b) Pair work: Analyse the language Shakespeare uses to convey Hamlet's attitude towards death. One partner works on lines 126-139, the other on lines 275-284.
c) Analyse to what extent Hamlet's attitude towards mortality has changed in comparison to his earlier reflections on death ("To be or not to be", Act III, Scene I, ll. 89-122).

3. Yorick

a) Sum up the information Hamlet gives about Yorick.
b) Describe Hamlet's attitude towards Yorick.
c) Read the info box about jesters in Shakespeare's time and speculate about the reasons why Shakespeare mentions Yorick here.

Info: Jesters
A jester was a popular type of character in Elizabethan drama. Jesters were also known as clowns or fools. They were employed for entertainment in royal and noble households. They usually enjoyed a high reputation and were regarded as witty and wise. In Shakespeare's plays they often function as prophets and wise men who, behind their folly, speak the truth. But there were also natural fools, who were exposed to pratfalls, misfortunes and humiliations in the plays, and whose mere function was to amuse the audience.

4. The funeral procession

a) Outline the major incidents that take place during the funeral procession.
b) Explain the compromise over Ophelia's burial that the priest has found.
c) What might Laertes be thinking when he talks to the priest? Note down your ideas in the right-hand column.

LAERTES What ceremony else? PRIEST Her obsequies have been as far enlarged As we have warranty. Her death was doubtful, And, but that great command o'ersways the order, She should in ground unsanctified have lodged Till the last trumpet. For charitable prayers Shards, flints and pebbles should be thrown on her. Yet here she is allowed her virgin crants, Her maiden strewments, and the bringing home Of bell and burial. LAERTES Must there no more be done? PRIEST No more be done. We should profane the service of the dead To sing a requiem and such rest to her As to peace-parted souls. LAERTES Lay her i' th' earth, And from her fair and unpolluted flesh May violets spring! I tell thee, churlish priest, A ministering angel shall my sister be When thou liest howling.	

d) In class, discuss where you would stage the fight between Laertes and Hamlet: inside or outside the grave? Give reasons.

e) Discuss why Shakespeare makes Hamlet finally declare his love for Ophelia.

5. Claudius and Laertes

Go back to Act IV, Scene VII, task 3 in order to recap what Claudius and Laertes have planned for Hamlet. Then re-read what Claudius says to Laertes at the end of the scene. Behind each line, note down what Claudius might be thinking.

What Claudius says	What Claudius thinks
Strengthen your patience in our last night's speech.	
We'll put the matter to the present push.	
Good Gertrude, set some watch over your son.	
This grave shall have a living monument.	
An hour of quiet shortly shall we see;	
Till then in patience our proceeding be.	

SCENE II. A hall in the castle.

Enter HAMLET and HORATIO

❍ Fate vs.
free will
❍ **Questions
of morality**

HAMLET
So much for this, sir. Now shall you see the other.
You do remember all the circumstance?

the other the rest of the story
circumstance details

5 **HORATIO**
Remember it, my lord?

HAMLET
Sir, in my heart there was a kind of fighting
That would not let me sleep. Methought I lay
10 Worse than the mutines in the bilboes. Rashly –
And praised be rashness for it – let us know
Our indiscretion sometimes serves us well
When our deep plots do pall, and that should teach us
There's a divinity that shapes our ends,
15 Rough-hew them how we will –

fighting agitation
methought I thought
mutines mutineers
in the bilboes in ankle shackles (*Fesseln*)
   fixed to an iron bar
rashly impulsively · **know** acknowledge
indiscretion impulsive action
deep planned in detail · **pall** fail
divinity God
shapes our ends determines the outcome
rough-hew plan only carelessly or roughly

HORATIO
That is most certain.

HAMLET
Up from my cabin,
20 My sea-gown scarfed about me, in the dark
Groped I to find out them, had my desire.
Fingered their packet, and in fine withdrew
To mine own room again, making so bold,
My fears forgetting manners, to unseal
25 Their grand commission; where I found, Horatio –
O royal knavery, an exact command,
Larded with many several sorts of reasons
Importing Denmark's health and England's too,
With, ho! Such bugs and goblins in my life,
30 That on the supervise, no leisure bated,
No, not to stay the grinding of the axe,
My head should be struck off.

sea-gown seaman's coat
scarfed about me wrapped loosely
   around me
groped searched around with my hands
to find out them to discover their plan
had my desire succeeded
fingered pickpocketed
packet letter · **in fine** finally
making so bold not hesitating
unseal open
commission letter with instructions
knavery trickery
larded decorated, elaborated
importing concerning
such bugs and goblins in my life such ter-
   rors and dangers should I remain alive
on the supervise upon reading
no leisure bated without delay
stay await · **grinding** sharpening

HORATIO
Is't possible?

35 **HAMLET**
[*Giving it to him*] Here's the commission; read it at more leisure.
But wilt thou hear me how I did proceed?

HORATIO
I beseech you.

I beseech you. I beg you.
benetted surrounded by a net
villanies evil deeds
I could make a prologue to my brains I
   could make an outline for the coming
   action in my head
devised invented
fair in formal handwriting

40 **HAMLET**
Being thus benetted round with villanies,
Ere I could make a prologue to my brains,
They had begun the play – I sat me down,
Devised a new commission, wrote it fair.

hold it consider it · **statists** statesmen
baseness a lower-class skill
laboured much made a great effort
yeoman's service the service of a faithful attendant
effect substance

conjuration request
England i.e. the Anglo-Saxons
tributary country paying tribute
as peace so that peace · **still** always
wheaten made of wheat
stand a comma [...] amities serve to connect their friendship
"as"es repetitions of phrases with "as" at the beginning
charge weight
without debatement further without further debate
bearers those carrying the document
shriving-time time for confession

ordinant directing events
signet small seal
model replica
writ written document
the other the original
subscribed it forged the signature
gave't (gave it) **the impression** sealed it
changeling substitute
was sequent followed

did make [...] employment did it willingly
defeat destruction

the baser nature inferior men
pass thrust of a sword
fell incensèd points greatly angered sword points

Does it [...] upon It is now my obligation to act?
whored made into a whore
popped in intervened
angle fishing hook · **proper** own
cozenage deception, trickery
Is't not perfect conscience Isn't it perfectly justifiable
quit him repay him

---

45 I once did hold it, as our statists do,
A baseness to write fair and laboured much
How to forget that learning, but, sir, now
It did me yeoman's service. Wilt thou know
The effect of what I wrote?

50 **HORATIO**
Ay, good my lord.

HAMLET
An earnest conjuration from the King,
As England was his faithful tributary,
55 As love between them like the palm* might flourish,
As peace should still her wheaten garland* wear
And stand a comma 'tween their amities,
And many such-like "as"es of great charge,
That, on the view and knowing of these contents,
60 Without debatement further, more or less,
He should the bearers put to sudden death,
Not shriving-time allowed.

HORATIO
How was this sealed?

65 **HAMLET**
Why, even in that was heaven ordinant.
I had my father's signet in my purse,
Which was the model of that Danish seal.
Folded the writ up in form of the other,
70 Subscribed it, gave't the impression, placed it safely,
The changeling never known. Now, the next day
Was our sea-fight; and what to this was sequent
Thou knowest already.

HORATIO
75 So Guildenstern and Rosencrantz go to't.

HAMLET
Why, man, they did make love to this employment.
They are not near my conscience. Their defeat
Does by their own insinuation grow.*
80 'Tis dangerous when the baser nature comes
Between the pass and fell incensèd points
Of mighty opposites.

HORATIO
Why, what a King is this!

85 **HAMLET**
Does it not, think thee, stand me now upon?
He that hath killed my King and whored my mother,
Popped in between the election and my hopes*,
Thrown out his angle for my proper life,
90 And with such cozenage. Is't not perfect conscience,
To quit him with this arm? And is't not to be damned,

To let this canker of our nature come
In further evil?

HORATIO

95 It must be shortly known to him from England
What is the issue of the business there.

HAMLET

It will be short. The interim is mine,
And a man's life's no more than to say "one".
100 But I am very sorry, good Horatio,
That to Laertes I forgot myself;
For, by the image of my cause I see
The portraiture of his. I'll court his favours.
But, sure, the bravery of his grief did put me
105 Into a towering passion.

HORATIO

Peace, who comes here?

Enter young OSRIC, a courtier, taking off his hat

OSRIC

110 Your lordship is right welcome back to Denmark.

HAMLET

I humbly thank you, sir. [*To HORATIO*] Dost know this waterfly?

HORATIO

[*Aside to HAMLET*] No, my good lord.

115 **HAMLET**

[*Aside to HORATIO*] Thy state is the more gracious, for 'tis a
vice to know him. He hath much land, and fertile. Let a beast be
lord of beasts, and his crib shall stand at the King's mess. 'Tis a
chough, but, as I say, spacious in the possession of dirt.

120 **OSRIC**

Sweet lord, if your lordship were at leisure, I should impart a
thing to you from his majesty.

HAMLET

I will receive it, sir, with all diligence of spirit. Put your bonnet
125 to his right use.* 'Tis for the head.

OSRIC

I thank your lordship, it is very hot.

HAMLET

No, believe me, 'tis very cold. The wind is northerly.

130 **OSRIC**

It is indifferent cold, my lord, indeed.

HAMLET

But yet methinks it is very sultry and hot for my complexion.

OSRIC

135 Exceedingly, my lord. It is very sultry, as 'twere – I cannot tell
how. But, my lord, his majesty bade me signify to you that he
has laid a great wager on your head. Sir, this is the matter.

---

canker cancer
come in further evil develop into a greater evil

issue result
The interim is mine I still have time.

portraiture mirror image
court his favours try to regain his friendship
bravery exaggeration
towering passion extreme emotion

waterfly i.e. a superficial person

state circumstances · **gracious** blessed
crib *Futtertrog* · **mess** table
chough jackdaw, a bird that seems to chatter a lot
spacious [...] dirt owns a lot of land

were at leisure have some free time
impart a thing inform you about sth.

with [...] spirit most attentively
bonnet hat · **his** its

indifferent rather

sultry *schwül*

as 'twere so to speak
bade asked · **signify** indicate
wager bet · **the matter** the situation

remember remember your courtesy, i.e. to put on your hat

nay no
for mine ease because it is more convenient for me
in good faith I mean well.
differences distinguishing qualities
of very soft society socially very agreeable
great showing impressive appearance
feelingly appreciatively
card [...] gentry model of gentlemanly behaviour
continent embodiment
of what part [...] see every gentleman would like to see
definement description
suffers no perdition in you suffers no loss in your words
divide him inventorially list all his qualities separately
would [...] memory would be too complicated to calculate
yaw not be able to sail in a direct course
in the verity of extolment in truthful praise
a soul of great article the essence of greatness
infusion [...] rareness mixture of qualities that are precious and rare
to make true [...] of him to speak truly of him
his semblable is his mirror the only person like him is his mirror image
trace him rival him • **umbrage** shadow
infallibly accurately
concernancy relevancy
Why [...] breath? Why do we use such crude language that is inadequate for this excellent gentleman?
Is't [...] tongue? Isn't it possible to use a simpler language?
do't succeed
What imports [...] gentleman? What's the significance of speaking of this gentleman?

ignorant Osric means "unaware". Hamlet interprets it to mean "lacking education".

would wish
would not much approve me would not make much difference to my reputation

HAMLET
I beseech you, remember.

140 *HAMLET gestures to him to put on his hat.*

OSRIC
Nay, good my lord; for mine ease, in good faith. Sir, here is newly come to court Laertes, believe me, an absolute gentleman, full of most excellent differences, of very soft society and great
145 showing. Indeed, to speak feelingly of him, he is the card or calendar of gentry, for you shall find in him the continent of what part a gentleman would see.

HAMLET
Sir, his definement suffers no perdition in you, though I know
150 to divide him inventorially would dizzy the arithmetic of memory, and yet but yaw neither, in respect of his quick sail. But in the verity of extolment, I take him to be a soul of great article, and his infusion of such dearth and rareness, as, to make true diction of him, his semblable is his mirror, and who else would
155 trace him, his umbrage, nothing more.

OSRIC
Your lordship speaks most infallibly of him.

HAMLET
The concernancy, sir? Why do we wrap the gentleman in our
160 more rawer breath?

OSRIC
Sir?

HORATIO
Is't not possible to understand in another tongue? You will do't,
165 sir, really.

HAMLET
What imports the nomination of this gentleman?

OSRIC
Of Laertes?

170 **HORATIO**
[*To HAMLET*] His purse is empty already. All's golden words are spent.

HAMLET
[*To OSRIC*] Of him, sir.

175 **OSRIC**
I know you are not ignorant –

HAMLET
I would you did, sir. Yet, in faith, if you did, it would not much approve me. Well, sir?

180 **OSRIC**
You are not ignorant of what excellence Laertes is.

HAMLET

I dare not confess that, lest I should compare with him in excellence. But to know a man well were to know himself.

185 **OSRIC**

I mean, sir, for his weapon. But in the imputation laid on him by them, in his meed he's unfellowed.

HAMLET

What's his weapon?

190 **OSRIC**

Rapier and dagger.

HAMLET

That's two of his weapons – but well.

OSRIC

195 The King, sir, hath wagered with him six Barbary horses, against the which he has impawned, as I take it, six French rapiers and poniards, with their assigns, as girdle, hangers, and so. Three of the carriages, in faith, are very dear to fancy, very responsive to the hilts, most delicate carriages, and of very liberal conceit.

200 **HAMLET**

What call you the "carriages"?

HORATIO

[*To HAMLET*] I knew you must be edified by the margent ere you had done.

205 **OSRIC**

The carriages, sir, are the hangers.

HAMLET

The phrase would be more germane to the matter, if we could carry cannon by our sides*. I would it might be "hangers" till

210 then. But on, six Barbary horses against six French swords, their assigns, and three liberal-conceited carriages – that's the French bet against the Danish. Why is this "impawned", as you call it?

OSRIC

The King, sir, hath laid, that in a dozen passes between yourself

215 and him, he shall not exceed you three hits. He hath laid on twelve for nine; and it would come to immediate trial if your lordship would vouchsafe the answer.

HAMLET

How if I answer "no"?

220 **OSRIC**

I mean, my lord, the opposition of your person in trial.

HAMLET

Sir, I will walk here in the hall. If it please his majesty, 'tis the breathing time of day with me. Let the foils be brought, the

225 gentleman willing, and the King hold his purpose, I will win for him an I can. If not, I will gain nothing but my shame and the odd hits.

I dare […] in excellence. I cannot presume to know how excellent Laertes is for fear that I might imply I am his equal.

But to know […] himself. Only with self-knowledge can you judge another man.

imputation reputation

laid on him by them given him by others

meed specialty • **unfellowed** unrivaled

rapier light, sharp-pointed sword in the right hand

dagger sharp, pointed knife for the left hand

wagered with him put a bet on him

Barbary Arabian

impawned wagered

poniards daggers • **assigns** *Zubehör*

girdle belt

hangers straps (*Riemen*) to the girdle

so so forth

carriages fashionable word for hangers

very dear to fancy elaborately decorated

responsive to the hilts fitting very well with the hilts (handles of a sword)

delicate skillfully made

of liberal conceit ingeniously designed

I knew […] margent I knew you would want an explanation

germane to the matter appropriate

I would I would prefer

on to go on

French bet i.e. Laertes' bet

the Danish i.e. mine

laid placed his bet • **passes** rounds

he shall not exceed you […] twelve for nine he will not be able to hit you three times more than you will hit him

it would come to immediate trial the fencing match would immediately take place

vouchsafe the answer accept the challenge

I mean […] in trial I mean your presence in the match, not the answer to any yes/no question

'tis the breathing time of day with me. It is the time for my daily exercise.

hold his purpose keep to his plan

an if

odd occasional

Shall I [...] so? Shall I convey your response in this way?
to this effect just so
after what flourish [...] will in whatever elaborate language you choose to use
commend my duty dedicate my service

OSRIC
Shall I re-deliver you e'en so?
230 **HAMLET**
To this effect, sir; after what flourish your nature will.
OSRIC
I commend my duty to your lordship.
HAMLET
235 Yours, yours.

Exit OSRIC

He does well to commend [...] for's turn. It is good that he praises himself since nobody else will do it.
This lapwing (newly hatched chick) **[...] the** (egg) **shell on his head.** This bird-brain runs away with his hat back on.
He did comply [...] sucked it. He made compliments to his mother's breast before sucking from the nipple.
bevy sort
drossy age present time, which is worthless
dotes on adores
only got the tune of the time only uses the jargon that is now popular
outward habit of encounter coming together with like-minded people
yesty collection collection of clichés
fanned and winnowed trendy and unsubstantial
out burst
commended him to you sent his greetings

He does well to commend it himself. There are no tongues else for's turn.
HORATIO
240 This lapwing runs away with the shell on his head.
HAMLET
He did comply with his dug, before he sucked it. Thus has he – and many more of the same bevy that I know the drossy age dotes on – only got the tune of the time and outward habit
245 of encounter; a kind of yesty collection, which carries them through and through the most fanned and winnowed opinions; and do but blow them to their trial, the bubbles are out.

Enter a LORD

LORD
250 My lord, his Majesty commended him to you by young Osric, who brings back to him that you attend him in the hall: he sends to know if your pleasure hold to play with Laertes, or that you will take longer time.
HAMLET
255 I am constant to my purpose; they follow the King's pleasure: if his fitness speaks, mine is ready; now or whensoever, provided I be so able as now.
LORD
The King and Queen and all are coming down.

follow obey
his fitness speaks he is ready

260 **HAMLET**
In happy time.
LORD
The Queen desires you to use some gentle entertainment to Laertes before you fall to play.
265 **HAMLET**
She well instructs me.

In happy time. The time is opportune.

use some gentle entertainment be courteous
before you fall to play before you begin to fence
She well instructs me. That's good advice.

Exit LORD

HORATIO
You will lose this wager, my lord.

● Fate vs. free will

270 HAMLET

I do not think so. Since he went into France, I have been in continual practice. I shall win at the odds. But thou wouldst not think how ill all's here about my heart. But it is no matter.

at the odds with the conditions of the bet

HORATIO

275 Nay, good my lord –

HAMLET

It is but foolery, but it is such a kind of gaingiving, as would perhaps trouble a woman.

foolery foolish thoughts
gaingiving misgiving, doubt

HORATIO

280 If your mind dislike anything, obey it. I will forestall their repair hither, and say you are not fit.

forestall delay · **repair** coming
hither here

HAMLET

Not a whit. We defy augury. There's a special providence in the fall of a sparrow*. If it be now, 'tis not to come. If it be not to

285 come, it will be now. If it be not now, yet it will come. The readiness is all. Since no man has aught of what he leaves, what is't to leave betimes? Let be.

Not a whit. Not at all.
defy reject
augury predicting the future by interpreting omens, such as the flight of birds
providence God's direction for a certain event
sparrow *Spatz*
The readiness is all. You must be prepared to die at any time.
aught anything · **leaves** leaves behind
what is't what does it matter
leave betimes die sooner

Enter KING CLAUDIUS, QUEEN GERTRUDE, LAERTES, LORDS, OSRIC, and OTHER ATTENDANTS with trumpets, drums, cush-
290 *ions, foils and gauntlets, a table and flagons of wine on it*

gauntlet heavy glove

KING CLAUDIUS

Come, Hamlet, come, and take this hand from me.

KING CLAUDIUS puts LAERTES' hand into HAMLET's.

☉ Questions of morality

HAMLET

295 Give me your pardon, sir. I've done you wrong;
But pardon't, as you are a gentleman.
This presence knows,
And you must needs have heard, how I am punished
With a sore distraction. What I have done

pardon't (it) forgive it
presence royal company
must needs have must have
sore distraction serious mental problem

300 That might your nature, honour and exception
Roughly awake, I here proclaim was madness.
Was't Hamlet wronged Laertes? Never Hamlet.
If Hamlet from himself be ta'en away,
And when he's not himself does wrong Laertes,

nature natural feelings
exception resentment, anger

Was't Was it
from himself be ta'en away divided from himself

305 Then Hamlet does it not, Hamlet denies it.
Who does it then? His madness. If't be so,
Hamlet is of the faction that is wronged;
His madness is poor Hamlet's enemy.
Sir, in this audience,

faction party

310 Let my disclaiming from a purposed evil
Free me so far in your most generous thoughts
That I have shot mine arrow o'er the house
And hurt my brother.

in this audience with the witnesses present
my disclaiming from a purposed evil my denial of deliberate evil intention
play fence
that I have [...] the house that what I have done was accidental

in nature as far as my feelings are concerned
motive motivation • **stir** be the cause of
in my terms of honour as far as my honour
   is concerned
I stand aloof I am undecided • **will** wish
reconcilement reconciliation (*Aussöhnung*)
Till by [...] of peace Until men of authority
   come to an agreement on the basis of
   tradition so that I can make an honorable
   peace.
my name ungored my reputation intact
receive accept
wrong it do anything to challenge it
embrace welcome
frankly in good faith
foil 1. fencing sword, 2. thin piece of shiny
   metal in which a precious stone is set to
   add brightness

LAERTES
315 I am satisfied in nature,
Whose motive, in this case, should stir me most
To my revenge. But in my terms of honour
I stand aloof, and will no reconcilement,
Till by some elder masters, of known honour,
320 I have a voice and precedent of peace,
To keep my name ungored. But till that time,
I do receive your offered love like love,
And will not wrong it.
HAMLET
325 I embrace it freely;
And will this brother's wager frankly play.
Give us the foils. Come on.
LAERTES
Come, one for me.
330 **HAMLET**
I'll be your foil, Laertes. In mine ignorance

stick fiery off indeed shine out brightly in
   contrast

Your skill shall, like a star i' the darkest night,
Stick fiery off indeed.
LAERTES
335 You mock me, sir.
HAMLET
No, by this hand.

by this hand i.e. I swear

KING CLAUDIUS
Give them the foils, young Osric. Cousin Hamlet,
340 You know the wager?
HAMLET
Very well, my lord
Your grace hath laid the odds o' the weaker side.
KING CLAUDIUS
345 I do not fear it. I have seen you both.
But since he is better, we have therefore odds.

laid the odds o' (on) **the weaker side** bet
   on the weaker fencer

we have therefore odds I have arranged
   the odds in your favour

HAMLET and LAERTES choose foils.

LAERTES
This is too heavy, let me see another.
350 **HAMLET**
This likes me well. These foils have all a length?
OSRIC
Ay, my good lord.

This likes me well. This pleases me very
   much.
have all a length have all the same length

They prepare to play.

355 **KING CLAUDIUS**
Set me the stoops of wine upon that table.
If Hamlet give the first or second hit,

stoop large bottle, jar

**◑ Questions
of morality**

Or quit in answer of the third exchange,
Let all the battlements their ordnance fire.
360 The King shall drink to Hamlet's better breath,
And in the cup an union shall he throw
Richer than that which four successive Kings
In Denmark's crown have worn. Give me the cups,
And let the kettle to the trumpet speak,
365 The trumpet to the cannoneer without,
The cannons to the heavens, the heavens to earth,
"Now the King drinks to Hamlet."

Trumpets the while. He drinks.

Come, begin.
370 And you, the judges, bear a wary eye.
HAMLET
[*To LAERTES*] Come on, sir.
LAERTES
Come, my lord.

375 *They play. HAMLET scores a hit.*

HAMLET
One.
LAERTES
No.
380 **HAMLET**
[*To OSRIC*] Judgement?
OSRIC
A hit, a very palpable hit.

Drum and trumpets sound, and cannon shot off

385 **LAERTES**
Well, again.
KING CLAUDIUS
Stay. Give me drink. Hamlet, this pearl is thine.
Here's to thy health.

390 *He drinks.*

Give him the cup.
HAMLET
I'll play this bout first. Set it by awhile.
Come.

395 *They play again.*

---

or quit [...] exchange wins the third bout to repay Laertes for his earlier hits
battlements i.e. the soldiers standing at defensive positions at the top of the outside wall
ordnance cannons
union pearl

kettle *Kesselpauke*
speak start playing with the next instrument then following
cannoneer person in charge of the cannons
without outside

bear a wary eye watch attentively

Judgement What is your decision?

palpable definite

stay stop

the cup Note: King Claudius presumably puts the pearl (union), which contains a deadly poison, into the cup for Hamlet to drink.
by aside

Another hit. What say you?

LAERTES

touch touché, hit

A touch, a touch, I do confess.

KING CLAUDIUS

400   Our son shall win.

QUEEN GERTRUDE

fat sweaty · **scant of breath** out of breath
napkin handkerchief
carouses drinks a toast

He's fat, and scant of breath.

Here, Hamlet, take my napkin. Rub thy brows.

The Queen carouses to thy fortune, Hamlet.

405   **HAMLET**

Good madam.

KING CLAUDIUS

Gertrude, do not drink.

QUEEN GERTRUDE

410   I will, my lord, I pray you pardon me.

She drinks, then offers the cup to HAMLET.

KING CLAUDIUS

[*Aside*] It is the poisoned cup. It is too late.

HAMLET

by and by eventually

415   I dare not drink yet, madam – by and by.

QUEEN GERTRUDE

[*To HAMLET*] Come, let me wipe thy face.

LAERTES

My lord, I'll hit him now.

I do not think't (it). Perhaps it is not a good
   idea.
'tis almost 'gainst my conscience I am
   beginning to have doubts about what I
   am doing
you but dally you are not taking this match
   seriously
pass make a thrust
with your best violence with as much
   force as you can
wanton spoiled child

420   **KING CLAUDIUS**

[*Aside to LAERTES*] I do not think't.

LAERTES

[*Aside*] And yet 'tis almost 'gainst my conscience.

HAMLET

425   Come, for the third, Laertes, you but dally.

I pray you, pass with your best violence.

I am afeard you make a wanton of me.

LAERTES

Say you so? Come on.

430   *They play.*

OSRIC

Nothing, neither way.

LAERTES

Nothing, neither way. No advantage on
   either side.

[*To HAMLET*] Have at you now!

scuffling short fight without much violence

435   *LAERTES wounds HAMLET; then in scuffling, they change rapiers, and HAMLET wounds LAERTES.*

○ **The roles(s)
of women**
○ **Questions
of morality**

KING CLAUDIUS
Part them! They are incensed.

HAMLET
440 Nay, come, again.

QUEEN GERTRUDE falls.

OSRIC
Look to the Queen there, ho!

HORATIO
445 They bleed on both sides. How is it, my lord?

OSRIC
How is't, Laertes?

LAERTES
Why, as a woodcock to mine own springe, Osric;
450 I am justly killed with mine own treachery.

HAMLET
How does the Queen?

KING CLAUDIUS
She swoons to see them bleed.

455 **QUEEN GERTRUDE**
No, no, the drink, the drink – O my dear Hamlet! –
The drink, the drink! I am poisoned.

QUEEN GERTRUDE dies.

HAMLET
460 O villainy! Ho! Let the door be locked.
Treachery! Seek it out.

LAERTES falls. Exit OSRIC

LAERTES
It is here, Hamlet. Hamlet, thou art slain.
465 No medicine in the world can do thee good.
In thee there is not half an hour of life.
The treacherous instrument is in thy hand,
Unbated and envenomed. The foul practice
Hath turned itself on me. Lo, here I lie,
470 Never to rise again. Thy mother's poisoned.
I can no more. The King, the King's to blame.

HAMLET
The point envenomed too?
Then, venom, to thy work.

475 *Stabs KING CLAUDIUS*

---

incensed angry

How is it How are you

woodcock a bird thought stupid because it was easy to catch
to mine own springe in my own trap
treachery *Verrat*

swoons collapses, faints

◑ **Questions of morality**   **villainy** evil act

slain *here:* mortally wounded

unbated with the point unprotected
envenomed poisoned
foul practice shameful plot • **lo** see

venom poison

to stab sb to push a sharp instrument such as a knife into a person's body to injure or kill this person

but hurt only wounded

incestuous committing incest (*Inzest*)

union pearl or Claudius' incestuous marriage

He is justly served. He is getting what he
deserves.
tempered prepared

Mine […] thine on me. If we forgive each
other, then we can no longer be held
accountable [in the eyes of God] for our
murders.

make thee free of it absolve (*freisprechen*)
you of your crime
I am dead I am dying.
this chance What has happened here.
mutes actors without a speaking part,
onlookers
fell cruel
sergeant officer responsible for arrest
report me and my cause aright give an accurate account of what I have done and
of the reasons
the unsatisfied those who feel the need for
an explanation
Never believe it. Don't believe I will do so.
liquor i.e. the drink with poison

what a wounded name what a damaged
reputation

ALL
Treason! Treason!
KING CLAUDIUS
O, yet defend me, friends. I am but hurt.
480 **HAMLET**
Here, thou incestuous, murderous, damnèd Dane,
Drink off this potion.

He forces CLAUDIUS to drink.

Is thy union here?
485 Follow my mother.

KING CLAUDIUS dies.

LAERTES
He is justly served.
It is a poison tempered by himself.
490 Exchange forgiveness with me, noble Hamlet.
Mine and my father's death come not upon thee,
Nor thine on me.

Dies

HAMLET
495 Heaven make thee free of it. I follow thee.
I am dead, Horatio. Wretched Queen, adieu!
You that look pale and tremble at this chance,
That are but mutes or audience to this act,
Had I but time – as this fell sergeant Death,
500 Is strict in his arrest – O, I could tell you –
But let it be. Horatio, I am dead.
Thou livest. Report me and my cause aright
To the unsatisfied.
HORATIO
505 Never believe it.
I am more an antique Roman than a Dane.*
Here's yet some liquor left.

*He attempts to drink from the poisoned cup, but HAMLET
restrains him.*

510 **HAMLET**
As thou'rt a man,
Give me the cup. Let go. By heaven, I'll have't.
O God, Horatio, what a wounded name,
Things standing thus unknown, shall live behind me.
515 If thou didst ever hold me in thy heart,

Absent thee from felicity awhile,
And in this harsh world draw thy breath in pain,
To tell my story.

March afar off, and shot within

520 What warlike noise is this?

Enter OSRIC

OSRIC
Young Fortinbras, with conquest come from Poland,
To the ambassadors of England gives
525 This warlike volley.
HAMLET
O, I die, Horatio.
The potent poison quite o'ercrows my spirit.
I cannot live to hear the news from England,
530 But I do prophesy the election lights
On Fortinbras. He has my dying voice.
So tell him, with the occurrents, more and less,
Which have solicited – The rest is silence.

Dies

535 **HORATIO**
Now cracks a noble heart.* Good night sweet prince,
And flights of angels sing thee to thy rest.

March within

Why does the drum come hither?

540 *Enter FORTINBRAS, the English AMBASSADORS, with drums,*
colours, and OTHERS

FORTINBRAS
Where is this sight?
HORATIO
545 What is it ye would see?
If aught of woe or wonder, cease your search.
FORTINBRAS
This quarry cries on havoc. O proud Death,
What feast is toward in thine eternal cell,
550 That thou so many princes at a shot
So bloodily hast struck?
ENGLISH AMBASSADOR
The sight is dismal,
And our affairs from England come too late.

---

absent thee from felicity keep yourself from the happiness of death
harsh cruel
draw thy breath in pain as painful as it may be to speak

gives this warlike volley shoots off their cannons as a military salute

⊙ **Fate vs. free will**
⊙ **Questions of morality**

potent strong
o'ercrows (overcrows) **my spirit** triumphs over my spirit like a victorious cockerel in a cockfight
election the election of a king by the council of nobles
lights on falls on • **voice** vote
occurrents occurrences
more and less great and small
solicited prompted – Note: Hamlet does not finish the sentence.

⊙ **Fate vs. free will**

flights of angles companies of angels

hither towards this place

colours flags

would wish to
if aught of if either • **woe** great misery

This quarry cries on havoc. The pile of bodies proclaims a great slaughter.
toward being prepared

dismal dreadful

senseless unable to hear

555 The ears are senseless that should give us hearing
To tell him his commandment is fulfilled,
That Rosencrantz and Guildenstern are dead.
Where should we have our thanks?

HORATIO

560 Not from his mouth,
Had it the ability of life to thank you.
He never gave commandment for their death.

jump upon immediately after
question conflict

But since, so jump upon this bloody question,
You from the Polack wars, and you from England,

stage platform

565 Are here arrived, give order that these bodies
High on a stage be placèd to the view,
And let me speak to the yet unknowing world
How these things came about. So shall you hear

carnal connected with lust
accidental judgements impulsive decisions
casual happening by chance
forced cause invented reasons
upshot conclusion to it all
purposes mistook plots gone wrong
deliver report

Of carnal, bloody, and unnatural acts,
570 Of accidental judgements, casual slaughters,
Of deaths put on by cunning and forced cause,
And, in this upshot, purposes mistook
Fallen on the inventors' heads. All this can I
Truly deliver.

575 **FORTINBRAS**

Let us haste to hear it.
And call the noblest to the audience.

embrace accept · **fortune** good luck
rights of memory traditional rights
which the Danish kingdom
vantage position of strength
**from his mouth whose voice will draw
   on more** i.e. Fortinbras can expect more
   support in his election because of Hamlet's support (his dying voice)
this same Horatio's detailed report of the
   events and then with Fortinbras being
   quickly crowned king
presently immediately
wild excited · **mischance** misfortune
on arising from
put on tested, become king
most royal a capable monarch
passage death

For me, with sorrow I embrace my fortune.
I have some rights of memory in this kingdom,
580 Which now to claim my vantage doth invite me.

HORATIO

Of that I shall have also cause to speak
And from his mouth whose voice will draw on more.
But let this same be presently performed
585 Even while men's minds are wild, lest more mischance
On plots and errors happen.

FORTINBRAS

Let four captains
Bear Hamlet like a soldier to the stage.
590 For he was likely, had he been put on,
To have proved most royal. And for his passage
The soldiers' music and the rites of war
Speak loudly for him.
Take up the bodies. Such a sight as this

becomes the field is more typical of a
   battlefield
amiss unsuitable
shoot shoot their cannons
a peal of ordnance is shot off the shooting
   of a series of cannons takes place

595 Becomes the field but here shows much amiss.
Go, bid the soldiers shoot.

*Exeunt, marching and bearing off the dead bodies, after which a
peal of ordnance is shot off*

FINIS

Summary

Hamlet tells Horatio the full story of his adventurous ship voyage. A courtier arrives to inform Hamlet about the fencing bout that Claudius has arranged for Hamlet and Laertes. During the match, Hamlet and Laertes are both fatally wounded. Queen Gertrude dies because she drinks the poisoned wine prepared for Hamlet, and King Claudius is killed by his nephew. Fortinbras arrives with his army and ascends the Danish throne.

Tasks

1. Hamlet spoils his uncle's plan

a) Go back to Act IV, Scene VI and revisit what Hamlet tells Horatio in his letter about his journey to England.
b) Describe the steps Hamlet takes aboard the ship to spoil his uncle's plan.
c) Explain Hamlet's feelings about Rosencrantz and Guildenstern.
d) Extra: Imagine you are Hamlet. Write the document addressed to the King of England.

2. Osric and Hamlet

a) Bring the summaries into the correct chronological order and give line references.

	Summaries	Line references
	Hamlet deliberately misunderstands what Osric says.	
	Hamlet makes Osric give a coherent account of the arranged fencing match.	
	Osric praises Laertes' qualities.	
1	Hamlet points out that Osric is a wealthy landowner and as such welcomed by the king.	ll. 116-119
	Hamlet chides Osric for holding his hat in his hands instead of wearing it on his head.	
	Hamlet praises Laertes' qualities.	
	Osric explains the reason for his visit: Laertes has come back from France and the king has made a bet with him involving Hamlet.	

b) Briefly outline Osric's conversation with Hamlet.
c) Choose the adjectives that best describe Osric and Hamlet's attitudes towards each other and find examples from the text to support your ideas.

> creepy – slimy – beastly – grateful – admiring – humble – servile –friendly – mocking – ridiculing – flattering – respectful – supportive – sycophantic

d) Group work (4): Stage the part of the conversation from line 120 to 155:
   Have two people read out Osric and Hamlet's parts, pausing after each part, with two other students expressing their true feelings and thoughts about each other.
e) In class discuss the dramatic function Osric serves.

3. Preparing for the fencing bout

a) Explain the reasons for the fencing bout. You may use your results from Act IV, Scene VII, task 3.
b) Describe Hamlet's attitude towards death in lines 283-287.
c) Re-read the definition of dramatic irony in Act II, Scene II, task 3 and identify the dramatic irony in lines 268-287. Explain the effect on the audience.

4. Hamlet and Laertes

a) Take stock: Recap what you know about Laertes and Hamlet's relationship.
b) Pair work: Analyse two extracts: Partner A looks at Hamlet's speech (ll. 294-313), partner B at Laertes' (ll. 314-323). Exchange your results at the end.
   1 First summarize the most important contents of the respective speeches.
   2 Then analyse the language Shakespeare uses to show the two men's attitudes towards each other.

5. The fencing bout

a) Put the different causes and effects into the correct chronological order and give line references.

> Hamlet wounds Laertes. – Hamlet wounds the king. – The queen drinks from the poisoned cup. – Laertes poisons a rapier's tip. – The king dies. – Laertes dies. – Laertes and Hamlet swap their rapiers. – Hamlet makes the king drink from the poisoned cup. – Laertes wounds Hamlet. – Claudius poisons the drink. – Hamlet dies. – The queen dies.

	Causes and effects	Lines
1		
2		
3		
4		
5		
6		
7		

	Causes and effects	Lines
8		
9		
10		
11		
12		

b) Talk about the reasons why Shakespeare makes his characters die in this chronological order.
c) Compare Laertes' attitude towards Hamlet before and after their fencing match.

6. The ending

a) Sum up Hamlet's last wishes concerning Horatio and Fortinbras (ll. 510-518, 526-533).
b) Pair work: Hamlet dies by saying "the rest is silence". (l. 533) How do you understand Hamlet's last words? Exchange your ideas with a partner.
c) Look at what Horatio reports to Fortinbras and the English ambassador. His words are rather abstract. Explain the underlined phrases and find examples from the play. Then imagine you are Horatio and tell Fortinbras the whole story.

> And let me speak to th' yet-unknowing world
> How these things came about. So shall you hear
> Of carnal, bloody, and unnatural acts,
> Of accidental judgments, casual slaughters,
> Of deaths put on by cunning and forced cause,
> And, in this upshot, purposes mistook
> Fallen on the inventors' heads. All this can I
> Truly deliver.

d) Analyse the political impact of Hamlet's death.
e) According to Aristotle, a famous Greek philosopher and critic (384–322 BC), the ideal tragic ending is the necessary consequence of all the action that preceded it, in other words the final outcome somehow reflects the story as a whole. Discuss to what extent this is true for this play.

Looking back at Act V

1. The themes

a) Complete the mind-map you started in *Looking back at Act II*.
b) Choose one of the themes and write an essay about its presentation in the play. Make sure you give evidence from the play.
c) "Shakespeare uses comedy and ordinary people to provide alternative perspectives on his themes." Explain this statement and give examples from the play.

2. Hamlet's end

In some productions the play ends with a dying Hamlet saying "the rest is silence" (l. 533). In class, discuss what is won or lost when the play ends with this line.

3. News coverage

Group work (4): Prepare a modern-style news coverage of the major events of Act V:
• Decide if the coverage is for a newspaper, radio or TV station.
• In your group, talk about the passages you want to report on.
• Then write about, record or film the events.

Post-reading
Looking back at the play

1. The structure of *Hamlet*

a) Look at the diagram. A classical play usually has the following structure:

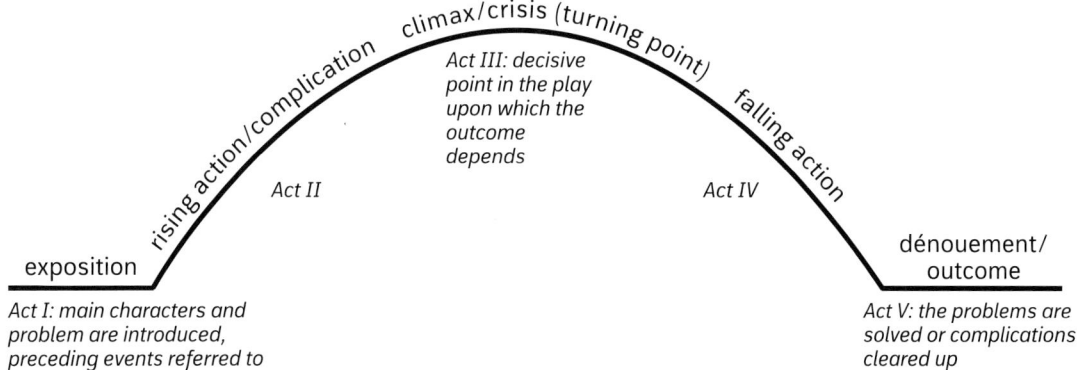

climax/crisis (turning point)

rising action/complication

Act III: decisive
point in the play
upon which the
outcome
depends

Act II

falling action

Act IV

exposition

dénouement/
outcome

*Act I: main characters and
problem are introduced,
preceding events referred to*

*Act V: the problems are
solved or complications
cleared up*

b) Identify the plot developments in *Hamlet* and give examples from the play to show how they fit into the structure.
c) Group work (4–5): Decide which are the most important passages in the play. Then act out the play in only 3 minutes. One student is the timekeeper. Explain why you chose the passages you did.

2. Inspecting Hamlet's relationships

Group work: Choose three characters and identify typical lines from the play that illustrate Hamlet's attitude towards them. Explain what the lines reveal about Hamlet's relationships with the respective characters. You can use the character map you started in the pre-reading section for help.

3. Looking back at Hamlet

a) Pair work: Hamlet's character is often described as elusive as he plays so many different roles. Choose the descriptions or attributes from the box below that best describe your understanding of Hamlet. Give evidence from the play to prove your point.

> ironic commentator – potential suicide – joker – angry son – lacerating self-critic – bloodthirsty revenger –
> alienated outsider – genuinely mad – elated – self-loathing – clever – dreamer – truly noble prince –
> impersonator of madness – reliable son – misogynist

b) Design a character poster in which you show Hamlet's different sides.

4. Famous quotes

Read the quotations below and on p. 192 and choose the one you like best. Briefly outline the context and explain your choice.
1 Frailty, thy name is Woman (Act I, Scene II, line 172)
2 Neither a borrower nor a lender be. For loan oft loses both itself and friend and borrowing dulls the edge of husbandry. (Act I, Scene III, lines 89-91)

3   Something is rotten in the state of Denmark. (Act I, Scene IV, line 134)
4   Though this be madness, yet there is method in't. (Act II, Scene II, line 291)
5   What a piece of work is a man. How noble in reason, how infinite in faculty, in form and moving how express and admirable, in action how like an angel, in apprehension how like a god – the beauty of the world, the paragon of animals. (Act II, Scene II, lines 433-437)
6   they [i.e. the players] are the abstract and brief chronicles of the time. (Act II, Scene II, lines 708-709)
7   To be, or not to be, that is the question. Whether 'tis nobler in the mind to suffer the slings and arrows of outrageous fortune, or to take arms against a sea of troubles, and by opposing end them? (Act III, Scene I, lines 90-94)
8   The lady doth protest too much, methinks. (Act III, Scene II, line 321)

Fate vs. free will

1. Fate vs. free will

Is life determined by fate or free will? In other words, have you ever wondered if you have control over your actions, and if so, to what extent? Or are your actions determined by other forces? Philosophers have been discussing these issues for thousands of years.

a) Pair work: Read the following scenarios. In your opinion, what role do fate and free will play in them? Discuss this question with a partner.

-   A man wakes up late for work, his phone died overnight and so his alarm didn't go off. Despite being awoken by the sun, he is still late getting up. He runs for his bus and misses it by a matter of seconds.
-   A woman has just finished her masters degree at a university and has a job offer from a company. The day before she is about to sign the contract, her university offer her a role on a PhD programme.
-   A deer walks out into a road in front of a speeding car. The driver of the car sees the deer and slams on the breaks. The car swerves off the road and into a tree. The deer walks off unharmed.

b) What are your personal views on fate vs. free will? Do you believe you have complete control over your life? Have a discussion in class.

2. What the Elizabethans believed in

a) Pair work: One student reads text A and the other text B. Then explain the main aspects of the two concepts to each other.

A | **The Wheel of Fortune** – It was widely believed that fate (or fortune) was the main controlling force in life. Just as part of a wheel moves from a low to a high position or from high to low, so does a man's life. A man in a high position could expect (owing to a change in fortune) to suffer some disappointment or fall. Similarly, a man in an unhappy, lowly position could hope for a change in fortune and consequently a rise to a higher position. However, there was no way of knowing where the wheel would stop, where fortune would lead.
Andrea Wilson, The Elizabethan World View

B **The Great Chain of Being** – Elizabethans believed that God set out an order for everything in the universe. This was known as the Great Chain of Being. On Earth, God created a social order for everybody and chose where you belonged. In other words, the king or queen was in charge because God put them there and they were only answerable to God (the Divine Right of Kings). This meant that disobeying the monarch was a sin, which was handy for keeping people in their place! It also led to the idea that if the wrong person was monarch everything would go wrong for a country, including whether the crops would be good, or if animals behaved as they should. The Elizabethans were very superstitious.
The Great Chain of Being includes everything from God and the angels at the top, to humans, to animals, to plants, to rocks and minerals at the bottom. It moves from beings of pure spirit at the top of the Chain to things made entirely of matter at the bottom. Humans are pretty much in the middle, being mostly mortal, or made of matter, but with a soul made of spirit. The theory started with the Greek philosophers Aristotle and Plato, but was a basic assumption of life in Elizabethan England. You were a noble, or a farmer, or a beggar, because that was the place God had ordained for you.
BBC Bitesize: Beliefs and Superstitions

b) Read the following two extracts from the play and explain how they relate to the Elizabethan world view.

A	B
I have of late – but wherefore I know not – lost all my mirth, forgone all custom of exercises and indeed it goes so heavily with my disposition that this goodly frame, the earth, seems to me a sterile promontory. This most excellent canopy, the air, look you, this brave o'erhanging firmament, this majestical roof fretted with golden fire, why, it appears no other thing to me than a foul and pestilent congregation of vapours. What a piece of work is a man. How noble in reason, how infinite in faculty, in form and moving how express and admirable, in action how like an angel, in apprehension how like a god – the beauty of the world, the paragon of animals. And yet, to me what is this quintessence of dust? *(Act II Scene II, lines 424-438)*	The single and peculiar life is bound With all the strength and armour of the mind To keep itself from noyance; but much more That spirit upon whose weal depends and rests The lives of many. The cease of majesty Dies not alone, but like a gulf doth draw What's near it with it. It is a massy wheel, Fixed on the summit of the highest mount, To whose huge spokes ten thousand lesser things Are mortised and adjoined, which, when it falls, Each small annexment, petty consequence, Attends the boisterous ruin. Never alone Did the King sigh, but with a general groan. *(Act III Scene III, lines 16-28)*

c) Explain how Elizabethan society regarded the issues of fate and free will.
d) Explain why Claudius had to die at the end of the play.

3. Hamlet – torn between fate and free will?

a) Pair work: Study the extracts that deal with Hamlet's attitude towards fate and free will (Act I, Scene IV, ll. 119-125; Scene V, ll. 23-140, 248-274; Act III, Scene I, ll. 89-122; Scene IV, ll. 249-255; Act IV, Scene IV, ll. 42-90; Act V, Scene II, ll. 10-73, 268-287). Then start a grid like the one on p. 194 to list examples that deal with the issue.

Actions/plans based on Hamlet's free will	Hamlet expressing his attitude towards fate
• Hamlet decides to obey the ghost's command and take revenge (Act I, Scene V, ll. 125–131) • …	• Hamlet feels fate commands him to talk to his father's ghost (Act I, Scene IV, ll. 119–125). • …

b) Discuss to what extent Hamlet tries to change his fate through his different ruses.

4. Fortinbras – the righteous successor to the throne?

a) Study these extracts that deal with Fortinbras: Act I, Scene I, ll. 145–174; Act II, Scene II, ll. 87–109; Act IV, Scene IV, ll. 1–47; Act V, Scene II, ll. 526–598. Collect arguments for and against his succession to the Danish throne.

b) Choose: Write a newspaper article in which you present Fortinbras as the rightful successor to the Danish throne.

OR

Write an article in which you argue against Fortinbras' succession to the Danish throne.

5. Group work (4–5): Fate vs. free will in *Hamlet*

a) Study the extracts in the play labelled *Fate vs. free will*. You find them on pages 14/15, 20-22, 36, 39-42, 44/45, 70, 82, 96, 106, 115, 132/133, 173-175, 178/179 and 185/186. Then create a poster in which you show the general attitude towards fate and free will as expressed in the play. Provide examples from the extracts to support your ideas.

b) Based on your findings in task a), explain what the player king means when he recites these lines:
"Our wills and fates do so contrary run
That our devices still are overthrown.
Our thoughts are ours, their ends none of our own."
(Act III, Scene II, ll. 293–295)

c) Gallery walk: Present your poster in class in the form of a gallery walk.

d) Choose:
Discuss the function of the different characters as regards the question of fate vs. free will.

OR

Host a talk show in which the characters come together and talk about to what extent free will and fate have played a role in their lives.

OR

Before their impending deaths, or in Fortinbras' case enthronement, the characters each reflect on the main events that shaped the course of their life towards their final destiny. Choose one of the characters and perform your ideas in the form of a soliloquy to the class.

The role(s) of women

1. The role of women in Shakespeare's time

Read the info box and outline what life was like for women in England during Shakespeare's time.

Info: Women in Elizabethan times
Ironically, despite women's often important roles in Shakespeare's plays, they weren't allowed on stage during his active years. At the time, most of the famous female characters from the plays would have been performed by young men. This fact perhaps sets the tone as to the status of women in Elizabethan times. Women belonged to men – either to their husbands, their fathers, or, if their fathers had died, to their brothers. Women were not able to own property. The only exception to this rule was widows. However, widows commonly re-married quickly so they had a man to protect them. Women were legally allowed to marry from the age of twelve, and many wealthy families took advantage of this rule to create a beneficial union between two families. Arranged marriages were particularly common among the upper class, with some girls being promised to their future husbands at a very young age. Women from the lower classes enjoyed a higher degree of freedom, but this was only due to the fact that they were seen as less important than women from the upper class.

2. The role(s) of women in *Hamlet*

a) Study the extracts of the play labelled *The role(s) of women*. You find them on pages 20/21, 22, 29/30, 31/32, 40/41, 51/52, 58-60, 81, 82-84, 93-97, 110-116, 121, 136-138, 141/142, 150, 154/155, 165-168, 182/183. Make a list collecting all the information about Queen Gertrude and Ophelia.

b) Choose the adjectives that best describe their characters and give evidence from the play.

sensual – shallow – lustful – self-indulgent – innocent – passive – intelligent – observant – enigmatic – sheepish – oblivious – mild – honest – ignorant – powerless – ambiguous – malleable – naive – compassionate

3. Gertrude

Imagine you are a director wanting Gertrude to voice her thoughts and feelings about her taking the poisoned cup that Claudius prepared for Hamlet. Did she know the drink was poisoned or was it a mere accident? Write her final soliloquy in which she reflects upon her action.

4. Ophelia

a) On the graph below, show where you would position Ophelia. Give evidence from the play.

filial obedience ←---→ true love

b) Explain the dilemma Ophelia finds herself in, which finally drives her into madness.

5. Hamlet's attitude towards women

a) Analyse Hamlet's attitude towards the women in the play.

b) Imagine you are a journalist writing for a newspaper. Carry out an interview with Hamlet about his attitude towards women.

6. Looking back at the role(s) of women in the play

a) Some scholars claim that the women in *Hamlet* are all powerless victims. Considering your findings from tasks 2–5, discuss this claim.

b) Stage a talk show in which Gertrude and Ophelia get the chance to talk about their roles in Hamlet's life.

7. Essay topics

Write an essay on one of these topics:

1 The role(s) of women in *Hamlet*
2 Hamlet: torn between love and hate towards women
3 "Frailty, thy name is Woman" (Act I, Scene II, l. 172): the image of women in Shakespeare's *Hamlet*

Questions of morality

1. Revenge: right or wrong?

a) Pair work: Have you ever thought about taking revenge? Where does revenge still take place? Can taking revenge ever be justified? Discuss these questions with a partner.

b) Group work (4–5): Team up with another pair. Pick one of the situations presented below and discuss them in your group.

   1 You own a small business and you discover that your accountant has been stealing money from you for the last five years – which is almost as long as the affair he's been having. Do you tell his wife?

   2 You learn that your ex has posted compromising photos of you online. You have photos of him/her that are even worse. What do you do?

   3 You work for a company and the person who bullied you unmercifully throughout school is up for a job there. You could anonymously prevent him/her from getting it. Do you?

c) Outline the major arguments discussed in your group.

d) Explain what made it easy or difficult for you to reach a decision.

e) Is your motto "An eye for an eye" or rather "Turn the other cheek"? Explain.

Info
The "an-eye-for-an-eye" principle or law of retaliation was used in early societies to seek punishment of wrongdoings according to a just system. With the growth of Christianity, the attitude of "turning the other cheek" became predominant, suggesting that vengeance should be left to God alone.

2. Revenge in Elizabethan plays

Although the Elizabethans regarded revenge as a crime and a sin and the revenger's soul was believed to be condemned to eternal torment, the genre of revenge tragedy was immensely popular during Shakespeare's lifetime.

a) Read the info box about revenge tragedies and apply the characteristics to *Hamlet*. Give evidence from the play.

Info: Revenge tragedy

The earliest English revenge tragedy, *The Spanish Tragedy*, was written by Thomas Kyd around 1582. Other well-known revenge tragedies are Christopher Marlowe's *The Jew of Malta* (1589–90), William Shakespeare's *Titus Andronicus* (1588) and Thomas Middleton's *The Revenger's Tragedy* (around 1606). The most common characteristics of a revenge tragedy are:

1. a play-within-a-play
2. madness
3. the supernatural (e.g. a ghost who forces the protagonist to avenge his death)
4. disguises
5. violent murders
6. a once-noble protagonist who degenerates
7. complex plotting
8. hesitant behaviour
9. the display of melancholy
10. a fifth act in which many characters are killed.

---

b) Extra: Research the revenge tragedies mentioned in the info box. Give a brief outline of the respective plays and compare them to *Hamlet*: Where do they show similarities and where do they differ?

3. Hamlet – a tragic hero?

a) Use the information from the info box to show to what extent Hamlet can be called a tragic hero. Give evidence from the play.

Info: Tragedy

According to the Greek philosopher Aristotle (384–322 BC), a tragedy is a play that possesses magnitude and imitates events that evoke pity and fear. Its plot is complex, involving reversal (a changing situation) and recognition (a change from ignorance to knowledge). The tragic hero is not of outstanding moral excellence but is held in great esteem and enjoys great fortune. He is nobler and more refined than ordinary people. The change to bad fortune that he must undergo is the result of an error of some kind (Greek: *hamartia*). This error has been interpreted in different ways. Some modern scholars call it a moral flaw or tragic flaw, others, however, interpret it as an intellectual error made in ignorance or through misjudgement, a misinterpretation of the circumstances.

---

b) Pair work: On the psychiatrist's couch: One of you is Hamlet, who seeks help from a psychiatrist for his troubled mind. The other one is the psychiatrist, who helps him come to terms with his problems. Write their dialogue. Then perform it in front of the class.

4. Claudius

a) Make a list of all the evil acts Claudius has committed and give evidence from the play.
b) Decide whether the statements on p. 198 are right or wrong. Give evidence from the play.

	Statement	right	wrong	Evidence
1	Claudius loves Hamlet.			
2	Claudius tries to calm Laertes' fury.			
3	Claudius is a hypocrite.			
4	He is a competent king.			
5	He loves Gertrude.			
6	Claudius ignores Polonius' advice.			
7	Claudius is tormented by his guilty conscience and tries to pray.			

c) Use your findings from tasks a) and b) to analyse the image of Claudius Shakespeare creates.

5. To kill or not to kill

a) Hamlet mentions four reasons for his revenge:
   1 Claudius has killed Hamlet's father.
   2 Claudius has slept with Hamlet's mother.
   3 Claudius has deprived Hamlet of the throne.
   4 Claudius has plotted Hamlet's death.
   Explain which reason you consider to be the most and least important ones to Hamlet.

b) Scan the extracts in which Hamlet contemplates his revenge (Act I, Scene V, ll. 23-140; Act II, Scene II, ll. 745-803; Act III, Scene III, ll. 50-122; Act IV, Scene IV, ll. 56-90). Collect arguments for and against the murder of Claudius or Hamlet's revenge in general. Then split the class into two groups, one group supporting the revenge, the other against taking revenge.

Choose two students, one takes Claudius' part and one Hamlet's. The two groups line up with the members facing each other, thus creating a corridor. Claudius stands at one end of the corridor and Hamlet at the other. While Hamlet slowly walks through the corridor towards Claudius, the students on his left encourage him not to kill Claudius, whereas the students on his right give him reasons why he should kill the king. Once he has passed through the corridor and reached Claudius, Hamlet has to decide which side he found more convincing.

6. Revenge in *Hamlet*

a) Hamlet is not the only character in the play who wants to take revenge or set right what he perceives is wrong. Sum up Fortinbras' and Laertes' reasons for wanting to take revenge.
b) Compare Hamlet, Laertes and Fortinbras in terms of the ways they deal with their desire for revenge.
c) Discuss the following statement: Through Hamlet's character, Shakespeare illuminates the different ethical implications of taking revenge.

7. Questions of morality

a) Read the extracts of the play that are labelled *Questions of morality*. You find them on pages 19, 22, 39-42, 55/56, 62-64, 71/72, 82, 107/108, 110-113, 114-116, 132/133, 139-141, 151/152, 153/154, 173-175, 179/180, 180/181 and 182-185. Then copy the grid below and collect information about the characters regarding their moral principles and general attitudes towards morality. Add other characters to the grid that you consider relevant in this regard.

	Hamlet	Claudius	Gertrude	...
moral principles/ attitude towards morality				

b) Rank the different characters according to a scale ranging from 1 (morally good) to 6 (morally bad) and explain your decisions.
c) Explain the functions of these characters and their moral attitudes for the play.
d) Extra: Group work (4–7): Host a talk show. Each of you plays a character you have analysed in a) and b) and one of you acts as the talk show host. The host and the other students from your class as the audience can ask the characters questions about their moral principles.

Additional Notes

Page	Line	
15	183	**A little ere the mightiest Julius fell,** **The graves stood tenantless and the sheeted dead** **Did squeak and gibber in the Roman stre**ets It was said that shortly before Julius Caesar was assassinated, graves were open and empty and the ghosts of the dead were wandering about.
15	188	**Neptune** the Roman god of the sea
15	191	**fates** the three goddesses who control the destiny of man
19	32	**Norway, uncle of young Fortinbras** Apparently, the dead king's brother has succeeded to the throne and not the son.
20	78	**a little more than kin** Hamlet is pointing out that, in a way, he is now more closely related to King Claudius because Claudius has married his mother.
20	82	**I am too much in the sun.** (pun) I feel uncomfortable as the stepson. Or: I feel I am too much under the influence of Claudius, the sun also serving as a symbol of the King.
21	126	**first corpse** According to the Bible, the first person to die was Abel, killed by Cain.
21	134	**Wittenberg** home to a university founded in 1502, connected with Martin Luther and the emergence of Protestantism; many Danes studied there
22	166	**Hyperion** Greek god of the sun
22	166	**satyr** creature half goat, half man; companion of Dionysus, the Greek god of wine and fertility
22	175	**Niobe** Greek mythological figure who continued to weep when her children were killed even when she was turned into stone
22	179	**Hercules** Greek mythological hero of great strength and courage
22	183	**incestuous sheets** At the time the Catholic Church considered it to be incest for a man to marry his dead brother's widow.
23	191	**Horatio, or I do forget myself.** It seems Hamlet is so preoccupied with himself that he doesn't immediately recognize Horatio.
29	12	**violet** as a symbol of love that is unlikely to last long
30	46	**moon** symbol of chastity (*Keuschheit*); women of the upper classes wore masks to avoid the rays of the sun
30	71	**There** When saying this, Polonius perhaps gives his son a pat on the back or on the head.
34	16	**A flourish of trumpets, and two pieces of ordnance shot off, within** King Claudius has requested the trumpets and cannons to celebrate Hamlet's obedience in staying in Denmark.
39	32	**like stars start from their spheres** Stars were thought to be fixed in spheres (*Umlaufbahnen*).
40	55	**Lethe wharf** banks of the river Lethe, in Greek mythology the river in Hades; drinking its water was thought to induce forgetfulness
41	97	**lazar-like** like Lazarus in Luke 16:20 in the Bible: a poor and sick man covered in sores

Page	Line	
42	152	**Illo, ho, ho, boy! Come, bird, come.** Hamlet seems to be mocking Marcellus and Horatio by using the call of a falconer when he wants his bird to return.
45	274	**let's go together** Hamlet is telling his friends not to wait for him to go first, but to leave together as friends.
62	335	**live about her waist, or in the middle of her favours** Fortuna grants you an average amount of luck; he could also refer to sexual favours
63	365	**ambition** Perhaps Rosencrantz thinks Hamlet is disappointed that he did not succeed his father as king.
63	386	**No such matter.** Hamlet seems to think "We'll wait upon you." means "We'll act as your servants."
64	438	**quintessence of dust** essence of man, that is dust; cf. Genesis 3:19: "for dust you are and to dust you will return"
65	452	**Adventurous Knight** the types of roles mentioned here were stock characters in plays at the time of Shakespeare.
65	466	**the late innovation** this fashion was prevalent in London at the time Hamlet was first performed
65	477	**little eyases** A company of boy actors flourished at the private Black Friars Theatre in London between 1600 and 1608.
66	504	**Hercules and his load too** Cf. Hercules bearing the globe to relieve Atlas – Hercules bearing the globe was also an emblem of the Globe Theatre.
67	548	**Roscius** Quintus Roscius, famous actor in ancient Rome at the time of Cicero
67	562	**Seneca** (4 BC-65 AD) Roman philosopher and writer of tragic plays
67	563	**Plautus** (254-184 BC) Roman writer of comedies
67	566	**Jephthah** Jephthah made a vow to God that if he defeated the Ammonites, he would sacrifice the first living thing that came to meet him. It turned out to be his daughter. Cf. Judges 11:9-40.
67	571	**"One fair daughter and no more,** **The which he lovèd passing well."** Shakespeare is probably referring to a contemporary ballad that begins: I read that many years ago When Jephithah, Judge of Israel, Had one fair daughter and no more, Who he loved passing well, And by lot, God wot, It came to pass most like it was Great wars there should be, And who should be the chief but he.
68	595	**my young lady and mistress** Hamlet is addressing a boy actor who plays female roles. In Shakespeare's time female roles were played by boys.
68	596	**By'r Lady** A mild oath (*Fluch*) not unusual in Protestant England at the time.

Page	Line	
68	601	**like French falconers** The English considered the French to be poor falconers because they made no effort to select the bird that should be hunted.
68	610	**caviary to the general** Caviar had just been introduced into England at that time.
68	620	**Aeneas' tale to Dido** Virgil's *Aeneid* tells the story of the travels of the Trojan Aeneas, who escaped during the fall of Troy. In books 2 and 3 he tells the Carthaginian Queen Dido about the Trojan War. Hamlet refers to the part where Pyrrhus avenges his father Achilles by killing the Trojan King Priam.
69	624	**Hyrcanian beast** tiger from Hyrcania near the Caspian Sea, which was famous for its tigers
69	638	**grandsire** Priam was thought to have 50 sons and grandchildren
69	650	**Ilium** the citadel (fortified building) of Troy
69	665	**Cyclops** the three one-eyed giants of Greek mythology who assisted Vulcan in producing armour and weapons such as swords for the gods – They are said to have made the armour and sword for Achilles.
69	666	**Mars**, the god of war – It appears the Cyclops also forged (*schmieden*) armour and weapons for Mars.
70	671	**wheel** Fortuna was said to sit or stand on top of the wheel of fortune, thus controlling human destiny by turning the wheel.
70	679	**Hecuba** Priam's wife, whose grief over her husband's tragic death contrasts greatly with Queen Gertrude's short period of mourning
70	715	**who should 'scape** (escape) **whipping** Whipping was the punishment for being an unlicensed player or a vagabond in Shakespeare's time.
71	724	**The Murder of Gonzago** Hamlet later claims it is an Italian play.
72	773	**pigeon-livered and lack gall** Pigeons were considered meek and gentle because they lacked gall (*Galle*) and were thus thought to be incapable of anger.
72	785-789	**I have heard [...] proclaimed their malefactions** A widow confessed to having murdered her husband after seeing *A Warning for Fair Women*, in which a wife murders her husband. It was performed by Shakespeare's company in 1599.
72	799	**he is very potent with such spirits** It was believed that people who suffered from melancholy (depression) were easily influenced by the devil.
82	109	**his quietus make** settle his accounts, i.e. die – from the Latin, "quietus est" meaning "The debt is paid."
83	153-154	**your honesty should admit no discourse to your beauty** Cf. saying: "Beauty and honesty seldom meet."
84	202	**your paintings** In Shakespeare's time, it was the custom of women to make excessive use of makeup. Even Queen Elizabeth plastered her face with makeup in old age. This practice was often satirized and attacked by dramatists.
85	236	**neglected tribute** Danegelt: protection money England had to pay to Denmark in tribute to the Viking raiders to ensure continuing peace and safety from pillaging.

Page	Line	
90	13	**groundlings** in Elizabethan times, members of the audience standing directly in front of the stage, where admittance was the cheapest – being from the lower classes, they expected to be entertained with bawdy humour
90	15	**inexplicable dumb-shows** Such pantomimes were outdated by the end of the 16th century in serious drama.
90	16	**Termagant** god believed by medieval Christians to be worshipped by Muslims; thought to be violent and arrogant
90	17	**out-Herods Herod** Herod of the New Testament, who ordered the massacre of children fearing that Jesus would later take his throne, was often portrayed as a raging tyrant in medieval plays.
92	123	**the air, promise-crammed** One can speculate whether "air" is meant to pun with "heir" (*Thronerbe*). King Claudius may have no intention of allowing Hamlet to inherit the throne, as he implied in Act I, Scene II, l. 130: "You are the most immediate to our throne." To Hamlet, Claudius' promise to allow his succession is just air.
92	123	**You cannot feed capons so.** A capon is a castrated cock overfed before being served as food. In its metaphorical sense it can also mean "idiot". You cannot feed capons with air. Perhaps Hamlet implies that Claudius considers him to be an idiot, or someone who will soon be slaughtered like a capon. He may also be suggesting that he is entirely stuffed with air (i.e. empty promises), more than anyone could ever stuff a chicken.
93	136	**Capitol** Caesar was actually killed in the Senate House. – Note: The killing of Polonius later in the play is anticipated.
93	145	**here's metal more attractive** By sitting next to Ophelia, Hamlet can better observe Claudius.
95	254	**For husband shalt thou** We can assume the next world would be "find", which rhymes with "kind".
96	261	**wormwood** *Artemisia Absinthium*; perhaps to mean that Hamlet's suspicions about his mother being an accessory to murder makes him feel very bitter
97	333	**A murder done in Vienna** Shakespeare seems to have used an actual murder in 1538 as the basis for Hamlet's playlet. The Duke becomes the King in Hamlet's playlet. It was Gonzago who was originally the murderer.
98	354	**"the croaking raven doth bellow for revenge"** a quote from *The Tragedy of Richard III* by an unknown playwright, published in 1594
98	358	**of midnight weeds collected** It was thought that poisonous herbs were most potent when collected at midnight.
98	383-386	**Why, let [...] world away.** These lines seem to be from an old ballad.
98	383	**let the stricken deer go weep** It was thought that a fatally wounded deer had tears in its eyes before dying.
99	431	**put him to his purgation** The phrase can have several meanings: (1) to cure him of his anger with bloodletting, which was thought to be a cure for all kinds of illnesses (2) to free him from the burden of sin through confession (*Beichte*) and absolution (*Sündenerlass*), or (3) to clear him of a crime in court.

Page	Line	
100	471	**by these pickers and stealers** I swear by my own hands, which I promise will not pick or steal. – a reference to the promise a person must keep as stated in the Catechism of the Book of Common Prayer, first published by the Protestant Church of England in 1546
101	487-488	**recover the wind of me as if you would drive me into a toil** A group of hunters would stand windward to the animal so it would smell them, thus causing the animal to run away. But on the other side there would be another group of hunters waiting to trap the animal in a net.
102	548	**drink hot blood** Drinking hot blood was thought to increase the desire to kill.
102	552	**Nero** Roman emperor who was said to have killed his mother, Agrippina, and to have ripped open her womb (*Gebärmutter*)
107	72	**Offence's gilded hand** the hand of the criminal holding gold to bribe the judge
107	84	**heart with strings of steel** The heart was thought to be held in place with tendons/sinews (*Sehnen*), the heartstings.
112	83	**sets a blister there** Prostitutes were threatened with being branded on the forehead, though this punishment was never carried out.
112	119	**hoodman-blind** a game where one player is blindfolded with a hood over his/her head – Hamlet is saying that his mother must have been blindfolded when she chose her second husband.
113	148	**a vice of kings** 1) the worst example of a king, 2) the representation of "Vice", a clownlike or villainous role in the Morality plays performed between the 14th and 16th centuries
116	272-275	**Unpeg the basket on the house's top.** **Let the birds fly, and, like the famous ape,** **To try conclusions, in the basket creep,** **And break your own neck down.** The story is from an unknown source: A curious ape steals a basket full of birds and carries it up unto a roof. The ape then opens it up, allowing the birds to fly away. The ape thinks it can imitate the birds and climbs into the basket and jumps out, thinking it can fly like the birds. It jumps out of the basket and falls off the roof and lands on the ground with a broken neck. Hamlet is saying: Don't try to be too clever and co-operate with the king; the results might be disastrous.
121		**O'er whom his very madness, like some ore** **Among a mineral of metals base,** **Shows itself pure. He weeps for what is done.** Note: Queen Gertrude is covering up for Hamlet. Hamlet admitted to her he was only faking his madness and she knows he didn't weep because of killing Polonius.
124	12	**Dust, whereto 'tis kin** Cf. "Dust thou art and unto dust shalt thou return." (Genesis 3:19)
124-125	40, 44	**The King is a thing […] Of nothing.** Perhaps a reference to Psalm 144: "Man is like a thing of nought; his time passeth away like a shadow."
127	136-137	**Your worm […] for diet.** Shakespeare seems to be making a joke about the Diet of Worms (*Reichstag zu Worms*) (1521), called by the Emperor of the Holy Roman Empire, Charles V, to challenge Martin Luther's views.

Page	Line	
129	96	**After the Danish sword** If we assume the play takes place in the 10th or early 11th century, reference is perhaps being made to the frequent raids of the Danes on England and its partial occupation. Even a "Danegeld" (tribute or protection money to fight off Viking raids) was regularly paid at that time.
136	39-40	**cockle hat [...] sandal shoon** an outfit often worn by pilgrims who visited the shrine of Saint James of Compostela in Spain, often people in love, seeking the help of the saint
141	221-222	**kind life-rendering pelican** **Repast them with my blood** At Shakespeare's time it was believed that the pelican pierced its own breast with its bill to feed its young with its own blood.
142	264	**pansy** symbol of love
142	268	**fennel** symbol of flattery
142	268	**columbine** symbol of infidelity (*Untreue*)
142	268	**rue** symbol of repentance (*Reue*)
142	270-271	**daisy** symbol of deception (*Betrug*)
142	271	**violet** symbol of faithfulness in love
150	21	**as the star** (planet) **moves not but in his** (its) **sphere** At the time it was believed that planets moved in hollow spheres that revolved around the earth. – Claudius is saying he feels his love for Gertrude is so great that he cannot bear not to be close to her.
150	26	**the spring that turneth wood to stone** a reference to a spring (*Bach*) that contains a lot of lime (*Kalk*) and would thus be able to cover a piece of wood floating in it with lime so that it would look like limestone (*Kalkstein*)
152	113	**Normandy** We can assume the play to be set some time before 1066, when William of Normandy, nowadays known as William the Conqueror, invaded England. The Normans were known for being excellent horsemen, as the description of Lamord confirms.
155	263-264	**her coronet weeds/Clambering to hang** It seems Ophelia wanted to hang her "coronet weeds" on a branch of the willow. In Shakespeare's time it was a custom for disappointed lovers to hang a garland on the branch of a willow.
159	9-10	**in her own defence** Normally, a court of law or the Church would accept self-defence as an acceptable reason for killing s.o. who is trying to kill you. In the case of suicide, this is of course absurd.
159	15-17	**if I drown myself wittingly, it argues an act, and an act hath three branches: it is, to act, to do, to perform: argal, she drowned herself wittingly.** The gravedigger is ridiculing the kinds of argument and the legal terms used by lawyers. Shakespeare is probably parodying the actual case of Sir James Hales' suicide brought before a court in 1554.
159	40	**gentleman** a person with a coat of arms (*Familienwappen*), having the right to bear arms, and in the social hierarchy socially above simple farmers; and unlike simple farmers, they had their own land

Page	Line	
160	47	**Adam digged.** The grave-digger is probably referring to John Ball, leader of a great peasants' revolt in England in 1381, who famously said, "When Adam dalf and Eva span who was than a gentilman?" (a German version goes, "Als Adam grub und Eva spann, wer war da der Edelmann?"). However, it is not specifically stated in the Bible that Adam "digged". Cf. Genesis 2:15: "The Lord God took the man (Adam) and put him in the garden of Eden to till (*den Boden bestellen*) it and keep it." and Genesis 3:19: "By the sweat of your brow you will eat your food until you return to the ground, since from it you were taken; for dust you are and to dust you will return." "Adam's profession" (mentioned a few lines above) as a gardener, ditcher, and grave-maker would be a logical conclusion.
160	80-83	**In youth, when I did love, did love,** **Methought it was very sweet** **To contract – O – the time, for – a – my behove.** **O methought there – a – was nothing – a – meet.** This verse and the one on the next page seem to be a corrupted form of poems by Lord Vaux, which were published in an anthology called *Tottel's Miscellany* in 1557.
161	102	**Cain's jawbone** According to medieval tradition, Cain, the first murderer, killed his brother, Abel, with the jawbone of an ass. However, this instrument of murder is not mentioned in the Bible.
162	138-139	**the length and breadth of a pair of indentures** Perhaps Hamlet is making an allusion to the grave being as long and wide as this document.
164	257-258	**Now get you to my lady's chamber and tell her, let her paint an inch thick, to this favour she must come.** In Shakespeare's time, engravings of Death in the form of a skeleton entering the bed-chamber of a young woman sitting at her dressing-table and applying make-up were widely distributed.
164	263	**Alexander** the Great (reigned 336-323 BC), creator of one of the largest empires of the ancient world
165	273	**dust** Cf. Genesis 3:19: "Thou art dust, and to dust thou shalt return."
166	338	**caught her [...] arms** Note: It seems to be an open coffin.
166	342	**Pelion** In Greek mythology, giants, rivals of the gods, piled Mount Pelion on top of Mount Ossa in an attempt to climb up to Mount Olympus, the home of the gods.
166	349	**Hamlet the Dane** It seems Hamlet is making his claim to be the next King of Denmark.
174	55	**palm** symbol of peace and prosperity, might be a reference to the Bible: "The righteous shall flourish like a palm." (Psalm 92:12)
174	56	**garland** also a symbol of peace and prosperity
174	88	**Popped in between the election and my hopes** Apparently the King of Denmark is elected by a council of nobles. We can conclude that had King Hamlet died a natural death or died in battle, his son Hamlet would have been elected the next king.
175	124-125	**Put your bonnet to his right use.** It was common to wear a hat even indoors. Perhaps Osric took off his hat as a sign of respect to Hamlet, but doesn't want to admit it, so claims he took off his hat because he feels uncomfortable wearing it in the hot weather.

Page	Line	
177	208-209	**if we [...] our sides** Hamlet is making a joke here. "Carriage" can also be the supporting structure with wheels that holds a cannon.
179	283-284	**in the fall of a sparrow** cf. Mathew 10:29-31: "Are not two sparrows sold for a farthing, and one of them shall not fall on the ground without your Father? [...] Fear ye not, therefore, ye are of more value than many sparrows."
184	506	**I am more an antique Roman than a Dane.** Ancient Romans committed suicide to avoid dishonour. Christians, however, in the play and in general, consider taking your own life for any reason a sin.
185	536	**Now cracks a noble heart.** The heartstrings (the tendons thought to support the heart) were thought to crack at the point of death.